The Unsound Convictions
of Judge Stephen Mentall

Stephen P. Smith

First Published 2018

ISBN: 978-1-7218022-5-8

By Stephen P. Smith

Fiction
The Unsound Convictions of Judge Stephen Mentall
The Veteran and The Boy

Computer Science
Thinking About Computer Programming?

Biography
The Charlie Chaplin Walk

1

Martin Palmer, clerk to the court, stepped towards the stand and placed a Bible before Mrs Jackson. The jury, mostly white, middle-class, and dressed to the nines, watched the proceedings in Court Room Three of the Albridge Crown Court.

"Repeat after me, 'I swear by Almighty God'," began Palmer.

"I swear by Almighty God," replied Mrs Jackson with a faint quiver in her voice.

"Now repeat, 'The evidence I shall give'," said Palmer.

Mrs Jackson's elderly face crumpled into a frown. "What – I've got to repeat your evidence?"

Judge Stephen Mentall, presiding, flicked through his notes, which informed him that this latest witness was one Mrs Ruth Jackson, aged seventy-three. She looked, to be frank, ridiculous in her huge blue glasses and purple crocheted hat, and judging by her expression had all the intelligence of a field-mouse. Although nothing surprised him these days, he'd make an exception if she had anything useful to add to the trial.

"No, Mrs Jackson," continued Palmer. "Can you say the words, 'The evidence I shall give shall be the truth'?"

"The evidence I shall give shall be the truth," Mrs Jackson repeated dutifully.

"Now say, 'the whole truth'." Palmer allowed his voice to trail off with his eyes still fixed on her.

"Well I was queuing in the bank when–" said Mrs Jackson.

"No, no, no Mrs Jackson," said Palmer, stopping her with a raised hand. "Can you say the words, 'the whole truth and nothing but the truth'?"

"The whole truth and nothing but the truth," she replied, drawing together her fluorescent green shawl.

"Thank you," said Palmer, with evident relief.

"I've not had your education, you know," said Mrs Jackson waspishly.

Or breeding, thought Judge Mentall, drumming his fingers on

1

the bench and gazing around the courtroom in the dullness of the post-lunch atmosphere. A beam of afternoon sun from the top window exposed dust in the air, and reflected from droplets of dried 'Mr Sheen' caked onto the imitation oak of the court furnishings. What with a round of golf booked for four p.m. not to mention the pressing engagement of that evenings lodge meeting, Mentall longed to call a recess.

PC Edward Sawman, indicted of murdering a bank robber, stood impassively behind a sheet of glass.

The prosecution barrister, James Wittley, began by taking Mrs Jackson step by step through her statement: what she had done that day, what she had seen, and, in somewhat greater detail, the details of the robbery she had witnessed at the bank in Albridge. Mentall exchanged a glance with the defence barrister when she went as far as describing each and every transaction she had intended to make.

"So, Mrs Jackson," continued Wittley, after skilfully moving her on from her financial affairs, "what exactly did you see when the bank robber was shot?"

"Well," she said with a fixed stare, "there was a young man in front of me in the queue. When it was his turn, he drew out a gun, pointed it at the counter clerk, and demanded she fill a bag with money." Lowering her tone, as if sharing a confidence, she added, "What with the other recent robberies I knew straightaway what was happening."

Wittley nodded. "Please continue, Mrs Jackson."

"Well, at that moment a lot of policemen appeared at the door of the bank, and one of them yelled 'Armed Police, hands up'."

"And then?"

She blinked. "Well, he put his hands up."

Mentall's ears pricked up: he hadn't been expecting this. There was no indication in Mrs Jackson's witness statement that the robber had at any point put his hands up.

"Just to clarify, Mrs Jackson," asked Wittley, "do you mean the young man with the gun put his hands up?"

"Yes, that's right," she replied, nodding briskly. "One of *them*."

Wittley let out a barely concealed sigh. "Mrs Jackson, just how many bank robbers did you see that morning?"

"Just the one."

"Then could you please explain to the court just what you mean when you say that *one of them* raised his hands?"

"I mean," she said, "it was one of the police."

"Mrs Jackson," Mentall interrupted, "do you mean to tell the court that on the command 'Armed Police, hands up', one of the police officers put his *own* hands up?"

"Yes," she replied, nodding.

Mentall heard a low murmur from the direction of the public gallery, and a quickly suppressed laugh. He pressed a fist against his mouth to conceal a grin, and took the opportunity to study Sawman's colleagues from the Special Operations Armed Police, all of whom were sitting in the public gallery – and, he didn't doubt, claiming overtime for the privilege.

All of them, he noticed, were grinning broadly – all except twenty-three year old PC Andrew Bloc, who stared down at his shoes like he was checking whether they needed a polish.

"Mrs Jackson," Mentall continued, "can you, for the court's benefit, identify *which* police officer put his hands up?"

"No," replied Mrs Jackson.

"And why not?"

"They were all wearing helmets with those window things stuck on the front," she replied, waving a hand in front of her face.

"I think she means a visor, your honour," suggested Wittley.

Blast, thought Mentall. "Your witness, Mr Wittley."

"Thank you your honour. Mrs Jackson, after the command 'Armed Police, hands up,' what did the young man, by which I mean the bank robber, do?"

"Well," she replied, sensing the need to be precise, "he swung around and they shot him."

"And did he have a gun in his hand when the police officers shot him?"

"Yes."

"And was he pointing the gun at the police officers?"

"Oh yes, definitely." She hesitated. "Though it might have been a bit to the left. Or was it the right?"

Wittley pursed his lips then asked, "But to your knowledge, did the young man make any attempt to put his hands up, throw the gun away, or let it drop to his side?"

"No. There wasn't time."

"Wasn't time, Mrs Jackson?"

She shook her head. "He swung around and they shot him."

One of the jurors gasped. Mentall eyed them up: a typical bunch of middle-class do-gooders basking in their self-importance from being called up for jury service. Twenty years ago and a case like this would have never come to court: the police had been clear in their instruction to the robber, and instead of obeying, he'd swung around until his gun was pointing at the members of the Special Operations squad. He scribbled a note to remind himself to labour this point in his summing-up.

"And then?" asked Wittley.

"Well, he sort of fell to the floor," she replied.

"And the gun, Mrs Jackson?"

"What about the gun?"

"I'll rephrase that," said Wittley. "What happened to the gun that belonged to the bank robber?"

"It fell on the floor beside him."

"And then?"

"Well, the nearest policeman went and stood over him."

"And which policeman was that?" asked Wittley.

"Him," said Mrs Jackson, pointing at Sawman in the dock.

"Please record that the witness identified the defendant," Mentall instructed the clerk.

"And that," Wittley continued, "is when the defendant shot the robber a second time?"

Mentall heard another murmur from the jury. This was the point on which Sawman's defence rested: according to testimony from the rest of the Special Operations squad, the assailant had appeared to reach for his gun. Sawman, concerned for his life and that of his thirty-seven colleagues, had then shot him a second time.

"Objection!" shouted the defence barrister, getting to his feet.

"On what grounds?" asked Mentall.

"It has not yet been established whether or not it was the defendant or another officer that shot the bank robber a second time," said the barrister. "Until that is, or is not established, the prosecution barrister must not make reference to it."

"Yes, quite right, the prosecution must not lead the witness," Mentall replied. As far as he was concerned the old bird needed a bit of leading, but justice had to be acted out, however long it took.

"Sorry, your honour," murmured Wittley. "I'll rephrase that." He turned back to Mrs Jackson. "When the defendant stood over the robber, who had at that time been shot by a member of the Special Operations squad, what next happened?"

"The policeman shot him again," she replied. She nodded at Sawman. "Him."

"Did the bank robber move at all *before* this happened?"

"Oh yes," Mrs Jackson replied with profound certainty. "He was definitely twitching."

"But was he actually reaching for his gun?"

"I don't know," she admitted.

Mentall eyed her up and down and figured this was her big day. She'd no doubt already bored all her PG Tips friends to death with the thrilling details of what she'd witnessed on the day of the robbery, a legacy that could only be curtailed by her death. *And the sooner the better*, he thought, wondering how much of his tax bill had already been wasted on her pension and NHS treatments: his respect for the welfare state measured even less than his respect for the rights of deceased bank robbers.

"Did the defendant say anything at this time?" Wittley probed.

Mrs Jackson regarded him with a cow-like gaze. "What sort of thing?"

"A warning, perhaps." Wittley splayed his hands. "Take your time now, Mrs Jackson."

"Well… I'm not sure I'd like to say." Her lower lip quivered.

"Don't like to say what, Mrs Jackson?"

"Say what he said," she hissed in a loud whisper.

5

"Mrs Jackson," Mentall asked her, "*did* the police officer say anything?" It was going to be easier to ensure a full acquittal if she could tell the court that Sawman had at least shouted a second warning before shooting the bank robber.

"Yes, he did say something," she replied, her tone a little more certain.

"And?" Wittley asked, barely concealing his exasperation. "*What* did he say?"

"Bye, bye Sooty."

Dead silence filled the court. "Recess until the morning," Mentall barked, bringing the gavel down on the bench. He needed time to think.

*

Stephen Mentall faced the mirror in his private chamber, removed his wig, twisted the ends of his handlebar moustache, plucked out a nasal hair, and smiled.

Ever since that unfortunate incident some years before during the Waterloo Porn Trial, his career had been on hold. A jury, wide-eyed and alert and awaiting the viewing of a DVD entitled 'Wet Girls Clam Up,' had instead found themselves watching 'Amelia rides Dolly', a home video of Mentall's granddaughter riding on her pony. By some enormous stroke of luck nobody had recognised her and, despite national appeals by the police, who had become convinced she was the victim of a paedophile ring, she had never been traced.

Mentall had survived the debacle by pulling in a few favours from fellow lodge-members and allowing them to make copies of 'Wet Girls Clam Up'. But he'd still had to pay a price; all the juicier trials had been allocated to other judges, and the case of the Crown versus PC Edward Sawman had been intended to do little more than dot certain i's and cross certain t's, all to keep the pesky civil-rights types quiet. An open-and-shut-case, if there ever were one.

Instead, and rather unexpectedly, PC Sawman's watertight defence appeared to be leaking faster than an incontinent old man after a skinful in the pub. And furthermore, Sawman had been exposed as a racist – and racism, Mentall knew, thanks to an article he'd once read in The Telegraph, was far from acceptable.

Perhaps, if he handled the case right, there was a chance he might return to the High Court, where the smell of wax rubbed into real oak furnishings stamped the proceedings with authority, and battle-hardened prosecutors ran rings around stammering witnesses. He'd no longer need to suffer the embarrassment of the daily court lists and, even better, his ex-wife would be obliged to drop her snide remarks at family events.

The one regret he always felt during murder trials was not having been born half a century earlier. In those days, Britannia had still ruled the waves, and judges could don the black cloth, sending any number of poor wretches to their mortal ends on the gallows.

And however hard the prospect of prison might be for a hard-nut officer like Sawman, it was nothing compared to the social stigma Mentall had endured since the Waterloo Porn Trial.

2

"That's the man we want," said Aleksander Pawlak, speaking in his native Polish and pointing at an old fashioned television set in the corner of a shabby-looking lounge.

"Which man?" asked Krystyn, a short stocky, curly-haired male companion sat on a dilapidated sofa next to him.

"The judge," replied Aleksander, pointing at the screen. Shire News 24 had moved the trial to top billing.

"Are you sure?" asked a second companion, Tomasz, sat in a deep high-backed armchair.

Aleksander used a remote control to turn up the television's volume against the roar of traffic passing outside the house. "The man who paid us said, judge."

The television showed a young, well groomed, male studio presenter. "So, Angela, what was the mood in court like after the defendant's actual words were revealed?"

The picture switched to a mid-thirties, blonde reporter standing outside a red brick courthouse. She pressed a finger against her earpiece then looked into the camera. A passing car honked its horn. "Well Simon, you could say *tense*. This was a case that could have gone either way. Now there is key evidence to suggest the police officer may have summarily executed the bank robber and of course, this puts a different light on the case."

"Indeed it must. And with the recent tri-force merger this is a crucial time for the police."

"That's right, Simon," continued Angela, "it couldn't have come at a worse time with the recent merger of the old Eastshire, Westshire and Northshire constabularies into the newly-formed Shire Force. I think the chief constables were hoping they could draw a line under the past, but this brings the debate about police racism back to the top of the agenda."

"How did the judge, The Honourable Stephen Mentall, handle it?" asked Simon.

"He called for an immediate recess. Perhaps a bit hasty, but on reflection probably the best thing to do given the circumstances. I think everybody needed a cooling off period. The police officer, whose name we cannot release for legal reasons, needs to speak with his defence counsel."

"Yes. I expect it must be quite a worrying time for PC Sawman… oh shit," said Simon, "are we live?"

"Yes, we are, Simon," Angela replied with a pursed smile. The picture briefly switched back to the studio to show Simon looking aghast at his *faux pas*.

*

Aleksander turned away from the television to address his two friends. "We'll do it tonight."

"It's Eastenders tonight," said Tomasz. "Let's do it tomorrow."

The sooner the better, thought Aleksander. But he knew Krystyn and Tomasz wouldn't budge. He turned his attention back to the television.

"I believe there was another surprising incident during today's proceedings?" asked Simon.

"Yes indeed," replied Angela. "While questioning a witness it emerged that when one of the police officers shouted the words 'Armed Police Hands Up', one of the officers, presumably in panic, raised his own hands."

"And there we must leave it," said Simon.

Aleksander laughed and switched off the television.

"What's funny?" asked Krystyn.

"A policeman was foolish," replied Aleksander. He was in no mood to explain the nuances of British humour.

3

The next morning Judge Stephen Mentall strolled into court, called the editor of Shire News 24 to the stand, gave him a full dressing down for revealing the defendant's identity and, for good measure, threw in an accusation of opportunistically moving a racial revelation to top billing.

Sawman's defence began to collapse as the case proceeded. After the lunchtime recess everybody had had enough, so Mentall moved proceedings along to his summing-up.

"You are a racist and a disgrace to the national police force. It is officers like you that–"

Martin Palmer, clerk of the court, approached the bench with a bemused look. Mentall looked up and raised his eyebrows.

"I think you're reading the wrong script," Palmer whispered.

Mentall, realising he had started to read the media enticing, soundbite ridden sentencing speech he'd spent half the night carefully crafting, shuffled his papers, turned to the jury, and began to read from the correct set of papers.

One step at a time, thought Mentall. *You'll be back in the big time soon enough.*

He spent the next five minutes directing the jury regarding their expected verdict. "If you believe that this police officer acted without reason," he concluded, "then it's your solemn duty to protect the innocent and convict him." He sensed one or two members of the jury shifting with unease. "In this case the deceased wasn't innocent of attempting to rob a bank, but it is your duty to decide if he was the innocent victim of a man who overstepped the law."

That was another close call, he thought. *Don't want to say anything that'll get the blighter off on appeal.* He sent them for deliberation before he could foul things up any further.

After an hour he called them back, instructed them that the court would accept a majority verdict, and called a recess for the night.

*

Nailed it, Mentall thought, sliding into his Mercedes C-Class in the secure parking area behind the courthouse. *That boy's going down and I'll be back to working on the top cases.* He checked the dashboard clock; time enough to visit Madam Suzie's House of Pleasure before the evening rabble arrived.

A short drive and twenty minutes later, he tucked his car away on the Northbridge Industrial Estate and continued the rest of the way on foot. Although the local police were always obliging with tip-offs about raids, he still checked over his shoulder before entering through a nondescript red door.

The interior was softly lit. Madam Suzie emerged from behind a bead curtain and beamed at the man she knew to be her best customer. Mentall knew he could always rely on her discretion, and he appreciated her giving him the first pick of the new girls.

She led him into a lounge where several girls sat on soft leather sofas, talking amongst each other. He selected the leggy Petronella, whose services he'd enjoyed in the past, before being led upstairs for a thorough defrocking.

"That's the usual eighty quid, M'lud, plus shall we say, sixty-five for the little extras?" Petronella asked him precisely one hour later.

"That much?" Mentall grumbled, handing her a wad of scruffy bank notes.

"There's the laundry to consider," she replied tartly. "Most of the girls here wouldn't do them kind of things you want." She fumbled with the hook of her bra. "Not every girl can stand on one leg, and you cost me a fortune at the chiropractors, you do. Most blokes are happy just to have me on my back."

"Yes, yes, quite," he muttered. These surcharges were getting out of hand: the exhibit money from the East Castle Street Robbery Trial wasn't going to last for ever.

Petronella led him back down the dimly-lit grubby staircase and into the more palatial surroundings of the entrance lobby. The knowing goodbye smile of Madam Suzie and a sign reading *Cum Again* were the last memories Mentall were to have of freedom: the moment he stepped out of the building, hands roughly grabbed hold of him.

"What the-?"

He gagged as a handkerchief was thrust into his mouth. A cloth bag was then pulled over his head and drawn tight around his neck.

He heard the sound of a vehicle screeching to a halt and a door sliding open. Hands lifted him and he landed on something hard.

The same door slammed shut again, and it was only then he realised he was being kidnapped.

4

"You and your big ideas." Sandra Pughes glared into her husband's eyes from across a formica kitchen table. "Two grand a week this is costing us. Did you really think anybody would pay a ransom for a kidnapped judge?"

Jack knew he was in big trouble. "Well, my dear–"

"Don't you *my dear* me!" Sandra yelled, her face twisted up in rage.

"I didn't do it for any form of ransom," Jack replied, flustered. "It was meant to raise publicity for the Campaign Against Systemic Harassment."

"What?" She scowled at him. "The fake charity and *make your cheque payable to C-A-S-H* scam again?"

"It's worked before. What do you think is paying for this one?"

She slammed her empty coffee mug against the table. "Oh, you've really stepped up to the mark this time. A *charity* ad is one thing, but kidnapping is an altogether different prospect, wouldn't you say?"

"Sorry," whispered Jack. He pulled his own coffee mug closer and looked around their tired ex-local authority kitchen. "I never meant for them to kidnap the actual judge. I specifically told them to judge a key player in the case." He smiled ingratiatingly. "I'm afraid they took the word *judge* a bit too literally."

Sandra shook her head. "You and your schemes – how did you ever think kidnapping someone would win any kind of public sympathy?"

"I figured it would at least delay the trial and help raise awareness for the fact the courts were certain to acquit that copper. I was going to place an ad asking for funds so the Campaign Against Systemic Harassment could fight against police corruption. Then once we were in profit I'd release whoever those berks had grabbed." He shrugged. "It was supposed to be a bit of a giggle."

"But it didn't delay the trial, did it? And they convicted that copper against all expectations." She let out a snort. "What on earth were you thinking?"

13

Jack ran his bare foot along the edge of a cracked floor tile. "Well, you left it to me," he replied. "*You* said you needed a break after putting your mum in a care home, and next thing I knew you'd sodded off to Ibiza."

"And I've still to clear out mum's house," Sandra half-muttered to herself, ignoring everything Jack had just said. "It's not going to be easy to sell what with the dual carriageway next to it. Not to mention your idiotic attempt to create an ensuite bathroom."

Jack gaped at her. "Well, you didn't give me much time to build it!"

"We've been over this before. Mum was in hospital with all that bother with her waterworks. They said she needed an ensuite. So what did you do?"

"I built an ensuite."

"*No, you bloody didn't*, Jack. What you *did* was divide the bathroom in two and created an *en-bedroom*."

A blackbird landed on their kitchen windowsill behind Sandra. It cocked its head at him, and he noticed it had much the same expression as his wife. Then it flew off again, the flap of its wings somehow seeming to convey disgust.

Sandra sighed and brushed a lock of blond hair away from her ample forehead. "Where did you even get chatting to a bunch of Trotskyite students anyhow?"

"In a student union bar."

Sandra stared at him in disbelief. "What the hell were you doing hanging out with a bunch of students? Hoping to pick up a drunk teenager with a fetish for pig-faced, middle-aged men?"

"I was at university myself, remember," Jack bristled.

She barked out a laugh. "Two weeks at Brighton Polytechnic in 1983? A fat lot of good that did you."

"It's the *University* of Brighton now – it's where I learned how to spot a Trotskyite. And complain all you like, but the fact is they pulled it off. I wasn't to know they weren't following the trial when it became obvious that copper was going down."

Sandra groaned and rubbed her hands across her face. "I don't suppose for one moment these students are studying current affairs on their degrees are they?"

"There's no need to be sarcastic," he muttered.

"But even that's hardly the point," Sandra continued. "I don't know why I'm even trying to explain it to you. Conviction or no conviction, didn't it occur to you that even the most warped leftie might have thought twice before making a contribution on the back of an *abduction*?"

"If you aren't happy let's release him."

She shook her head. "As long as the authorities don't know where he is, we're probably safe. But the moment he talks to them, we're as good as in for a twenty-year stretch."

"He might not go to the law."

"He *is* the bleeding law, you prat."

Jack fumbled with his coffee mug. "What do we do, then, kill him?"

"Oh don't be so stupid. Kidnapping him is one thing, killing him another. So where is he?"

"I've got him well hidden," Jack replied with clear satisfaction.

"He's hardly incognito with that Heseltine hairdo and handlebar moustache, is he?"

Their ginger moggy clattered its way through the cat flap, made a quick assessment of the situation, then beat a hasty retreat.

"Well–" he started to say.

"No." She shook her head. "You'd better leave this to me. Give me the address and the names of the people holding him and I'll think of something."

"I… don't know their addresses."

Sandra closed her eyes for a moment. "I mean the address where they're holding him, Jack." She got up and fetched a pen and a spiral bound notebook from the dresser and placed them on the table before him. "Their names and the address, Jack."

Jack's hand shook and wrote down the details. She then snatched the pad back and placed a pair of glasses hanging from a chain around her neck onto her nose. "Alex, Tom and Chris," she read, then glanced at him over the top of her glasses. "Well, that really fills me full of hope."

"Look I realise all my schemes haven't worked out," Jack said.

15

Sandra flashed her eyes up at him. "You can bloody well say that again."

Jack was tempted but decided not to try his luck. Her eyes moved down to the address. He cringed, knowing there was no more delaying the inevitable.

"You bastard," she seethed, looking back at him. "You total, total fucking bastard."

"Well," he stammered, "it made sense. No point in renting a safe house when your mum's place was vacant. Gives us a nice little return."

Until that moment, Jack had never really appreciated the phrase *if looks could kill*. "My poor old mum in a home, and you use *her* house, the house *I* grew up in – as a *safe house* for some judge you've kidnapped!"

"I didn't kidnap–"

"You disgust me," she said, leaning over him until he was forced to shrink back. "Why I ever married you I'll never know. Even worse, it's a connection straight back to us. If the police ever figure out he'd been held there, don't you think they might have one or two questions for us? And what's more, I need to sell the place. What if I'd arranged to meet an estate agent there? It's hard enough to put a positive spin on a dual carriageway, but I think even the most optimistic estate agent would struggle to describe a resident kidnapped judge as an original feature."

"I'm sorry," Jack whined, his hands pressed between his legs. "I didn't think."

"Right," said Sandra, standing back up again. "From now on I'm in charge. You do everything I say, and be thankful I don't just sod off to Ibiza again and leave you to sort this mess out. The only reason I'm not going to do exactly that is I need to sell mum's place to pay for her care home."

"I was just trying to make some money for us," Jack grumbled petulantly. "And for Wayne, too."

"Leave my son out of this!" she barked at him.

"My son too."

"Stepson," she corrected, stabbing a fleshy finger towards him. "And not a word to him when he gets home on leave."

5

Judge Mentall was sitting alone in Jack's en-bedroom, accessed via the family bathroom, when he heard people moving around downstairs. The floor was covered by ancient, chipped linoleum and the walls, apart from the modern plasterboard partition, were covered in a stained, mustard-coloured wallpaper.

His left ankle had a chain wrapped around it and secured with a padlock, while the other end was affixed to a steel bracket held against the floorboards with four heavy screws. No matter how much he pulled on the chain, the bracket wouldn't budge so much as a millimetre. The chain, he had quickly discovered, was just long enough so he could sit on the toilet in the bathroom next door, but too short to get anywhere near the boarded-up window. There was a bowl of water for washing and drinking, and food was brought once a day.

"Who are you?" he yelled, thumping the floor with his fist. "Did my bloody ex-wife send you? Does the bloody cow want more alimony? Is that it? Or did that Copper's mates send you?"

He thought furiously, trying to think of anyone who might have any reason to wish him ill-will; unfortunately, there was no lack of them. There was that Margaret Wainscott-Bruce woman, for instance, who lived in his road and was about as neighbourly as a sewer full of rats. She was always complaining about something or the other – the height of his fence, the beech trees depriving her of sunlight or the rust on his satellite dish.

He bent back a piece of the brittle, patterned lino until a chunk snapped off with a crack. He touched it, realising suddenly it was actually quite sharp. He broke more pieces off until he had one, quite long piece he thought might serve as a very crude blade.

He wondered who else might hold a grudge. There'd been a few ungracious remarks at the lodge recently about his bar bill; and his deft kick of a golf ball on the ninth green had raised a few eyebrows. But surely even that wouldn't elicit such a violent response.

Then there was Tom Norman, a childhood acquaintance who'd

got hold of his email address and sent him a long and bitter screed about Mentall's treatment of him at school. Mentall had written back, reminding Norman that at the time he had confessed to the theft of some tuck, a misdemeanour for which the standard tariff was having one's head flushed down the toilet. He'd assumed Norman would have appreciated the sardonic wit of his reply, but perhaps, given his current predicament, it hadn't gone down as well as he'd hoped.

"Who are you?" he yelled again, thumping both heels against the floor until the chain chafed his ankle.

No answer.

He hobbled into the bathroom and inspected himself in the tiled mirror above the toilet. He smoothed down his eyebrows, ruffled his mop of hair then worried an ear hair until it gave way with a satisfying pop.

He stiffened at the sound of somebody running up the stairs, then heard the door between the landing and the bathroom click open.

"Put bag on head," said a kidnapper's voice in broken English.

Mentall knew if he saw any of their faces he'd be as good as dead. The fact they disguised their voices with those ridiculous fake Eastern European accents was surely sufficient evidence he was dealing with professionals.

He returned to the en-bedroom, squatting back down on the floor and pulling the musty-smelling bag back over his head. At the same time he reached down, fumbling around until his fingers found the improvised knife, holding it close against his side where, he hoped, the kidnapper wouldn't see it. Then he waited, listening.

"Why you shouting?" the kidnapper demanded.

"What do you bloody well expect?" Mentall barked in response. "I demand to know why you're holding me!"

"None your business."

"None of my business! You deny me my liberty, and you say it's none of my business?" He turned his head towards the other man's voice, and wondered if the kidnapper was still standing directly in front of him in the doorway.

"You deny other liberty."

Bloody Anarchists, he thought. He'd sent a few of those down in his time. Could *this* be the reason for his kidnapping?

"So you don't believe in penal servitude then, do you?" Mentall sneered. "Let them all out, eh?. Murderers, rapists, muggers, bank robbers – oh yes, you'd love to see them all back on the streets, wouldn't you? Well, let me tell you, the country would collapse in no time at all. There'd be rioting, anarchy, looting."

"Yah."

"It's all very well you being indifferent," he thundered. "All you types know is left wing claptrap fed to you by idealistic morons. It's *my* class that's given you the freedoms you enjoy. You'd not have had the time to go round kidnapping people in my day! You'd be fighting disease and famine with a polio-withered leg. That'd have you leaning a bit more to the right, I could tell you."

"Not polio," replied the kidnapper.

He heard the creak of a floorboard, directly in front of him. He took his moment, springing forward with his improvised weapon clutched in one hand.

6

Toby Peers took his seat at the head of the conference table, adjusted the sleeves of his Savile Row suit and nodded to the senior officials lining either side of the table before him. Portraits of former Home Secretaries decorated the oak panelled walls. Yesterday he had been little more than a ministerial bag-carrier; now, having been promoted to Home Secretary in a late-night cabinet reshuffle, his first task was to chair a meeting between the National Crime Agency and the three chief constables of the newly-formed Shire Force.

"All right, I'd like to call this meeting to order," he began. The distant sound of a car horn cut the air from the direction of Parliament Square. "Item one on the agenda is–"

"The Chief-Constable's driver," interrupted Simon Nortly, the former chief constable of the newly-defunct Northshire Constabulary.

Peers frowned. "What about the Chief-Constable's driver?"

"There's only one," said Nortly.

"So?"

"So there's only one driver, but three chief-constables. How are we all going to get about?"

In that moment, Peers found himself rueing the legislation that made it illegal to make any police officer redundant. "Item one," he repeated, staring hard at Nortly, "is the apparent disappearance of Judge Stephen Mentall."

"Can't we deal with that later?" Adam Edgeson, former chief constable of the newly-defunct Eastshire Constabulary, peered at him from behind a pair of designer glasses. "We need to sort out this driver situation."

"Can't you sort it out amongst yourselves?" Peers protested, already starting to wonder if the tri-force merger was worth the money it was intending to save.

"Not when there's a disagreement between officers of the same rank," Nortly replied stiffly. "If that happens, we have to push it up to the next level."

"And that's *me* I suppose, is it?" asked Peers unenthusiastically.

"Yes," said Nortly. "With respect, Sir, it is."

"Do tell me," said Peers, drawing the words out, "*why* we only have one driver for all three chief constables?"

"The driver for a chief constable is a civilian position," Robert Wytton, former chief constable of the newly-defunct Westshire Constabulary explained in a thick Yorkshire brogue. "The tri-force merger was all about cutbacks, so we're only allowed one, instead of three."

"So, just to be clear," asked Peers, "there's three of you, but only one driver?"

"And one car," added Edgeson.

Across the table, Hamilton-Smith, representing the National Crime Agency, visibly bit back a laugh.

Peers stared at Edgeson's lean figure. "Can't you all travel around in the same car?"

"That's far from practical, Sir," said Nortly. "We each cover quite different roles. It'd look a bit odd."

"It's already a bit bloody odd having the three of you running one police force," thundered Peers. "My God, can't you drive your own cars and take it in turns to use the official car and driver when you need them?"

Nortly shook his balding head in apparent horror. "And then what happens if we all have official engagements at the same time?"

"The only answer," said Wytton, tapping one finger on the table, "is returning to a car and driver each."

"Can't you do that?" asked Peers.

Wytton shook his head. "Not with how the new force is structured, Home Secretary. It only allows for the one post of civilian driver to the chief constable. We need you to sanction a change."

The audacity of the man, thought Peers. The three of them sounded like children squabbling over who should have first go on a new Nintendo game. "The terms of the merger are quite clear," he said levelly. "There are no circumstances under which I am prepared to sanction a driver for each of you."

"In that case we'll have to go back to the old system," said Edgeson, "and use police constables for our drivers."

"Well, do that then," said Peers, wearily.

"And a car each?" asked Edgeson, sitting up straight.

"If that lets us get onto item one," said Peers, his voice thick with irritation, "then by all means, yes."

The three of them exchanged smug and satisfied looks. "Item two," said Wytton, smoothing one bushy eyebrow with his thumb.

"I *think* you mean item one," snarled Peers.

"No, item one was the Chief Constable's driver," said Wytton, "so that makes the next point item *two*."

"Fine," Peers shouted, slamming his left hand down on the table hard enough to make Hamilton-Smith jump, "item two is therefore the apparent disappearance of Judge Stephen Mentall."

"Actually," said Nortly, "item two is the Chief Constable's parking space."

"Oh, for *God's sake!*" Peers flung his hands up in exasperation. "*What about* the Chief Constable's parking space?"

"There's only one and you've just sanctioned three cars, Sir"

"Can't you make two more?"

Nortly made a sucking sound with his lips in the traditional manner of a cowboy plumber giving a cost-estimate. "That's difficult, you see, because the designated parking space is an extra-width bay out front of the Headquarters building. It wouldn't be good for morale if one chief constable was seen to be privileged over the others."

Wytton nodded. "There's a certain… friction between the members of the different forces, and any indication of favouritism would be, well, catastrophic."

"With the Home Secretary's permission," said Nortly, "we could convert two of the extra-width disabled bays into additional spaces for the rest of us."

"Are any of you disabled?" asked Peers.

"No," Nortly replied.

"Presumably that only applies to being physically disabled," chipped in Hamilton-Smith.

"Go ahead then," groaned Peers. "Anything for an easy life. Item two."

Hamilton-Smith smiled wryly. "Item three, actually."

Peers regarded him stonily. "Item three," he said, "is the apparent disappearance of Judge Stephen Mentall." He looked around for signs of interruption and found none. "All that we currently know is that he disappeared immediately following an adjournment during the trial of PC Edward Sawman, at that time seconded to SOAP."

"What does SOAP stand for?" asked Edgeson.

"Special Operations Armed Police," Nortly explained. "It's our crack armed response team."

Peers, clearly annoyed at the interruption, gave Nortly a sideways glance. "Mentall's current whereabouts remain unknown and a cause for concern."

"We're pretty certain he's been kidnapped," said Nortly.

"How have you worked that out?" asked Wytton.

Nortly became suddenly evasive. "We have our sources."

"If your force had run SOAP properly," said Wytton, "we'd not be in this mess!"

"One rogue officer doesn't define a police force," Nortly snapped.

"I'd say it bloody defined yours," Wytton snapped back.

"Gentlemen, gentlemen," said Edgeson, "We're all one big force now. Let's not misbehave on the Home Secretary's first day."

"A kidnapping is certainly something we have to consider," said Peers, ignoring Edgeson. "What have you found?"

"We tracked his final movements down to a brothel."

"Oh dear," groaned Peers, "not another sex scandal."

"Unfortunately, the trail goes cold after that," added Nortly.

"And based on that and that alone, you think he's been kidnapped?" asked Wytton, his voice rich with scorn.

"Yes."

"Have you checked the brothel?" asked Peers.

"Yes," Nortly replied. "In fact a number of my officers volunteered to go undercover and check the place out."

"I bet they did," said Edgeson, peering at him from behind his glasses. "My officers have been carrying out their own investigation, and it seems he's known to his colleagues as a bit of a rogue. Various rumours, least of all call girls." He regarded them all with a bemused smile. "I think it far more likely he's gone into hiding because of something really shady that was about to be exposed."

"Of course," said Hamilton-Smith, "it's equally possible he was simply murdered. If it pleases the Home Secretary, the National Crime Agency are happy to take this entire case on."

All three chief constables began to shout at Hamilton-Smith. "You always want to pinch the best cases," Wytton snarled at him. "This is a police matter!"

"Gentlemen, gentlemen!" Peers shouted, standing until they had all quietened down again. "Which is it? Has he been kidnapped, hiding, murdered or what?"

"Either way," said Edgeson, as Peers resumed his seat, "we need to flush him out."

"Bit difficult if he's been murdered," Hamilton-Smith muttered under his breath.

"Flush him out?" asked Wytton.

"Look," said Edgeson, "if Mentall was up to something really shady, he could be a major embarrassment to us. The nation's already been rocked by the sexual shenanigans of supposedly respectable members of the establishment. The last thing we need on top of all that is a dodgy Judge. I think we have to be prepared for that possibility."

"*If* he's been up to something dodgy," Peers reminded him. "That still leaves murder or kidnap."

"We can't yield to kidnappers," said Wytton.

"And if he's dead?" asked Peers.

"If he's dead," said Edgeson, "and he's really as corrupt as everyone seems to be suggesting, then quite frankly all our problems are solved. Bunch of flowers to the family – that kind of thing." He looked around them all then added, "I have a suggestion, if I may. But I think it best it doesn't leave this room."

The rest of them muttered and nodded. Peers folded his arms wearily and shrugged. "The room is yours, Chief Constable."

"I suggest," continued Edgeson, "that we invent a few crimes, claim Judge Mentall committed them, and say he went into hiding once he knew he was on the verge of being found out."

"A moment ago," said Peers, "you were worried it would rock the nation's confidence if a member of the judiciary was revealed as being shady."

"I meant *really* shady. What I'm suggesting here is something only slightly *shady*. Something the public won't hold against the entire establishment. Something they can believe was down to just the one rotten apple."

The chimes of Big Ben striking midday came through the open window. Peers glanced at his watch. "May I make an alternative suggestion?" he asked. "Why don't we just tell the truth?"

Wytton laughed. "What that we haven't got a bloody clue?"

"We'd have to reveal the brothel connection," added Edgeson. "And you did say you were afraid of another sex scandal, Home Secretary."

"Point taken. But the one thing no one here seems to be addressing is whether or not he might in fact have been kidnapped. What if he *was*, and we'd only gone and invented a bunch of entirely spurious charges against him? Wouldn't that backfire on us, Chief Constable?"

Edgeson blew his cheeks out. "Well for one," he said, raising his left thumb, "if he's kidnapped and we discredit him, he'll be worthless to his kidnappers, and either they'll let him go or they'll kill him. Two," he continued, raising his index finger, "if he's gone into hiding because his dodgy past finally caught up with him, we've discredited him first. And as for number three," he added, raising his middle finger, "if he's in hiding because he's done something *really* bad, we can still lock him up on the basis of our fabricated charges and he'll be well out of harm's way."

Peers nodded. "I see your thinking."

Wytton flicked a piece of dust from his jacket sleeve. "Which force is going to lead on this?"

"You're all one force now," Peers reminded him.

"He disappeared in Albridge," said Nortly, "so I should take the lead."

"But we have a better track record of solving complex crime," protested Wytton.

"I can offer more manpower," said Edgeson.

"Let's leave worrying who's going to lead until we have some more information," said Hamilton-Smith.

Wytton leaned back and grasped his lapels in the manner of a man who feels his work is done for the day. "What charges are we going to make against him?"

"I suggest," said Nortly, "we all go away and come up with suggestions."

"Very well," agreed Peers, shuffling his papers and cracking open his case, "we'll meet again in seven days' time and all bring our ideas."

"And our drivers," added Hamilton-Smith, with barely a hint of a grin.

7

Mentall was startled awake by the sound of loud voices and banging coming from downstairs. He leapt up from where he had been sleeping curled up on the bare floorboards, convinced that at last rescue had come, and dusted himself down, the chain around his ankle rattling as he turned towards the attic door in trembling anticipation.

The banging was followed by a shriek, and then laughter, and he came to the slow realisation it was nothing of the kind. He slumped back down onto the floor and contemplated his predicament. His earlier attempt at escaping had been foiled when he had leapt forward, wielding his improvised knife made out of lino, only for the kidnapper to close the door without even being aware of Mentall's intentions. His hand and arm still ached from when he had slammed them into the door.

He listened to the different voices from downstairs, all shouting joviality to each other, and tried yet again to work out just how many kidnappers there were. It seemed like there were never less than two or three of them.

He tugged futilely at the chain that bound his left ankle, but he'd long since given up any hope of being able to force or pick the padlock that held it in place.

He stared at the boarded-up window, listening to the sound of traffic droning by outside. Sunlight seeped around the edges of the window. He'd long since guessed that it faced south, and had also noticed that the traffic flowed west to east in the mornings. That put him somewhere near the main road into town. Even so, the van they'd used to kidnap him had taken about half an hour to get here, by his estimation, and that made it impossible to figure out just where the house they were keeping him in was located.

He tried for the thousandth time to reach the window, but as always, his hands fell just short of the board that covered it. He yanked his shackled foot in frustration and felt a jolt of pain shoot up his leg in response. Could there, he wondered, be some way to frustrate his captors into making a mistake? He had even gone so far as to consider a dirty protest, like those IRA fellows had back in the nineteen-eighties, but it felt a bit on the unhygienic side. He had briefly flirted with the idea of a hunger strike, but he liked his food far too much to ever seriously consider the idea, shackled to the floor or not.

He froze in place, a sudden idea rising in his mind: perhaps, he wondered, his captivity might be some form of IRA retribution? He recalled that back in 1993 or thereabouts he'd signed a search warrant for an IRA safe house, and two years later his name had been discovered on a hit-list.

But then his shoulders slumped as he recalled there was hardly any nuance of an Irish accent about his captors. And they certainly didn't sound like those Islamic State chaps either.

"Bloody anarchists," he muttered, returning to one of his earlier theories.

But then again, he thought, once again struck by inspiration, perhaps there *was* a way to outwit his kidnappers, by creating a false emergency of some kind. He grabbed up the hood they always made him wear, and began to pinch and worry at a patch of the material: perhaps if he could wear some of it thin enough, he might be able to get at least a partial look at his kidnappers without them being any the wiser.

He worked steadily at it for most of an hour, then pulled it over his head, adjusting it until he could just about peer through one worn-out patch of dark cloth that didn't look too obvious from the outside. He found he could more or less make out the room around him. He pulled it back off, then shuffled into the bathroom where he eyed the loo thoughtfully for a moment. Then he brushed clumps of cobwebbing away from the cistern's lid, and watched as a spider scuttled out of sight behind it.

He lifted the cistern lid up. Inside, he saw that the ballcock was an old-style copper one, stained green and crusted in calcite. He pulled it up by its connecting arm and stuck a thumb across the overflow. Water began to hiss and spout, and the reservoir filled, then gently overflowed. The water soon lapped onto the floor, wetting his feet. He watched it run across the lino before disappearing between the skirting board and the floor.

"This'll teach the anarchist bastards," he muttered. If they were forced to call a proletariat plumber, there was no way they'd be able to keep him chained up there where he could be seen. And that, in turn, might give him an opportunity for escape.

It wasn't long before he heard a sudden change in the tone of the revelry coming from downstairs.

He removed his thumb from the overflow, replaced the lid, and quickly made his way back through to the room, pulling the bag back over his head and carefully adjusting the worn area so he could watch the door between the landing and the bathroom.

Somebody knocked on the door, then opened it a crack. "Put bag on head," commanded a familiar voice.

Mentall watched closely. After another moment, he saw the face of a young man peer past the door to make sure he had complied. The door opened further and three young men entered, their faces flush with anger.

"You do this?" demanded the one who had spoken first.

"Do what?" asked Mentall, adopting a tone of baffled confusion.

"Make water!"

"It's nothing to do with me," Mentall replied. He studied them as best he could, given the circumstances, and noted their distinct Eastern European features. He began to doubt his anarchists theory. "Perhaps you should call a plumber?"

"We are plumber."

Blast, thought Mentall. *Just my bloody luck.*

"You keep bag on head. We fix."

"So much for Brexit," muttered Mentall as the interconnecting door was pulled to. He listened as the three men got to work cleaning up and fiddling with the cistern. There was no more noise from downstairs, which rather suggested the three men had no other accomplices.

An hour passed before there was a knock on the interconnecting door. "Hey judge man, we finished. We fill cistern for you when you need."

Mentall waited until the three of them had gone back downstairs before pulling off his hood and hobbling through to the bathroom to inspect their handiwork. The feed-pipe to the cistern had been cut and capped, the floor had been mopped, and the lino taped down at the edges.

"Blast," huffed Mentall, although he was forced, somewhat begrudgingly, to concede they'd made a neat job of it.

He returned to his room, dragging his chain after him, and began to tug dejectedly at a yellowing piece of newspaper that had been used as lining paper beneath the lino. It gave way with a tear, and he found himself reading the headline from the Albridge Evening News dated May 19th 1987: 'TOWN NEARING ZERO UNEMPLOYMENT CLAIMS MAYOR.'

The eighties and the days of Thatcher, thought Mentall. Now *there* was a real leader, unlike that weakling Major or that ridiculous actor Blair. And as for the lot since, they changed their minds as often as the pollsters voiced an opinion.

He managed to make out the gist of the mayor's words from the half-torn page. He declared his pride in his town, and sang the praises of the young people who had found work, thereby making it one of the lowest youth unemployment regions in the country.

Not like the modern youth always playing games on their phones, thought Mentall, listening sourly to the voices from downstairs. *If they'd pulled their fingers out we'd not have been overrun by immigrants.*

He turned the musty paper over, finding half a cartoon and an advert for a local tyre centre. He lifted the lino up more, and pulled out the remainder of the newspaper. *Nothing of interest in the personal columns*, he thought, paging through it. For all its faults, when his former wife had withdrawn her sexual favours, the Albridge Evening News had led him to discover Madam Suzie's House of Pleasure.

And now, Madam Suzie's House of Pleasure had led him here, trapped in a house full of nefarious Eastern-European plumbers with ransom on their mind.

8

Sandra Pughes turned off the dual carriageway before pulling-up outside her mother's house. She sat there in her car for a few minutes, gazing sourly at the articulated lorries thundering past just metres away, and recalled the days when it had been little more than a minor road where she had been able to play outside with her friends. She sighed, her fingers tapping the wheel. Back when the road had been upgraded her father had made a series of fruitless attempts to get compensation from the council. After he'd passed, her mother had stayed on in the old house, growing gradually deaf from the day-and-night thunder of Spanish olives and German bratwurst bound for the aisles of supermarkets up and down the country; and as if it wasn't bad enough she had to try to figure out some way of selling a house nobody in their right mind wanted, she also had to deal with a resident kidnapped bloody judge and his captors.

She got out, slammed the door shut and let herself into the garden through a side gate before walking up the path towards the back door. She paused by an apple tree where, long ago, her dad used to lift her onto a lower bough so she could jump down into his arms. All the while her beloved Jack Russell, Charlie, would run around barking excitedly while urinating over every stationary object he could find.

The back door opened a crack, and a dark-haired young man looked out at her with suspicion.

"So are you Alex, Tom or Chris?" Sandra asked him.

"Tomasz," he replied, in what was clearly an Eastern European accent. His eyebrows knitted together. "Who you?"

Trotskyites my arse, she thought, regarding Tomasz's dim expression: the idea they were even students let alone anything else was about as plausible as there being any supporters of Trotskyism left anywhere in Eastern Europe.

"I believe," she said, "that you're working for my husband."

The young man looked blank for a moment, and then his eyes

widened in sudden realisation. "Oh," he said, "you are wife of pig-face?"

Her face coloured with indignation. "Less of your cheek about J…" She caught herself before she could say Jack's name. "You'd better let me in," she finished instead.

Tomasz eyed her dubiously for a moment, then stood to one side.

Sandra stepped into the hallway and cast an eye around. "So this is the house my husband rented?" she asked.

Tomasz responded with a puzzled shrug.

"Where are the others?" she tried instead.

"This way." Tomasz reluctantly led her into the kitchen where she found two other men sitting at the kitchen table. She glanced around: at least nothing else looked out of place.

"Where are you all from?" she asked, looking around at all of them. "Poland?"

None of them said anything, but then again, she thought, none of them denied it either.

"And you were all hired by my husband to keep the judge here?"

The three exchanged glances, their eyes wild with worry.

She stepped towards the kitchen table. "All right then, so which one is Chris and which one is Alex?"

"Krystyn and Aleksander," said Tomasz, pointing at each in turn.

Aleksander spoke angrily in Polish to Tomasz, then turned to her. "How we know who you?" he demanded. "We expect man, with money."

Sandra drew herself up and regarded him with a steely eye. "From now on I'll be taking charge. We won't be needing you lot anymore." Aleksander's face stiffened and he stood, glaring back at her. "Oh, don't worry," she reassured him, "we'll pay you what you're owed – but only to clear off."

"Hold it," said Aleksander, taking a step forward. "We make money. We happy with things." He looked at the others who stared impassively back at him.

"My husband and I will come and collect the judge tomorrow,"

Sandra continued regardless, her voice calm and steady and to the point. "You'll be paid, as I promised. But after that we never want to see any of you again."

Aleksander opened his mouth to make a retort, then fell silent when Tomasz stepped forward and put a hand on his shoulder. He glared at her in mute anger.

"Have him ready at eleven tomorrow morning," said Sandra, moving back towards the door. "And you'd better all have your bags packed."

As she turned towards the door, her eyes stopped suddenly at the mantelpiece.

"Charlie!" she exclaimed in shock.

"Charlie?" muttered Aleksander.

She whipped back around, glaring at all three of them. "What have you done with Charlie?" she demanded. She stabbed one trembling finger towards the mantelpiece. "There's supposed to be a pot with Charlie written on it!"

Aleksander's face screwed up in abject confusion. "What have I done with Charlie?"

"You have been here before?" asked Tomasz with a puzzled frown. "I thought…"

"Well, I grew up here," said Sandra, realising she'd given too much away. "Charlie's ashes are gone."

"You said house was rented," Tomasz insisted doggedly.

"Where is he?" Sandra demanded, her tone taking on a vicious edge.

"Who?" asked Aleksander, still deeply confused.

"There was a pot, there, on the mantelpiece," said Sandra, her throat ragged with emotion. *Oh, you fool, Jack. This is all your fault.* "It contains the ashes of Charlie. He was my pet dog when I was a girl."

"I broke," said Tomasz. "It was accident. Sorry."

Sandra stepped up close to him. "You're lying to me," she shouted. "I know you've done something with him, and I want to know *now*!"

"Well," began Tomasz, "Pig-face–"

"I'd thank you not to keep referring to my husband as *Pig-face!*"

"Sorry. You see, your husband stock house well. Food in freezer, beer in fridge and duty-free cigarettes in cupboard."

No surprise about the duty-free fags: one of Jack's schemes had been to rent a van, take it across the channel, and stock it with duty-free fags to sell back home. It wasn't long before their garden shed bulged with unsold Marlboro Lights as testament to an already flooded market. The biggest profiteers, as far as she could see, were the van rental companies.

What did surprise Sandra, however, was her husband's apparent ability to stock a freezer with food: a fridge filled with beer was a Jack speciality, but food? Well, that was a surprise.

"And when we saw pot marked *Charlie*," Tomasz continued, "we thought…"

"You thought what?"

"We thought husband left caine."

"Caine?" She stared at him in utter confusion. "What the hell is 'caine'?"

"Caine. Cocaine. *Charlie*. English slang, yes?"

Sandra stared at him in outright horror.

"So we put it in lines and snort," said Tomasz, staring at the ground like a naughty schoolboy.

"You did *what*?"

"We…snort."

"You *snorted Charlie*?"

"Many times," agreed Tomasz. "But this stuff it make eyes runny and throats bad."

"I'll give you more than sore throats," she shouted, her voice trembling with rage. "Where is the rest of him?"

"In bin," said Tomasz, pointing towards a pedal bin.

"And the pot?"

Wide-eyed delight filled Tomasz's face. "Pig-face left pot, too?"

He recoiled in terror when Sandra snatched a handful of his shirt, pulling him close, the blood throbbing in her head. "When I said *pot*, I meant the pot *marked Charlie*, i.e. the container what has sat on my mother's mantelpiece for the last three decades, longer than you have been on this planet and at this rate a duration you will *never see*."

She let go of him and pushed him away again, taking a deep breath. There were more pressing problems at hand, she reminded herself. "Now tell me, where is the judge?"

"In room on bathroom," said an ashen-faced Aleksander.

Sandra was about to ask him what the hell he meant when she remembered Jack's pathetic attempt to create an ensuite. She made her way back through to the hallway and climbed the stairs and was about to open the pink bathroom door when Tomasz called up to her.

"You need bag," he shouted. "Bag for head."

"I need what?" Sandra bellowed back down.

"Bag for head," he shouted. "So judge not see."

"I'm not putting any bag on my head!"

"No," yelled Tomasz. "Judge need bag for *his* head. Otherwise he see."

"Oh right," said Sandra, letting go again of the white plastic handle.

Tomasz ran up the stairs, opened the door an inch and shouted, "Hey, judge man! Put bag on head!"

Sandra huffed impatiently until Tomasz finally stood aside and allowed her to step into the bathroom. Light came from a window to her right, but the bedroom was mostly in shadow. Through the interconnecting doorway she could make out the shoes of a man, chained by one ankle.

"Oh my God," she whispered as the full horror of what her husband had done finally struck home.

"Who are you?" demanded Mentall.

"Never you mind," Sandra replied, her voice quavering slightly.

She heard him move suddenly. "I'm being held captive," he shouted through to her. "Please help me!"

Sandra stepped back out onto the landing and pulled the door shut again, ignoring Mentall's repeated demands for help. "Right," she said to Tomasz, quickly regaining her composure, "I'll see you all tomorrow at eleven a.m." She waved a warning finger in his face.

"Bags packed, judge ready to go, and after that I don't want to see any of your faces ever again." She paused and thought for a moment. "Oh, and give him a haircut. And shave off that stupid moustache of his while you're at it."

Tomasz regarded her with frightened confusion. "But he'll see, with no bag on head."

"You'll manage," snarled Sandra.

9

"Gentlemen, thank you all for attending again." Toby Peers, Home Secretary, glanced cautiously around the conference room at his crime-fighting colleagues; the last meeting seven days before had been a testy affair, with the three chief constables of the newly-formed Shire Force seemingly more concerned with fighting over their individual privileges than locating Judge Stephen Mentall.

"Did we have any choice?" asked Simon Nortly, reaching for a tin of assorted biscuits the catering staff had put out with the coffee and tea. The overhead strip-light shone brilliantly on his bald patch.

"So," began Peers, ignoring him, "have any of you come up with suitable charges to pin on Judge Mentall?" He looked towards Hamilton-Smith, grateful that the National Crime Agency had sent the same representative.

"Is that item one on the agenda?" asked Robert Wytton.

Peers flicked through his papers. "Not in so many words, no."

"Then might I suggest we make item one the question of the chief-constable's office," said Nortly.

"Good lord," groaned Peers, "I thought we sorted all that nonsense out last time!"

"That, if I may interject," said Hamilton-Smith, "was in regards to the question of whether they should have one official driver to share amongst the three of them, or each have their own driver."

Adam Edgeson raised a finger. "And not forgetting the question of official parking spaces."

"I thought that had all been resolved?" Peers asked somewhat testily.

"Not quite," said Nortly. "We've taken two police officers off front-line duty because you wouldn't sanction two additional civilian drivers. But there is still the matter of our office."

Peers twisted the signet ring on his little finger and seethed with frustration. "What about your office?"

"There's only one for the three of us," Nortly replied in a manner suggesting he was surprised by the question.

"Surely," asked Peers, "the new headquarters has enough spare offices for all of you?"

"Well, that's true," said Edgeson, "but only one has its own washroom."

"And the deep pile carpet with the new force emblem," added Wytton in his booming Yorkshire accent.

Peers blinked. "Do you mean to say the *washroom* is carpeted with the force emblem?"

"No," Wytton replied somewhat tersely. "It's the office that's carpeted with the force emblem. The washroom floor is tiled."

"With the force emblem," added Nortly.

Peers wondered how on Earth any of the former chief constables had managed to advance quite so far in their careers as they had. "Well, can't you just share this office?"

"Hardly," Nortly replied, looking offended. "A chief constable needs his privacy."

"Isn't that what the washroom is for?" suggested Hamilton-Smith with a smirk.

"That's not very helpful," said Nortly. Wytton and Edgeson both nodded in agreement.

"My understanding," said Peers, raising both palms, "is that since the Shire Force now covers all three counties of Eastshire, Westshire and Northshire, you're meant to function as one big happy family, so the question of whomever gets a particular office should be entirely irrelevant."

"With respect, Home Secretary, you're not valuing the traditions of the original three forces," said Wytton. "It's not good for morale if one force is shown favour over the other two."

"But they don't *exist anymore*," Peers shouted, thumping the table hard with his fist. "You're one force now!"

"In name, yes," agreed Nortly. "But the rank and file still owe a great deal of their loyalty to the original force structure."

Peers regarded him balefully. "Which, I feel compelled to point out, isn't exactly helped by having three chief constables to run the new force."

"It's a condition of the 1919 Police Act that no police officer can be made redundant," Nortly said firmly.

"Something I am painfully aware of," Peers replied. "And what *do* you all do? You can't *all* perform the role of chief constable, can you?"

"Robert maintains responsibility for Professional Standards, Adam is in charge of Crime and I take care of Operations," explained Nortly.

"Surely those are ACC positions?" asked Peers.

"The ACCs deputise for us," said Nortly, helping himself to a chocolate digestive.

"But who is in overall charge?"

"You are Sir," Nortly replied, catching a crumb in his hand. "We are all of equal rank."

"So," asked Wytton, raising bushy eyebrows, "what are you going to do about our office, Home Secretary?"

Peers momentarily closed his eyes. "Given that we could discuss this for a very long time, I suppose it would be easier to go ahead and build two more."

"Each with its own washroom?" asked Edgeson.

"If you must," Peers replied wearily.

"And the force emblem on the tiles?" chipped in Hamilton-Smith.

"Yes, that too." Peers shuffled his papers. "Can we now please get on with item one – no, I mean item two?" He shook his head. "I can barely remember it myself now."

"The question of some fabricated charges against Judge Mentall," Hamilton-Smith reminded him.

"So." Peers cast a look around the room. "Any ideas?"

"We could put it out he's been spying for a Middle Eastern state that sponsors terrorism," suggested Nortly.

"Utterly ridiculous," said Edgeson. "With all due respect, Stephen Mentall was hardly in a position to supply information to anyone in the Middle East, let alone anywhere else. He was a crown court judge, dealing with domestic issues." He formed his fingers into a steeple. "Now, *we* think–"

"With all due respect," hissed Nortly, "you've not heard me out."

"Gentlemen, gentlemen," said Peers. "I think state-sponsored terrorism is a bit farfetched, don't you? And don't forget it only need be sufficient to flush him out of hiding or to force the hand of a kidnapper. Let's briefly hear each idea. Adam next, I think."

"Well," said Edgeson, adjusting his designer glasses, "I suggest we create a rumour he took a bribe to swing a case."

"Your turn, Robert," said Peers, pointing to Wytton.

"My suggestion is he's been drug-trafficking."

"Even a false drug-trafficking charge would require hard evidence of some sort," said Peers, trying hard to be diplomatic. "I'm not quite sure it would fly."

Hamilton-Smith cleared his throat loud enough to get all of their attention. "Do you recall the robbery in East Castle Street? He was presiding over that trial when some of the exhibit money went missing. We could say there's evidence he stole it."

"What'd be the motive, on his salary?" asked Peers. "Greed?"

"Precisely," nodded Hamilton-Smith.

Peers sat back in his chair. "I prefer Adam's idea. Taking a bribe to swing a case sounds more plausible to me."

"Any case in mind?" asked Hamilton-Smith.

"I seem to recall that the defendants got off remarkably easy in the Waterloo Porn Trial," said Edgeson, taking his third custard cream of the afternoon.

"Does it have to be porn?" asked Peers, looking pained. "The press won't like it."

Edgeson laughed. "They'll love it."

Peers shook his head. "My in-tray is bulging with sex scandals. What about the trial of that SOAP officer? That was more recent."

"That officer went down fair and square in the public's eyes," said Nortly. "They wouldn't wear it. And what's more, Mentall disappeared before the trial had even ended."

"That was one of your officer's, wasn't it, Simon?" asked Edgeson, his voice rich with sarcasm. Nortly glared back at him with pursed lips.

"In the Waterloo Porn Trial," said Hamilton-Smith, "there was talk of a missing exhibit, a DVD or something. There was a suggestion he might have taken it himself. He's been on easy cases ever since."

"Let me make myself clear," Peers replied, "no sex scandals! Now, what's the other case you mentioned?"

"The East Castle Street robbery. Some of the exhibit money went missing from the court building."

"Is it possible Mentall actually took the money?" Peers wondered just what he'd inherited by becoming Home Secretary.

Hamilton-Smith shrugged. "It's not without the bounds of possibility."

Peers thought for a moment. "Let's go with that one."

"Very well." Hamilton-Smith nodded in agreement. "But we still need to find out where he is. Implying he's on the run from something dodgy in order to flush him out is one thing, but we still have no idea whether he's actually been kidnapped or murdered. And of equal pertinence," he continued, nodding in turn to each of the three chief constables, "You need to decide who precisely is going to lead the investigation."

"You could leave it to us to decide," said Wytton.

Peers stared around the room, wondering how a roomful of senior civil servants could remind him so much of the kindergarten his four-year-old son attended. "We'll decide at the next meeting," he concluded.

10

Mentall stirred in the early hours to the sound of feet running up the stairs. He stretched out his stiff legs then sat up and folded his arms to try and keep warm.

He heard the door to the landing click open. A few moments later the light, in the adjoining bathroom, was turned on and he froze with horror as he saw three figures advancing towards him. Each had a lady's stocking pulled tight over his head.

"Oh God no, please," he gasped in no more than a hushed whisper. He started to back away in utter panic. As the chain pulled tight around his ankle two of the figures stepped forward, grabbed his arms and then dragged him back to the centre of the room.

The third fumbled in his pocket and pulled out an orange-handled pair of kitchen scissors.

"No!" Mentall yelled.

"We no hurt you," replied the familiar voice of one of his captors. "We cut hair."

Mentall felt his heart rate drop back a few beats.

The two men, holding his arms, pressed down firmly until he sat still. He caught the whiff of stale alcohol from their sweaty bodies. The third man stepped forward, grabbed a clump of his hair and chopped it off with the scissors. Mentall tried to shake himself free but the men only tightened their grip. The 'barber' continued yanking and cutting clumps of his hair until he returned the scissors to his pocket and pulled out an electric razor. He switched it on and Mentall felt its cold, metal blade being pressed against his head.

The 'barber' drew the razor back and forth across his scalp until the man, holding Mentall's left shoulder spoke in his native tongue. The razor was then switched off and the men let go their grip and filed out the room. Mentall brushed his hands over his tingling scalp and face. His head felt cold and the short bristles tickled his fingers. A pile of hair laid to his left.

A few hours passed before he heard footstep on the stairs and people gathering on the landing. The bathroom door opened an

inch and a familiar voice called out, "Judge man, put bag on."
Mentall picked the hood up off the floor and pulled it over his head.
He then became aware of a number of people entering his room. He
felt the chain being undone then a multitude of hands lift him up.
His feet were pushed together and his ankles bound. The same was
then done to his wrists.

He was jostled out of the bathroom, half carried down the stairs
then pushed out through the front door. He was then shoved into
the rear footwell of a car and then ordered to keep his head down.
He started to shake and felt icy tendrils envelop his stomach.

The car doors were banged shut, the engine started and the car
accelerated away. His bound legs and arms felt cramped and the
back of his head felt every bump in the road. A ridge in the car's
floor poked into his shoulder blades and his right hip squeezed
uncomfortably against the front passenger seat.

They travelled for about half an hour before the car pulled up
and the front doors opened. Mentall felt his heart pounding inside
his chest. Was the severe haircut, and the removal of his distinctive
moustache, a ploy to make his body harder to identify?

The rear doors opened, Mentall was hauled up into the seat and
the hood was yanked off his head. The air smelt fresh and clear; a
notable improvement over his days of imprisonment. He blinked
and allowed time for his eyes to adjust to the bright daylight.

A middle-aged man was stood next to him holding the hood.
They had stopped in a deserted country lane. *Oh Christ,* he thought,
this is a quiet spot. He felt his heart begin to race and the blood
pounding in his ears.

"Are you going to kill me?" he blurted.

The man, whose facial features resembled that of a pig, stepped
back from the opened rear driver's door and shook his head. A deer
barked in a distant wood and a bird flapped in a hedgerow.

Through the front windscreen he made out a large, blonde,
heavily made-up, fifty-something woman wearing a brown, fake-fur
coat. She took a long drag on a cigarette before tossing it onto the
ground and stubbing it out with her foot. He then figured, with the
addition of a poodle and a cigarette holder, she could easily pass for

the type of woman he was more accustomed to meeting in a remote layby.

Mentall watched the man take a small bottle of Bells Scotch Whisky from his pocket, open it and then pour a generous measure into a Starbucks coffee cup. "Drink this," he said, holding the cup to Mentall's lips.

Mentall took a gulp, grimaced, coughed then spat. "That stuff tastes like gasoline."

"Come on drink it. We won't hurt you."

"I only drink single malts," scoffed Mentall.

The woman joined the man. "Try these," she said, taking a couple of pills from her purse and handing them to him.

"What are they?" he asked.

"Mirtazapine. Sleeping pills. They'll keep him quiet for a bit."

Mentall lifted his bound wrists and started to shake his head. But the man grabbed his chin, pulled down hard then pushed the pills onto his tongue. His head was then tipped back and the bottle was upended into his mouth. Mentall felt the whisky drench his tongue before it hit the back of his throat. He kecked then swallowed.

"That'll do," said the woman. "Better he doesn't stink too much of whisky." The man withdrew the bottle then slammed the rear door shut.

The couple got back into the front of the car. The man didn't look the brightest and, from what he'd seen and heard so far, the woman would hardly hold her own in a debating society. Mentall figured they were merely the next layer up in a highly organised criminal gang.

The man started the car and pulled back onto the road. Mentall gazed out of the window and attempted to memorise every feature they passed.

After a few minutes the car pulled up at a set of tall metal gates through which Mentall could see a curved gravel drive. The driver's window was lowered and, with a surveillance camera trained on his face, the man spoke into a microphone. The gates slid open, and the car pulled forward.

Mentall froze as he saw the woman take a vegetable knife from her bag. She leaned into the back of the car. "No," he yelled.

"Shut up," she hissed. "I'm only going to cut your bindings. Do as you're told and we won't harm you."

The car followed the drive to an imposing double-gabled, Victorian mansion house. His kidnappers got out and opened the rear passenger door. They both smiled gently at Mentall and helped him out.

"Take your time now, that's it," said the woman kindly.

"I don't need your help," scoffed Mentall. The cool air struck him and he stumbled then steadied himself against the car door. He shook his head to try and rid himself of the wooziness: the whisky and Mirtazapine were starting to kick in.

"Nice isn't it?" she said.

A weasel-like figure of a man walked down a slope leading from the front door to the driveway. An unfortunate hair transplant, to a continual receding hairline, had left an isolated tuft of thatch. With an outstretched arm he approached them.

"Mr and Mrs Pughes I presume? I'm Foster, Colin Foster."

"Sandra," said the woman, shaking Foster's offered hand.

"Jack," said the man, taking his turn.

"And you must be Mr Miles," Foster said, turning towards Mentall. "Welcome to the Smoking Chimneys Care Home." Mentall ignored the offered hand and tried to comprehend what the hell was going on.

A woman joined them from the direction of the front door. Foster introduced her as his wife, Ellie.

Mentall went to speak but Sandra Pughes caught the conversation.

"Now Dad, let's go inside."

Did she just call him *Dad*? Desperate to keep awake, he took a deep breath.

"Where are you taking me?" he demanded.

"Don't you remember what we talked about?"

"We never talked about anything."

"We've been through this a dozen times," Sandra replied, glancing at the Pughes. "We agreed it was for the best. You've been unwell, remember?"

Ellie smiled knowingly.

"We've agreed nothing," Mentall snapped.

"Now Dad, this is your new home," said Sandra, taking his arm.

Mentall shook her hand off and yelled, "You are not my *fucking* daughter!"

Sandra burst into tears and looked at Colin Foster, "See what *I* have had to put up with? It's been terrible these last few months, he doesn't even recognise his own daughter now, and he's become so angry and abusive."

"Yes, yes I do understand," said Colin Foster, patting her hand and offering her a paper tissue from his pocket. "This is common I'm afraid, we find our guests do improve once they have the stability of the care home but I'm afraid dementia is an irreversible process."

"He used to be so happy. He was such a good father – always taking me to the cinema and playing with me in the garden…" Sandra sobbed.

"My name is Stephen Mentall and I *am* a crown court judge," Mentall barked, fighting off the desire to lie on the ground and sleep.

"That's his latest fixation," sniffled Sandra. "Last week he was the prime minister now he's a crown court judge."

"I *am* a crown court judge," Mentall repeated.

"Now Dad, you're eighty-three, it's hardly likely you're a crown court judge is it?"

"That's because I'm sixty-three," Mentall blurted.

"He gets confused, 1963 was the year he married mum," said Sandra.

Colin Foster didn't appear in any mood to discuss ages and Mentall, having lived life to the full and been through a stressful divorce, knew he did look older than his years. Either way he couldn't make up his mind whether this weasel-faced idiot was in on this conspiracy or not. He took a chance and shouted, "These people have kidnapped me. The police will be looking for me."

Everybody but Mentall, exchanged a glance.

"Come now," said Ellie, taking his arm.

Mentall blinked and felt himself sway. The Mirtazapine wasn't all bad. In fact he was suddenly beginning to feel rather content.

He was led through the deep-set arched doorway with a level of courtesy and care at complete odds with his weeks in captivity. Faced with the cavernous Victorian entrance hall he took a deep breath; the smell of disinfectant was so strong he could taste it. The cream and red Victorian mosaic tiles echoed beneath his feet. The walls and ceiling were painted magnolia and the decorative detail of the cornicing, was highlighted in bright pink.

Ellie pointed out a large, gilt framed portrait of an imposing looking man. "That's our grandfather, Colinrick Thomas Kipling."

Sandra glanced at the painting. "He looks very stern."

"He *was*," Ellie replied. "Colin is really a Colinrick too, but you prefer Colin don't you love?"

"Definitely," Foster replied.

"This was the family home," continued Ellie. "Lots of our family have lived here, but Colin and I are the last of the line and three years ago we inherited it and converted it into a care home."

"So you're brother and sister then?" asked Sandra, smiling at the Fosters.

"No, husband and wife," Ellie replied.

Mentall yawned.

"But what about the same grandfather?" asked Sandra, looking confused.

"We are also cousins," explained Ellie with a slow nod and a smile.

"Inbreeds," Mentall whispered, feeling his eyes start to close.

"Dad!" said Sandra. She then turned towards the Fosters and added, "I'm so sorry about that."

Foster laughed and shook his head. "Please don't worry." He then pointed towards a half-opened door and added, "I'll show you the lounge."

Mentall followed the others into a high ceilinged room with tall sash windows. Pale faced residents sat motionless in high-back winged chairs; Mentall wondered if one or two of them might actually be dead. A fifty-two inch television was on autopilot in the corner.

47

"What was the fee you mentioned?" asked Jack as they left the lounge.

"Eight hundred a week," Foster replied, "payable monthly in advance but refunded, er… if there is cause to well er… terminate the contract during any one month."

Mentall felt the words echoing off the walls and penetrating his mind through a fuzzy haze. An old man shuffled by on a zimmer frame: he was well aware of what was meant by terminating a contract in this place.

"And you have the funds available to cover his stay?" asked Foster.

"Oh yes we've let his house, and Dad has a few savings too," said Sandra.

Mentall blinked rapidly and yawned. He tried to comprehend this. *They've let my house. This must be an extensive organisation to have faked the paperwork.*

"Let's show you to your room, Mr Miles," said Ellie.

They were led back out into the hall then to a room with a bed, a television, a nice view of the garden and an en-suite.

Mentall eyed the bed, longingly. "I'll just have a lie down, if you don't mind."

Jack turned to face Ellie. "You're fairly new to this game then?"

"Oh no," she replied. "This is actually the third care home I've ran. But we're really pleased to be back in the family home. We both love this area and feel the importance of engaging with the village. We encourage people to bring their pets in to visit the residents, and at Christmas time pupils from the local primary school call in to sing carols. That's always a popular afternoon."

Can't bloody well wait for that, thought Mentall. His head felt as if it was for ever sinking further into the pillow.

"Why the tall gates and fence then?" asked Jack.

Sandra shot him a glance.

"That's for security," said Foster. "You must remember our guests are vulnerable people. It stops them wandering off and undesirable types getting in. We thought it for the best after a gang of distraction burglars were targeting the elderly in Maston–"

"Shall we adjourn and let Dad sleep?" asked Sandra hurriedly.

So we are near Maston, thought Mentall, *she didn't want me to know that.* The voices were becoming ever fainter.

"Yes, we'll go to my office to complete a few formalities," Foster replied.

Mentall felt his body yield to sleep.

*

Sandra Pughes glanced around Foster's office then settled herself into a brown, leather armchair. She gave Jack an irritable glance as he slumped into an identical chair next to hers.

Foster parked himself in a green, button-backed swivel chair behind a desk and closed the lid on a laptop computer. "Are you happy with the room?" he asked. Before Sandra could answer she was distracted by shouting from the direction of the main entrance hall.

The door flew open and in burst a matronly, middle-aged woman.

"They are at it again," she yelled. "Oh sorry, Mr Foster," she continued, looking aghast, "I didn't realise you had company."

"That's quite all right Madge, always here in a crisis," said Foster, raising himself from his chair. He then directed his voice towards Sandra and her husband, "Please excuse me." Sandra and Jack, intrigued by what was going on, followed him and Madge out into the hall and met Ellie arriving from the direction of the kitchen.

An elderly man, bare legged and wearing a dressing gown, stood in the doorway to one of the bedrooms. An old lady, in an electric wheelchair, hurtled towards him. "No, no Mrs Syms," cried Madge, "and you should know better too Mr Handcross." She then turned towards Ellie, "You've got to stop them."

Ellie shook her head. "Give them a minute, we'll never get them to settle otherwise."

"Vroom, vroom," said Mr Syms.

Handcross leapt into the hall. Mrs Syms braked sharply. "Excuse me Ma'am, you're driving in excess of the speed limit," he said in an officious tone. "Do you have your driving licence?"

Mrs Syms rummaged around in her handbag, pulled out a bus ticket and handed it to Handcross. The old man inspected it, gave her a stern warning and waved her on. She went as far as the kitchen, swivelled her wheelchair around then headed back towards Mr Handcross.

"Excuse me Ma'am," he said leaping out in front of her again, "you're driving on the wrong side of the road. Can I see your logbook please?"

She dug around in her handbag, pulled out a diary and handed it to him. He examined it, gave her another warning and waved her on her way. She took off again up and down the hall weaving erratically. As she came to the old man's room for a third time he leapt out and opened his dressing gown revealing an age-defying erection. Mrs Syms, still in her wheelchair, screeched to a halt. At this point Madge and the Fosters flew forward.

"Stop them," yelled Madge.

"If the good officer Handcross says I must take the breathalyser test then that is what I *must* do," Mrs Syms said indignantly.

"Grab the fire extinguisher," Madge screamed, dragging Handcross to the ground. "I can't keep washing this uniform every time he gets it up."

"Which one?" asked Ellie.

"The water one, it's the red one," said Madge.

Madge pinned Handcross to the floor by his shoulders and chest. His skinny legs punched back and forth like a sewing machine. Ellie took aim.

"Now," yelled Madge.

Ellie squeezed the handle of the extinguisher. A jet of water sprayed into Handcross's groin.

"Has it done the job?" Madge asked, shaking her soaked arm.

Ellie peered down. "Yes, it's on the wane."

"Right, grab his legs."

And with that Handcross was bundled into his room and the door firmly closed behind him. Mrs Syms began to cry like a child called in when the game she was playing was just reaching its climax.

"Why don't you spend more time with Squadron Leader Jenkins?" asked Ellie.

"Mr Handcross *is* not a nice man," added Madge. "Squadron Leader Jenkins is a nice man, a perfect gentleman in fact."

"And he's had his prostate gland removed," said Ellie.

"Just my point," whispered Madge.

"My bottom set's come out," mumbled Mrs Syms fumbling with her teeth.

"Come on, let's get you to your room," said Madge softly.

Colin Foster returned to his office. Sandra followed with Jack trailing behind her.

"As I was saying," said Foster, forcing a weary grin, "we find people with dementia benefit from the surroundings here. We pride ourselves on the Victorian ambience of Smoking Chimneys. Its many original features give a sense of the past."

"We'll take it," said Sandra Pughes without hesitation.

*

"He's out for the count," said Foster, peering down at Mentall.

"Well he can't stay in here," said Ellie, "we've just had the room decorated."

She shook him by the shoulder. Mentall didn't even murmur. She rolled him to edge of the bed and, with her husband lining up a wheelchair, they slipped him onto the seat. Mentall's head tipped forward.

"That'll have to do," said Foster.

"It's almost as if he's been drugged," said Ellie, wheeling him out into the corridor. Foster followed and pulled the door to.

A dapper, elderly man stopped them.

"Oh heck," whispered Foster, "that's all we need, bloody Squadron Leader *Ginger* Jenkins."

"He looks a bit dopey," said Jenkins, tapping the wheelchair's footplate with his walking cane. "New boy is he?"

"Yes," Foster replied.

"Well, do the decent thing old boy. Introduce us," said Jenkins.

"I don't think he's quite ready for that," said Ellie.

Jenkins smoothed down his blazer, adjusted his Royal Air Force silk tie and offered a hand. "Jenkins, Squadron Leader Jenkins, but most people call me Ginger Jenkins."

"I really don't think–" started Ellie.

"Shy, is he?"

"You'll have other chances to get to know him," she said.

"What's the fellow's name?" asked Jenkins.

"Miles."

"Not Freddie Miles from RAF Merston?"

"No."

"Oh well, I'm sure I'll get to know him when he's sobered up. Mind you," continued Jenkins, lowering his voice, "the CO's doing his rounds. You'd better get him to bed. They're cracking down on this sort of thing."

"We'll do that," said Foster.

"Good show," Jenkins replied.

Foster slid open the door to the lift and Ellie wheeled Mentall in.

11

Jack braked sharply at the foot of Smoking Chimney's driveway. "Come on, come on," he huffed, staring at the closed gates and tapped his fingers on the steering wheel. "I don't want to become a resident of your bleeding care home too." Sandra clipped on the passenger seatbelt and sighed with irritation: the kind of sigh he'd become all too familiar with in their twenty years of marriage.

The gates slid back and he pulled his X-Type Jaguar out onto the country lane. Only when he reached the main road did he find the courage to speak to his wife again. "Well, that's the judge safely out of harm's way then."

"Don't bet on it," snarled Sandra. "And I can do without the cheery voice, thank you very much. I've just bought us some time, that's all."

Jack's stomach tightened: it always did when he was trying to pacify his wife. "It's a shame that Foster fellow let on the place is near Maston."

"You should've stopped him," snapped Sandra.

"How?" Jack snorted defensively.

"You could've changed the subject or something," said Sandra.

Jack took a sharp intake of breath and fished around for a reply. "I suppose there's no harm done. If he'd asked around he'd have soon found out."

Sandra stared out of the windscreen. "If he could get any sense out of that *crowd*," she muttered. "I was worried they'd give him a good slap for that inbred remark. If that's the state of the judiciary God help us all."

"Well it's a bit odd cousins marrying," said Jack. "Smoking Chimneys ain't the only thing they're *keeping* in the family." He then let out a laugh to test his wife's mood.

Sandra shook her head and took a boiled sweet from the glove box.

"I didn't know you'd rented his house," said Jack. "That gives us more time."

53

"I haven't let his house," Sandra replied with a hiss. "It was just a ruse to convince them that we're okay for funds."

"Oh."

"I don't even know where he bloody well lives. You are thick, Jack."

Jack thumped the accelerator and overtook a heavily-laden lorry. She always got the better of him in an argument.

"And there's no need to have a tantrum."

"I'm not having a bloody tantrum," hissed Jack.

"And why do you always have to be so disparaging of people? That Foster couple struck me as decent sorts, and you're now making wisecracks about inbreeds. There's nothing wrong with cousins marrying."

"I thought it was funny that's all," said Jack letting his speed slip back to the legal limit. "Nice room they gave him."

"Oh we're praising the Fosters now are we?"

"Well it was a nice room."

"Yes, yes it was a nice room. Perhaps he's the lucky one, in a nice room without anything to worry about. Nicer than my room at home."

"Our room," Jack replied cautiously.

"It's my room from now on," spat Sandra. "I've just about had it up to here with you Jack Pughes."

"Oh bloody hell," Jack protested. "And Wayne's home from the army tonight. Where am I going to sleep?"

"I think you're confusing me with somebody that gives a shit."

"But–"

"You can go in with Wayne," said Sandra, curling her upper lip. "I don't want you anywhere near me."

"It's not fair on Wayne."

"Well I'll go in with Wayne if that's bothering you," Sandra replied.

Jack squeezed the steering wheel. "What sleep with your own son?"

"Share a room is not quite the same as what your filthy mind is implying."

"But there's only one bed."

"We'll manage."

"There's bloody laws against what you're proposing," exploded Jack.

"Since when have you been concerned with what is and isn't the law? And let me make it *very* clear, you filthy little cretin, I ain't shagging my own son. Got it?"

"Yes," Jack replied.

"There's only one mother fucker in that house, and I'll tell you now Jack Pughes it isn't Wayne."

12

Aleksander, Krystyn and Tomasz, having just hitched the twenty miles into Albridge, sat in the central park swigging on Tesco own-brand cider and counting out their spoils.

"Four thousand pounds," said Tomasz, watching Aleksander tuck the money into an inside pocket of his jacket.

"Speak English," replied Aleksander. "We don't want trouble close to Brexit with people hearing we Polish."

"We go back to Krakow now?" asked Tomasz hopefully.

"We have one month until they make us leave. We make more money first then go home," replied Aleksander.

"How?" asked Tomasz, drawing in his eyebrows.

"From judge man's home. We go there and sell things."

"What!" said Krystyn, lowering his can of cider.

"Is it safe at his house?" asked Tomasz.

"Yes, TV said he lived alone," explained Aleksander.

"Where does he live?" asked Tomasz.

"We have address on driving license, and keys too," said Aleksander.

"Then we go home?" asked Krystyn, with almost childlike hope.

"Yes, if we make more money," replied Aleksander.

Tomasz nodded, clearly relieved.

"Let's look at video on judge man's phone again," said Krystyn.

Aleksander passed it to him and Krystyn flicked and tapped the screen then peered intently at it.

"You watch *Wet Girls Clam Up*?" asked Tomasz.

Krystyn nodded.

"*Amelia Rides Dolly* not working?" asked Aleksander.

"No, won't play."

"Amelia Rides Dolly," sighed Tomasz. "Wish I could see. Can we download?"

"Tried pornhub.com. Not there," said Krystyn.

"Let's try sex shop," said Aleksander, "perhaps judge man has DVD player at his house."

At the counter of the Albridge Adult Shop, and on a promise of a larger share of the payoff from the Pughes, Krystyn asked, "We want *Amelia Rides Dolly*."

"You want what mate?" asked the shopkeeper tugging his sweat-shirt down over his paunch. He was a young man, perhaps in his early thirties, with a fat round face, a scraggly beard and thick black hair tied back in a ponytail.

"Amelia Rides Dolly," Krystyn repeated.

"The dollies are over in the corner next to the handcuffs," he replied, pointing.

Aleksander followed the shopkeeper's outstretched arm. The shop was crowded with merchandise. He couldn't see any DVDs. "Films, we want films *Amelia Rides Dolly*."

"Never heard of it mate."

"You not have?"

"Nope."

"You order?"

The shopkeeper lazily picked up an iPad and tapped in the title with his stubby fingers. He looked at the screen for a few moments then shook his head. "No such film. They've got a whole bunch of Dolly Busters. We've got a couple of those. Doubt they're the Venus Awards one though."

"Where?" asked Aleksander.

"On the shelf, between the canes and the dildos," said the shop keeper, pointing.

"Did he say cocaine?" whispered Tomasz in his native Polish.

"You have cocaine?" asked Aleksander.

"Powder or rock?" asked the shopkeeper brightly.

*

They stepped out of the shop's musty interior onto the rain soaked concrete pavement slabs. Aleksander slipped the under-the-counter cocaine into his trouser pocket, tucked the DVDs inside his jacket and marched his protesting accomplices to the taxi rank across the road.

*

The cab, whose driver hadn't required any further explanation than a fist full of ten pound notes and a finger pointing at an address on a driving license, beat its way through the traffic. Pulling up on a crescent shaped driveway the three piled out and, as the taxi departed, Aleksander slipped the key into the lock.

"I'm not sure," said Tomasz.

"It'll be fine," replied Aleksander, "Judge man not here."

"What about the neighbours?" asked Krystyn.

Aleksander opened the door and kicked away a pile of post and takeaway flyers. "It's a detached house," he replied.

While Tomasz phoned for pizzas and a two litre bottle of Dr Pepper, Aleksander and Krystyn set up three lines of cocaine on the lounge carpet. After demolishing the pizzas and timing one another snorting the lines of coke, they watched their DVDs, had a night's sleep then proceeded to auction the contents of Mentall's house on eBay. With everything listed as a ninety-nine pence starting bid and 'Cash on Collection', the house was virtually clear within the week.

A few days later they disembarked from an easyJet flight and headed for downtown Krakow. With pockets crammed with money they convinced their friends, and every attractive woman they met in a bar, that indeed Britain had been the land of milk and honey.

Mentall became aware of a knocking on his bedroom door. He shook his head and tried to focus on where he was: the Mirtazapine was clearly good stuff.

"Come," he said.

A woman entered and placed a pale-blue cup and saucer on his bedside table. "Lovely cup of tea for you."

She walked across to the window and pulled back the curtains. Mentall cast his eyes down to her bottom and admired how it strained against the fabric of her light-pink tunic.

"Can you get yourself downstairs?" she asked.

"Downstairs? This room is downstairs."

"No, it's on the first floor."

It was then he noticed the paint was peeled, the carpet was rucked and the lampshade chipped. *Not the room I went to sleep in,* he thought.

"This is Smoking Chimneys?" he asked.

"Oh yes," she replied.

Mentall couldn't figure if this was good or bad news. Either way he was still a captive.

He decided to take a chance. "Listen you've got to help me," he said, then lowered his voice as if somebody was listening at the door, "I've been kidnapped."

"Of course you have, Mr Miles."

"I'm telling the truth," he protested. "I'm being held here against my will. I'm actually Judge Mentall."

"Yes, dear."

"I've been kidnapped."

"You drink up your tea now, and then I'll be back to help you down to breakfast."

"I'll manage," he sighed as she left the room. Given the circumstances his real name appeared to be more of a hindrance than a help.

He slid his legs onto the bedroom floor, picked up the cup and gulped back the lukewarm tea. He then hauled himself up and stepped out onto the landing. The bare walls were painted a bright white and the carpet had an industrial look about it. He ran his hand over the solid mahogany bannister rail then made his way downstairs. A domestic wheeled a Henry vacuum cleaner across the mosaic tiled floor. He tried the front door, but it was locked.

"Good morning, Mr Miles," said Foster, emerging from his office and greeting him with a rather limp handshake. "I trust you slept well."

"You've got a locked fire escape there," gruffed Mentall, pointing to the green sign above the door.

"Never mind that. The breakfast lounge is through there," said Foster, pointing in the general direction of the dining room.

Patronising weasel-faced idiot, thought Mentall, seething with the indignity. Figuring he needed sustenance he followed the direction of Foster's arm. Five fried eggs, seven sausages and a couple of rounds of toast later he decided to explore the house.

It was a standard Victorian layout, typical of the glebe houses his fellow masons liked to acquire: a grand hall and staircase for the guests and a narrow back stairway for the servants. In the hall some of the original wood panelling had been removed to make way for the lift. Mentall turned his back and grumbled, "They've made a bloody mess of that."

An elderly lady, using a stick shuffled towards him. She wore a pink quilted dressing gown over a white nightie and her hair, perched on a rotund, lined face, was a wavy grey.

"What did you say, sonny?" she asked.

"It was of no concern of yours," he replied.

As she came to within a yard of him she fixed him with a stare and asked, "Did you know Brian?"

"Don't mind our Mrs Somerbee," said a voice from somewhere behind him, "she's a harmless old thing, always asking if you knew her husband."

Mentall turned to the direction of the voice and there stood a well turned out gent with a neat moustache and thin mousy hair.

"Jenkins, Squadron Leader Jenkins, but most people call me

Ginger Jenkins," announced the man. He thrust his hand into Mentall's. Mentall presumed he'd once been ginger-headed but decided to not let that sway him. Instead he was relieved to meet a man of sanity and education; his voice was public school, one of his own type.

"You're a new boy. Fancy a cup of tea then?" enquired Jenkins.

"Yes," Mentall replied rather quickly.

"My room then, fifteen hundred hours," said Jenkins.

*

Mentall used the rest of the morning to explore the grounds. In the rear garden he took a look at an old wooden shed which had a door facing away from the house. He tugged on the handle, opened the door and stepped in. It smelt musty and was stacked with trestle tables and white plastic garden chairs. *Nothing there,* he thought before stepping out and pushing the door shut. He crossed the lawn towards a fence and stopped at an overgrown flower border. He reached across to the twelve foot high, diamond lattice fence and gave it a tug: droplets of rain water sprinkled his face. He jammed the toe of his right shoe into one of the holes and tried to haul himself up. His foot slipped out and he fell heavily onto his backside.

He listened to the distant clatter of a freight train and the hum of traffic on a nearby road: Maston had a railway station and he figured he now knew the direction.

He got back to his feet and walked around the edge of the grounds, occasionally giving the fence another tug. When he reached the driveway he rattled the main gates: they barely moved. On the other side was the entry phone system.

He reached through and pressed the call button. The speaker crackled for a moment before a soft voice answered, "Hello." He recognised Ellie Foster.

"Laundry," said Mentall, trying to sound like a gruff workman.

"Mr Miles, come away from the gates. I can see you on the security camera. And don't try climbing the fence either, you've triggered the motion detectors."

"Blast," said Mentall, looking up to the camera he had missed.

*

When three p.m. came Mentall positioned himself outside Sqn Ldr Jenkins DFC's door, knocked and waited.

"Come in, come in, and take a seat," said Jenkins, opening the door and revealing a room crowded with antique walnut furniture.

"It's good to meet you," began Mentall, sinking into a Bergere chair, "not many of our types in here."

"Not many of our types left full stop," Jenkins replied, "the upper sets are dying out or inbreeding with the lower middles. It's ruined the country."

"I couldn't agree more," Mentall replied.

"Though I have heard," said Jenkins with a twinkle in his eye, "there's still a breeding pair in South Buckinghamshire."

"Quite," Mentall replied. He glanced at an array of wooden photo frames on a chest of drawers. "Family pictures?" he asked.

"Yes. I'm the only one left," Jenkins replied. "Nobody to care for me in my dotage," he added with a mischievous grin.

"I'm sorry to hear that," said Mentall. "Is that you by the Spit-fire?"

Jenkins looked puzzled.

"The photo on the far left," added Mentall.

"Yes, taken at Tangmere in forty-three."

Mentall stood and surveyed the photos then looked around the room. An elaborate map, depicting the extent of the British Empire in 1889, was hung above a bed and an oil painting of a Spitfire in a dog fight, graced the far wall. *Those were the days*, thought Mentall.

"Did you see much active service?" asked Mentall, not quite believing Jenkins's age really qualified him for service in the Second World War.

"Fair bit. I was late for the Battle of Britain but still had a few pops at Jerry over the Channel. It was a good life. Had my own room and a batman."

"Did you really?"

"Yes, didn't get that again until I came in here," he replied, glancing round his room. "Did you have a woman to do for you?"

"I'm sorry?" Mentall replied, aghast. He wondered how Jenkins could possibly have known about Madam Suzie's House of Pleasure: unless he had been a regular too. Mentall always made a point of not catching the eye of fellow clientele, and he somehow doubted even Petronella could get this old boy back into active service. Either way he didn't want it getting around.

"Before you came in here," clarified Jenkins, "did you have a woman to come in? Carers?"

"Oh, oh I see," Mentall replied with relief. "No, straight in of my own accord."

"Your wife still alive then?" asked Jenkins.

"We're divorced I'm afraid," said Mentall, returning to his chair.

"That's nothing to be afraid of. Mine clung onto me until her last bloody breath. Though my carers were first rate, very kind. Miss them dearly, especially Liliana, the Polish one. She had a twin sister, she was Polish too."

"Right," Mentall replied, beginning to doubt Jenkins's sanity.

"Never talked about the war, mind. Said it was all in the past. Strange lot the Poles. The Mediterranean climate I suppose."

Mentall decided not to question this.

"Madge brought us some tea," he added, nodding towards a plastic tray decked out with paper doilies, pale blue cups and a black teapot. "Can you pour? I tend to slop it around a bit."

"Certainly," Mentall replied, grasping the handle of the teapot.

"What were you as a young man?" asked Jenkins.

"I was a barrister," Mentall replied, pouring the tea.

"Oh very good. Though I've heard the legal profession is full of Yids now."

"I wouldn't say that," said Mentall, trying to hide a smile.

"Jew boys then?" Jenkins replied.

"No, I mean you, I mean we, are not allowed to use such language now," said Mentall.

"Oh, what's wrong with it?" asked Jenkins.

"Well for better or worse, we are no longer allowed to use derogatory racial terms."

"Is that my tea?" asked Jenkins, pointing at a cup Mentall had just poured.

"Yes."

"Looks a bit strong."

"They were a bit jewy with the milk," Mentall replied before knocking back his tea and glancing at his watch. "I'd better be getting along."

"You off already?" Jenkins replied.

"Yes, one or two things to attend to," Mentall replied. Seeing the disappointment on Jenkins's face he added, "What'd you say to a sortie around the grounds this evening?"

Jenkins's eyes became distant and he turned his head towards the oil painting of the Spitfire. "Look out Johnny Bandits at one o'clock, Angels at three," he said excitedly.

Mentall emptied his lungs with one breath, slapped both knees with his hands and stood to leave.

"Of course that was in 1951 when my father was a lesbian," said Jenkins.

Mentall let himself out of the room and headed down the corridor.

*

Mentall visited the dayroom, slumped himself into a wingback chair and surveyed the scene. A middle-aged couple were fussing over an elderly man with a shock of thick white hair. The woman was thin and wore no makeup and the man had sloped shoulders on which hung a beige jacket. The walls were covered in cheap art, a television played to itself and the place stank of disinfectant.

When the visitors got ready to leave Mentall stood and greeted them. "Excuse me. Do you have a mobile phone? My battery's dead and I need to call a taxi."

"There's no signal here," said the woman.

"And that's on any of the networks," added the man. "We did get uncle a phone, but this place is in a dip."

Mentall figured this was a moot point: the old boy didn't look capable of using a phone. "Well, could you give me a lift to Maston station then?" he asked.

The woman shot her husband a glance. "We're not going that way."

"Which way are you going?" Mentall persisted.

"Albridge," replied the woman.

"That'll do, that's where my train's for," Mentall replied.

He followed them out to their Vauxhall Insignia. The woman furrowed her brow and reluctantly opened a rear door for him. He scrambled in. *Nicely done,* he thought, clipping on a seatbelt.

The man reversed the car out of the parking space and then set off down the drive. The gates slid back and the car pulled out onto the side road.

"Who were you visiting?" asked the woman.

"My mother, she's ninety-six," Mentall replied.

"Good innings," said the man.

"It's hard when they become infirm," said the woman, "though easier once they are in a home."

As the car took to the main road Mentall nodded and they fell silent. He watched the trees flicker by and wondered whether to tell them who he really was. He decided to keep quiet. No need to complicate the situation.

"There's a police car, flashing us to stop," said the man.

"What?" asked the woman sounding shocked.

He pulled up before a roundabout and switched on the car's hazard warning lights.

Mentall turned his head and watched a female police officer approaching their car. *Stroke of luck,* he thought.

The police officer tapped on the driver's window. The man lowered it and she asked, "Have you just visited the Smoking Chimneys care home?"

The man confirmed they had.

"Is this gentleman with you?" she asked, nodding towards Mentall.

"Well, he only asked us for a lift. Is there a problem officer?"

"The proprietor of the home has reported that a resident left with you."

"Oh dear," said the man.

"We haven't abducted him," said the woman sounding worried.

"Don't worry ma'am, I don't believe for a moment you have. There's not much ransom payable on an eighty-three year old."

The man turned his head and looked at Mentall. "He doesn't look it."

Mentall unclipped his seatbelt and then stepped out of the car.

The police officer noted the couple's details. "Purely routine," she said. She then waved them off and steered Mentall towards the police car. Placing a hand on his head she guided him into the rear passenger-side seat.

A male officer, with his hands on the steering wheel, turned his head and spoke to Mentall. "You've been a naughty boy then?"

"I didn't want to cause a fuss in front of that couple," began Mentall, "but actually I'm Judge Stephen Mentall."

"Really, sir?" he replied, glancing at his colleague slipping into the seat beside him.

"Oh yes," Mentall replied.

The police car circled the roundabout and headed back down the main road.

"We're heading away from Albridge," said Mentall.

"We'll soon have you safely back," said the female officer.

"But *I am* Stephen Mentall."

"Of course you are, sir," replied the male officer then added, in a low whisper for the benefit of his colleague, "He probably saw the news about that judge's disappearance and has got himself confused."

"I'm not bloody confused," shouted Mentall, "I *am* Judge Stephen Mentall."

"We believe you, sir. We'll soon have you back home."

Mentall thumped the headrest of the female officer. She turned to him and said, "Now *you* just stop that." She then picked up her radio, "M2GW this is U5. Have collected eighty-three year old male believed to be Mr Miles. Now on route to the Smoking Chimneys care home. Please call and advise the proprietors that their resident is becoming distressed and angry. Advise they have a team on standby pending our arrival. ETA three minutes."

"Roger that," came the reply.

"Over and out," replied the officer.

"Look," Mentall protested, "I was kidnapped during the trial of your colleague, Edward Sawman. I was held by a bunch of Eastern European plumbers before being transferred to Smoking Chimneys."

"Humour him," whispered the male officer.

"That's right," said the female officer, "we're freeing you now. That couple who gave you the lift were in on it too."

"No they bloody weren't," barked Mentall. "They were just some couple visiting their aged uncle."

"We'll soon have you home."

Mentall slumped back into his seat. *Bloody cretins*, he thought.

*

The police car turned off the main road and headed back down the country lane towards Smoking Chimneys. Colin Foster was stood at the open gates and waved them through. As they pulled up at the entrance to the house Mentall noticed Ellie and Madge waiting for them. Ellie opened his door and began to guide him out the car.

"Get your hands off me," yelled Mentall.

"I'm sorry about this," said Ellie to the police officers. "We are pretty tight on security here, not sure how it happened."

"He span them a yarn about needing a lift to Albridge," said the female police officer.

"Did he now," Ellie replied.

"I *am*," shouted Mentall with full force, "Stephen Mentall."

Foster approached from the direction of the gates. "Madge, get a sedative."

Ellie and Colin grabbed hold of his arms and bustled him into the hallway. He tried to break free but the police officers followed on and wrestled him to the floor. He saw Madge coming towards him with a wicked-looking syringe. Mentall felt a sharp pain in his left buttock, and within moments his eyelids grew heavy and he felt his body relax.

14

Home Secretary, Toby Peers looked nervously along the conference table at the former chief constables, of the defunct Eastshire, Northshire and Westshire Constabularies. He hoped they would be more grown up than they were at the last two meetings. "Let's begin with item one on the agenda," he began.

"On past experience," said Hamilton-Smith, representing the National Crime Agency, "I suggest we begin with item two."

Peers gazed at him blankly. "Item one—"

"The Chief Constable's secretary," said Nortly.

"Told you," said Hamilton-Smith, smiling thinly.

"What! Oh for God's sake," said Peers, "let me guess. It's a civilian post, and you made the other two redundant. I've sanctioned three offices, each one needs a secretary, and you can't sort it out amongst yourselves *because you need* my permission to hire two more."

"That's it!" said Nortly.

"Oh for God's sake," said Peers. "Hire two more."

"Well, there's a snag," said Wytton.

"What shag—" Peers made a show of clearing his throat, then looked around innocently. "I mean snag?"

"If we hire two more," said Wytton, "the two we made redundant could sue for unfair dismissal. To make somebody redundant you have to prove their job has disappeared. It's the law."

"I can't face any more industrial tribunals," said Nortly. "This tri-force merger has thrown up too many for my liking."

"Then re-instate the two you made redundant," said Peers curtly.

"Can't do that," said Wytton resting his cup of coffee back into its saucer.

"Why not?" asked Peers.

"Her Majesty's Customs and Excise takes a dim view of tax-free redundancy payments followed by reinstatement. It'll be seen as a tax-free bonus."

Peers took a sharp intake of breath. "Well ask these ladies – I assume they are ladies – to repay their redundancy money then."

"They won't go for that!" said Wytton. "They're all members of Unison. The only way round this is for the force to pay the tax."

Peers dropped his head into his hands. "And I suppose you need *me* to sanction that?"

"It'd be helpful – it'd save having to justify it to the commissioner."

"There is only one commissioner isn't there?" asked Peers cautiously.

"Well," said Nortly, "until the next election we still have three, but two of them are on gardening leave."

"Good! I couldn't face explaining it three times," Peers replied. "Okay item two, how are we getting on locating Judge Mentall?" He paused and looked around at the blank faces. "You *are* looking for him aren't you?"

"Well–" began Wytton.

"Have you even visited his house?" asked Peers. He had a sinking feeling about where this was heading.

"His house is on Northshire's patch," said Wytton.

Peers closed his eyes and let his left arm flop onto the table. "Look, you're *all* one force now." He stabbed a finger at Nortly. "You can't expect Simon to have instigated a visit to Mentall's house just because it's on his old patch."

"Thank you," Nortly replied.

"Do you even know his address?" asked Peers.

"Yes," said Wytton, flicking through some notes, "it's Three Oak Hill Drive, Albridge."

Nortly took a sharp intake of breath and shuffled uneasily on his seat.

"Something the matter, Simon?" asked Peers, looking concerned.

"Nothing," Nortly replied, recalling his recent visit to that address to collect a garden strimmer he'd bought for ninety-nine pence, on eBay.

"Right, well make sure somebody visits that address," said Peers. "Item three, based on what we agreed at the last meeting, is how are we going to publicise he is suspected of stealing exhibit money from the East Castle Street trial?"

"Can I suggest," said Edgeson, "we make a press release? That the evidence to this effect had just come to light and this is why he's made a dash for it. Then the press will have a field day and make up what they want. The least we say the better."

Peers looked around the room and watched his colleagues nod. "Very well, let's hope that flushes him out then," he said, raising his eyebrows and sighing. "I'll prepare the press release and leave it to Shire Force to call a press conference. The final item is to decide which one of *you three* is going to investigate whether he's kidnapped, in hiding or murdered."

Hamilton-Smith reached into his briefcase and retrieved a small cloth bag. Thumping it onto the table he explained, "It has three balls in it."

"You *are* joking," said Peers incredulously.

"What colours are they?" asked Nortly.

"White, red and black, they're snooker balls," Hamilton-Smith replied. "Toby, you can choose who has which colour."

"Very well," sighed Peers, "we'll have white for Robert, red for Adam and black for Simon. Bertie, you draw."

Hamilton-Smith drew out a rather battered cue ball. "Westshire it is."

"Let me see that bag," said Nortly.

"What?" asked Hamilton-Smith, rather surprised.

"How do I know you've not got three white balls in there?"

Hamilton-Smith upturned the bag and a red ball and a black ball rolled out.

"We'll meet again in seven days," said Peers.

*

A no-news day was selected for the press conference. Abuzz with speculation and activity, mobile phones were left open to editors. The story was sent shooting to newsfeeds, twenty-four hour news channels and the front pages of newspapers. Speculation as to Judge Mentall's whereabouts had long since withered but this new revelation had the entire country chattering. The press delved into his past, the search was on. 'Just where is the disgraced judge?' asked

The Daily Express. The Sun had probed further and gave the country, 'My night with kinky Judge Stephen and how he sent me down', and the Daily Star led with, 'Bishop's daughter in tits out garden party.'

*

Toby Peers groaned when he saw the front pages. "I was trying to avoid a sex scandal," he complained during a telephone conversation with Hamilton-Smith.

15

Detective Sergeant Tadler's desk phone rang with an ear piercing shrill. "Why does it always do that right at the end of my shift," he huffed. He reached across his desk for the handset and knocked over a mug of coffee. "Bollocks," he said, lifting the receiver to his ear.

"What did you say?" barked a voice from the other end of the line. Tadler's heart sank. He was in no doubt that his boss, Detective Chief Inspector Marjorie Stainthwaite, didn't particularly rate him, but now he'd just gone and put his foot in it again.

"Oh, sorry Ma'am," he stumbled into the mouthpiece.

"I expect better language from one of *my* officers, I could have been a member of the public."

"Sorry, Ma'am," said Tadler, wishing that she was in fact a member of the public.

"Can you make an appointment in my office?"

"When?"

"Now if it's not too much trouble."

"It's nearly the end of my shift," he replied. The following silence led him to the inevitable, "Okay." He raised himself from his chair and used the last page of a crucial witness statement to wipe dripping coffee from his arm.

As he turned towards the door admin assistant, nineteen-year-old Niky Smith, glanced up from her desk. "Horse Face?" she asked. Tadler nodded and made his way out into the corridor and up the stairs. Stainthwaite was waiting in the doorway to her office. She looked him up and down then beckoned him in.

"Take a seat Peter, take a seat," she said, employing the force wide patronising technique Tadler was only too aware of. He settled himself on the opposite side of her desk. Uneasy in the company of Marjorie Stainthwaite he viewed her: about forty-five, a long face, sticky out ears, a protruding chin and a mouth housing an impressive set of teeth. *Horse Face* indeed thought Tadler, smiling inwardly at Niky Smith's latest nickname for Stainthwaite.

He looked down at her desk: a laptop, mobile phone and a tray of coffee were so spotlessly clean they could have just stepped out of a catalogue.

"How are the family?" she asked, forgetting Tadler's wife had booted him out and moved her lover, a convicted felon, in.

"You tell me," gruffed Tadler.

"Oh I'm sorry," Stainthwaite replied, using a tone Tadler recognised from the force training video on dealing with distressed staff.

"Any contact?" she asked, raising her eyebrows.

"Not for a while now," Tadler replied, shaking his head mournfully. His shabby bedsit wasn't really setup for family life.

She lifted the coffee pot. "Coffee?"

"Thanks," said Tadler.

She poured him a cup, added milk and slid it across the desk towards him. She then straightened herself and looked him in the eye. "Have you read about the Mentall case?"

"What mental case?" asked Tadler wondering who she was referring to.

"Judge Stephen Mentall."

"Oh," he replied, adjusting his seating position to pacify a rather painful haemorrhoid.

"The Chief Super has been sat on by the Chief Constable."

"I'm very sorry to hear that, Ma'am."

"No, Sergeant Tadler," she replied with a sigh, "the Chief Constable–"

"Which one, Ma'am?"

"Our one, Westshire. He has instructed the Chief Super who has asked me to take a look at the case. It appears his disappearance has now to be viewed as suspicious. Previously it was felt he had just left to start a new life… he'd had certain family problems." Stainthwaite paused for a breath of emphasis and cast a mock look of understanding towards Tadler. "But," she continued, "the newspaper reports suggest he has been a bit of a rogue and gone into hiding."

"Shouldn't it be a case for Northshire?" asked Tadler, replacing the coffee cup on her desk. "After all he disappeared on their turf during the trial of one of their boys?"

"We are now one force, Sergeant. One territory."

Tadler felt a heavy heart, he knew what was coming. 'CDE' – Career Dead End. This kind of case should be managed at DCI level, or above, but transferring it to a lower rank meant only one thing – 'THTH' – Too Hot To Handle. He then imagined her as a horse, grazing in a field then he imagined a stallion approaching from the rear.

Her mobile phone vibrated on the desk. She glanced at the screen and killed the call. "And," she continued, "this will be a chance for you to show your leadership skills in the new force structure."

"Shire Horse, Ma'am."

"What Sergeant Tadler?"

"I mean Shire Force. Shire Police Force," Tadler replied hastily correcting himself.

"Good, that's what I thought you said," Stainthwaite replied, while eyeing him with suspicion.

Tadler knew if he didn't accept this path of opportunity she'd resort to threats about his future career.

"Also," she continued, "with the force merger there will be some interesting opportunities coming up."

"All right," said Tadler in resigned tones. The passive threats of non-compliance were all too familiar with his marriage. "Is it on the computer?"

"Not yet," Stainthwaite replied, "I need to be sure it's a real case before I'll sanction putting it on the *computer*."

She took a beige A4 document wallet from the top drawer of her desk and handed it to him. "It's mainly newspaper accounts, nothing really concrete apart from some interviews with the last people to have seen him."

"Very well, Ma'am," he replied, trying to shake off the image of a stallion shire horse. He couldn't help but think he was the mule straining for the carrot, which brought further ghastly images to mind.

"Apparently the Chief Constable has asked you check out his house first. The address is in the folder."

"Thanks," said Tadler, just managing to get the final throes of the stallion out of his mind.

Tadler returned to his office, dumped the case file on his desk, collected his jacket, drove home and picked up his post.

Slumped down on his brown, dralon fabric armchair he pulled his smartphone from his trouser pocket and began to flick through Facebook. He read a post tagging his ex-wife out on the town with some of the wives of his ex-drinking buddies: the very women who had put the kibosh on his Saturday nights out for fear his new found singlehood might lead their husband's astray.

He tore open the latest letter from her solicitor and read another list of demands and veiled threats. She was working him like a puppet by proxy and now Stainthwaite was pulling on all his strings too.

He shook his head at the latest demand for alimony. They'd cottoned on to his promotion and were wanting a slice of that too. And to emphasise the insult they were now citing his long hours, which had got him the promotion, as a reason for the irrecoverable breakdown of the marriage.

He cracked open a can of beer, cursed as it frothed and dribbled down his hand and then read on.

His complaint about her infidelity was now described as 'sought comfort in another man during her husband's frequent absences'. *Nice way to describe shagging a felon,* he thought.

He downed his can of beer, then another and another until he felt himself slipping off to sleep.

At four a.m. he woke to the heart thumping shrill of his smartphone. He tapped its screen and raised it to his ear. "What?"

"Oh what number is that?" asked the caller.

"Who is this?" asked Tadler.

"James."

"James who?"

"James Smethurst."

"Never heard of you, you just woke me up," Tadler replied.

"Why did you pick it up if you didn't recognise the number?"

"I was bloody half asleep."

Smethurst hung up.

Tadler, after no further sign of sleep, flicked on a light and noted Smethurst's name and the number on the back of his latest fag packet.

16

At nine a.m. Detective Sergeant Tadler drummed his fingers on his office desk and sighed. He looked through the file that his boss, DCI Marjorie Stainthwaite, had given him about some crown court judge having done a runner. So what? If he had been kidnapped surely his captors would have made contact by now. As he flicked through the pages he felt himself start to drift off to sleep. He pulled himself up straight rather too quickly and upset a mug of coffee over the file.

"Shit and blast," said Tadler.

"All not well, Sarge?" asked Niky Smith, looking up from her computer screen. "That's two cups over the desk in two days."

"About the only pair of cups I'll get anywhere with these days," he replied.

"Sarge!"

"Sorry."

"You should try some internet dating if you feel like that. You're a bit bitter and twisted, a date or two might lighten you up."

"It's just this bloody case," he continued, attempting to mop up the coffee. "No clues and if I don't solve it I'm for the high jump. And I don't think I'll make somebody a very good boyfriend – I didn't make much success of being a husband. Who's going to go for a guy living in a shabby bedsit and driving around in a thirty year old BMW he bought on eBay?"

"You never know. If you dyed your hair back to its natural brown colour, lost a couple of pounds and had a professional photo taken you might get them beating a path to your door."

Tadler screwed up his forehead. "You really think so?"

"It worked for my granddad."

"Thanks for that, Niky," Tadler replied curtly.

This was a new revelation to him: he'd always thought of himself as well-built with a full head of hair. He did enjoy working in the same office as Niky but sometimes she did lack tact. It was okay for her: with those bright blue eyes and curvaceous figure she didn't have any problems getting hitched up.

"You never know what's around the corner," she replied. "Any idea why the judge might have disappeared?"

"Nope, nobody else has either that's why I've been landed with it."

"Tried asking his family?"

"Worth a try I suppose," he replied. He then went through the Nescafe dripping pages and found the address of Mentall's wife, called directory enquiries then dialled her.

"Jennifer Mentall how can I help you?" came the reply from the other end of the phone.

"Are you the wife of Judge Stephen Mentall?"

"No, ex-wife. And before you ask, no he isn't here." And she slammed the phone down.

Tadler hit the redial button and the phone was answered after one ring.

"I'm fed up with you press," said Jennifer Mentall.

"Hold on, I'm a police officer, madam."

"Oh. You're the first to call me. And before you ask I haven't seen him recently and barely at all since our divorce came through. Even when we were married we saw each other infrequently."

"I'm sorry, any reason?"

"Well not that's it your business but spending time together was playing havoc with our marriage."

Tadler snorted out a laugh. "I'm just trying to get some background. Build up a picture. May I come and see you?"

"When?" asked Jennifer Mentall, with a distinct note of caution.

"Now, if possible?"

"Yes, all right then. Do you have the address?"

"Yes."

"It's a bit tricky to find, I'm tucked away so you–"

"Don't worry I'll find it. I'm a policeman after all."

Tadler spent forty-five minutes cruising the one-way system while glowering at the pool car's Sat-Nav. Conceding defeat he drove up the ramp of a multi-storey car park and headed for the one remaining parking space.

"Bastard," yelled Tadler as he was beaten to it by a battered old blue Ford Focus.

The driver leapt out and flicked the V sign.

Tadler pressed a button on the car's radio and spoke. "PNC check on a Ford Focus registration number, LV53MMV."

"Identify yourself," asked a voice from the radio.

"DS1553 Tadler."

"Password?"

"Moonraker."

"One moment."

"That vehicle is registered to an Edward Lovering, 73 Damegarten Rise."

"Thanks."

The line went quiet then, after a call to directory enquiries, an electronic voice announced, "The number you require is 442177." He noted this in his pocket book along with a brief description of Lovering.

Tadler continued around the car park and, on reaching the roof, spotted the one remaining space. A concrete post, multi-coloured by years of being scraped, made for a narrow bay. After a succession of forward and backward manoeuvres, accompanied by the acrid, sweet smell of a protesting clutch, he cut the engine, got out the car and proceeded on foot. He flipped open his smartphone and used Google Maps to locate Jennifer Mentall's house. He pressed the bell push and she immediately opened the door. She was elegant, in her mid-fifties, but if this was what Niky meant by something just around the corner he could give it a miss.

"Come through into the lounge and take a seat Sergeant…"

"Tadler, madam. Nice place you've got here," he said, glancing around the room before lowering himself onto a two-seater leather sofa.

Jennifer took a seat in a bottle green wing backed chair directly opposite him. "It's the best I could manage after the divorce."

"Oh, I'm sorry…"

"Don't be," she snorted. "I'm well shot of Stephen and if he's done a runner then the world is a better place without him. He could be playing a round of golf with Lord Lucan for all I care."

"So you've not really been in touch with him?"

"No, the odd family event. We have two daughters." Tadler's heart lifted, perhaps Niky was right and there was something around the corner.

"Three grandchildren too," she said proudly.

"Both married are they?" asked Tadler.

"Yes, Veronica is married to a Group Captain in the RAF and Philippa to a chief superintendent in your line of business."

"Oh, that's a shame." said Tadler, feeling his heart sink.

"I don't follow you, Sergeant."

"Oh, I mean such a shame you can't all be together. One happy family," Tadler hastily replied.

"Happy family! That'd be the day. Anyhow I'm not sure I can be of much help to you," she replied.

"When did you last see him?" asked Tadler.

"About five months ago, at Rupert's christening. That's my youngest grandchild."

"Do you have any photos of him?"

"Yes, on the sideboard."

Tadler followed her glance to the highly polished walnut cabinet. "No, I meant your husband, not little Rupert."

"No. I left them all behind when we divorced. He always took the photographs, never let me use anything technical. Anyhow it suits me not to have a picture rubbing shoulders with him."

"I see," said Tadler.

"I'd have thought you'd have lots of photographs anyhow, Sergeant."

"We do, we do, but they all show him in his capacity as a judge. Do you have one of him doing something he enjoyed outside of work? We find the personal touch gets a better result from the public."

"No, sorry, I'm afraid I'm not being much help. Oh wait a minute, I might have something," she said standing up and heading towards a walnut veneer bureau. She spent a few moments rifling through a drawer.

"Ah here we are," she said handing Tadler an A4 sheet with an inkjet photograph on it.

"It's not a very good picture," said Tadler.

"Well it's got him in it," she replied.

"I mean it's not very clear. What's the background for this photo?"

"It's a brothel, taken with a long range telephoto lens by my private detective. That's why I divorced him."

"I was actually meaning the background for having the photo taken," Tadler replied, "but I think I get the picture." He stood to leave. "Perhaps if you hear of anything you could phone me?" he asked, taking a card from his pocket and offering it to her.

"Yes, I will Sergeant. I'll see you out."

*

Tadler drove to Mentall's house, walked around the overgrown grounds and, by cupping his hands around his eyes, peered through the lounge window.

"Can I help you?" came a voice from behind him. It was a woman, and her tone was accusatory.

Tadler stopped peering, straightened himself, turned and faced a ferocious looking woman in a mauve tweed twinset.

"Do you have permission to be on these grounds?" she asked.

"I'm a police officer, madam," said Tadler. He enjoyed watching her manner change.

"Margaret Wainscott-Bruce," she said offering a hand, "chair of the local neighbourhood watch."

I bet you are, thought Tadler.

"Are you looking for our judge?" she asked.

"I'm just checking out his house for any signs of life."

"I'm surprised you lot haven't been here before," she said.

Tadler was surprised too.

"Any idea when the house was emptied?" he asked.

"Emptied?" she asked, sounding rather surprised.

"Yup, the place is bare."

Margaret Wainscott-Bruce placed a green wellie on a forget-me-not and steadied herself against the windowsill.

"My word," she said, "the place's been cleaned out."

"When did you last check the property?" asked Tadler, knowing she'd be more expansive on the back foot.

"Well, we don't do that as a policy."

"But you knew he'd disappeared?"

"Well, yes but we only look out for suspicious behaviour."

Tadler wondered what might be more suspicious than a house being cleared after the occupier had disappeared.

"You didn't see any removal vans at the property?"

"No."

"No smaller vans, tradesmen or the like?"

"No, but I have been away."

"What dates were you away?" asked Tadler, flipping open his pocketbook.

"Between the fifth and the fifteenth."

Tadler made a note.

"And who was keeping an eye out then?" he asked.

"How do you mean?"

"Well which other neighbours are in your local neighbourhood watch team?" he asked, looking up from his pocketbook.

Wainscott-Bruce paused and Tadler sensed this was going to be good.

"Well there's only me at the moment."

"Only you? How come?"

"Well there's been a bit of friction and the other members have stood down."

"Why's that?"

"Search me," she replied.

As invitations went Tadler decided to give that one a miss.

17

Mentall sat on a hard, orange plastic chair at the lunch table. It was three days since he'd last been sedated and he could still feel where the needle had been roughly injected into his left buttock.

He chased a piece of boiled carrot around his plate then viewed the scene: those with dementia-ridden brains appeared to be able to stuff their faces with food while those that were merely infirm could barely summon the effort to be spoon-fed. A toothless man, sat on the opposite side of the table, dribbled onto a plastic tablecloth. *This is utterly depressing,* he thought.

He cast his mind back to his first week at boarding school when, as a socially outcast new boy, hiding away from the taunts of 'Mentall by name, mental by nature', he'd found comfort in a book, from the school library, describing heroic accounts of British prisoners of war escaping from Colditz Castle. Mentall nodded as he realised that escaping from this place would also need some good old British guts and determination.

Squadron Leader Jenkins had fought in the war and Mentall held him in total admiration. He imagined himself as a Spitfire pilot looking out for German bombers heading towards England's cities. Incensed he'd climb steeply and, with the sun behind, take his plane into a momentary stall before swinging it down towards the enemy. With the super-charged Rolls Royce Merlin engine under full throttle he'd scream his kite towards a German plane. With his face grimacing, heart pounding, and the bomber growing in size in his canopy window, he'd count five, four, three, two, one then press the button to operate the machine guns. With inches to spare he'd swing out of the dive and, during the victory roll, watch the German plane explode in the air and fragment into the sea below. Round he'd go again, and again picking off the enemy then return to a hero's welcome, medals and the prettiest girl.

Mentall scuffed his shoes against the washable nylon carpet, chewed on a rather bland potato and reviewed his escape plans. The fence was out, the front gates were out, anybody he spoke to didn't believe him and there was no mobile phone reception. And to cap it all a poster had been put up in the entrance instructing visitors not to give him a lift.

He knew that his disappearance would have initially made headline news but he also knew the press – by now he'd be yesterday's news. He needed to get his case across, so he resolved to break into Foster's office and make a call to The Telegraph. The good old British press would take his story.

He recalled the art of picking a lock from night-time raids on his school's tuckshop. He looked around the room, he needed a hairpin with which to pick the lock on Foster's office door. He noticed that Mrs Somerbee's wavy grey hair was pinned back from her face. Furthermore she had conveniently nodded off.

*

Back in his bedroom Mentall straightened out the hairpin and rehearsed creeping along the corridor, down the stairs, picking the lock, letting himself into Foster's office and phoning the press: 'Hello I'd like to speak to the editor please?' 'One moment, sir, putting you through.' 'Editor here.' 'This is Judge Stephen Mentall speaking.' 'Well I'll be blowed! We've been running bigger stories on you than we did for John McCarthy, and you know how that captured the public's imagination. Where are you? Are you okay? How can we rescue you?'

Mentall had it all planned out, a rescue, a press conference, dismissing offers of counselling followed by an RAF flypast to celebrate his release. The inevitable book and newspaper stories of how wonderful it was to be able to take up his career again. This could be his making: promotion to Sir Stephen Mentall as a high court judge then onwards to Lord Chief Justice Stephen Mentall.

*

At eleven p.m. and desperate to keep himself awake, Mentall sat on his bed and listened to the groans of his fellow inmates. At eleven thirty he let himself out onto the landing, made his way towards the top of the stairs and smacked his shin into a small mahogany table.

Taking each stair at a time he descended until he reached the tiled floor of the hall. He tried the door to Foster's office: it was locked so he slipped the hairpin into the keyhole, raised and lowered the handle and worked the hairpin until the lock gave way with a satisfying click.

He switched the light on, crossed to the desk, called directory enquiries and asked for 'The Telegraph'. He then accepted the premium rate option of being automatically connected: he felt relieved when the phone rang and was then answered by a softly spoken man.

"Hello I'd like to speak to the editor please," said Mentall.

"Who is this?"

"Judge Stephen Mentall."

"Who?"

"Mentall, Judge Stephen Mentall," he replied, running a hand across his forehead.

"Wait one moment."

His heart pounded and his anxiety rose with the premium rate telephone bill. After a few minutes Mentall considered hanging up and trying a different paper. But 'The Telegraph', that was the paper. All British and the best to help him out.

Mentall jumped when a tree branch brushed against the office window. A few moments later a voice from the other end of the phone announced, "Deputy assistant editor here."

"This is Judge Stephen Mentall," he replied, thinking the editor would have been more appropriate.

"I've just been told that and have spoken to the editor. It's a strict policy of the paper not to buy stories from felons or support them while on the run."

"What?" exclaimed Mentall, feeling his heart rate begin to soar. "I'm no felon. I'm being held captive."

"That's not what the police are saying. If you'll give yourself up and agree to a deal, giving us an exclusive, we'll put your side of the story. But no payments. So, do you want to meet to talk?"

"I can't do that," said Mentall.

"Try one of the gutter press then," continued the deputy assistant editor, "they'll probably give you some form of nest egg for when you have done your stretch. But likely they'll sensationalise it. With us we'll promise to put your case."

Mentall returned the handset to its cradle and stood up, shaking. What was this about? He opened the lid on Foster's laptop and pressed a few keys. "Blast," he uttered as the computer asked for a password. He cast his eyes around the room. A copy of The Daily Mail was poking out of a wastepaper basket. He retrieved it and read the headlines: 'Still No Sign of Disgraced Judge'. He continued reading and learnt they were on to him about the theft of the exhibit money from the East Castle Street trial. He shook his head in despair and took little comfort in there being no mention of the mix up with the DVD from the Waterloo Porn Trial.

He made his way back to his room, sat on his bed and, with his head in his hands, listened to the distant cries of 'Angels at three o'clock', 'Did you know Brian?' and 'I'm afraid I'm going to have to ask you to blow into this breathalyser, madam'. His resolve strengthened; he had to get out of this place and clear his name.

From what he could see Foster didn't have a clue about anything, let alone he had a kidnapped judge on his hands. If confronted Mentall hoped the ignorant ass would panic and let him go. If not he reckoned he could strike a deal with him. Foster looked dodgy and doubtless calculated the care home fees by taking the address of any potential new resident, finding similar properties on Rightmove and dividing the value by the number of weeks they were expected to live.

Based on trials he'd presided over, potential benefactors readily signed over their inheritance to avoid the pointless conversations and the daily changing of bed linen. And, in his experience, not enough questions were ever asked when a loved one died shortly before the money ran out.

It was worth working on Foster. With that sniff of hope he drifted off to sleep.

*

"Come in," said Foster in response to a knock at his office door. When the door opened he was surprised to see his newest resident, Mr Miles, step into the room. He folded away his newspaper and straightened himself in his chair.

"Ah, what can I do for you, Stephen?" he asked. He'd restricted the old duffer's privileges for his escape attempt and that impertinent remark about inbreeds: he didn't want a scene over it. He pointed to a chair on the opposite side of his desk. "Take a seat."

"I'm not here of my own free will," began Miles, lowering himself into the chair. "The people who brought me here weren't my daughter and son-in-law."

"Who were they then?" asked Foster sceptically.

"They were my kidnappers."

"Oh I see," Foster replied, reaching below his desk and pressing the silent alarm button.

"My name is not Stephen Miles, it is Stephen Mentall. Judge Stephen Mentall in fact. You'll be familiar with some of my wider known cases such as the Waterloo Porn Trial," he said in a tone implying everybody should have heard of the Waterloo Porn Trial.

"I barely get a chance to read the paper and then only the sport," Foster replied, gesticulating towards the newspaper on his desk.

"I was also interviewed on Panorama about the East Castle Street robbery." Mentall then nodded in a fashion that left Foster thinking he should be agreeing to something.

"Running this place is full-on," said Foster. "I don't have time for the TV." He paused and then added incredulously, "So you're saying you've been kidnapped and put here against your will?"

"Yes," Mentall replied.

"I'll look into this for you, Stephen. Just leave it with me."

"Thank you," Mentall replied and got up to leave. As he left the room Ellie Foster appeared and gave her husband a quizzical look.

Foster waited for her to close the door. "Poor old sod, hopeless case," he said shaking his head. "He was in here just now convinced he's a judge. Do you remember old Pearson we had in here the other

87

year, convinced he was from the House of Lords? Both barking irreversible cases."

"Mr Miles's family warned us about that," said Ellie.

"What?" asked Foster.

"That he'd claim he was a judge."

"Why didn't you tell me?" he asked, furrowing his brow.

"You were there when they told us," she said testily.

"Was I?"

"Yes dear, when they brought him in."

18

Sergeant Tadler returned to his desk and read a yellow sticky note attached to his computer screen. "Need to see you right away – Stainthwaite (Horse Face)."

Tadler checked his watch, it was two minutes to the end of his shift. "Sod it," he grumbled, pocketing the sticky note and then heading for his car.

After a frustrating drive, in heavy traffic, he parked outside his local pub, The Red Lion, and spent the evening sat in a corner drowning his sorrows with a succession of pints of Guinness and vodka shots.

When the barman called for last orders he staggered out onto the street and stumbled by the Golden Dragon Chinese Takeaway, the Prima Doner Kebab Shop and Mr Fry's Chip Emporium. He then negotiated an overflowing black litter bin and steadied himself as he entered the Spice Paradise Indian Takeaway.

Back in his bedsit, and munching through a Bombay Curry, the spices got the better of him and he sneezed. He pulled a handkerchief from his pocket and found the yellow sticky note that he'd taken from his desk. *Funny she signed it Horse Face*, he thought. He suddenly got a pang of guilt; she was trying to be friendly and he'd ignored her and gone to the pub. He pulled his smartphone from his other pocket and, with one hand spooning curry into his mouth, he keyed:

Dear Ma'am, or should I say Horse Face,

So nice of you to address yourself by the nickname we have for you at the station. I did not realise you knew, it makes for a more relaxed environment if one can rib oneself, does it not?

Sorry I was unable to see you straight away, I had an urgent lead on the Mentall case to chase up and had to dash.

Will see you in the morning.
Pete.

Even with his few sober brain cells firing off some unsettling feelings, Tadler pressed SEND and retired to his bed. Waking with a dry mouth, he showered, drank a pint of water and headed for work with an eerie unease that the day wasn't going to start out well.

At his desk, with his curry blasted haemorrhoids making his back passage feel like a thoroughfare for a tribe of sandpaper headed pygmies, he clenched his buttocks, closed his eyes and, with his mouth pursed, let out a sigh.

"You all right, Sarge," asked Niky entering the office.

"Oh yeah, just an itch."

"I've heard that one before. Anyhow good morning DS Tadler. I just saw Horse Face in the corridor, she told me to send you up to her office."

"Okay, I'll go and see her in a minute."

"She looked very angry to me, muttering something about you sending an email."

"Dunno why she's angry. I sent it in the early hours after following up an, ahem, lead."

"She wants to see you straightaway," said Niky, settling herself into her chair.

"Okay, we'll have to think of another nickname. It doesn't feel so much fun now she calls herself Horse Face."

"Is she calling herself Horse Face now then?" replied Niky, pressing the power button on her computer screen.

"Yep, she signed a Post-it note with it yesterday."

"The one on your desk at the end of yesterday's shift?" asked Niky, glancing up.

"Yep, that one. I sent her an email saying I didn't realise she knew."

"Oh!" replied Niky, turning back to her computer screen.

"What's the problem?"

"Well," stumbled Niky, "she phoned that message down, I just added the *Horse Face* in brackets for fun."

"Oh shit!"

"Sorry Sarge."

"Fuck, fuck, fuck."

"Guess you're in for it now."

"In for it, in for it – I'm as good as dead."

"Sorry. I never thought you'd think she'd written it. I did it as a joke to cheer you up."

"Yeah, I know," said Tadler.

*

After twenty minutes on the receiving end of a lifetime's anger at being called Horse Face, Tadler emerged, rather shaken, from Stainthwaite's office. Knowing the undercurrent of a tribunal would be to reference 'Horse Face' at every opportunity he was not surprised she'd stopped short of threatening him with a disciplinary.

He returned to his desk. "Bloody tosspot of a woman," he said under his breath.

"I guess it didn't go well, Sarge," said Niky.

19

Mentall woke the next morning suspicious that Foster hadn't believed his story about the kidnapping. He cast his mind back to the fence that surrounded Smoking Chimneys. One way or another he had to get through it, over it or under it. A knock at his door diverted him from his thoughts.

"Come," he called.

"Lovely cup of tea?" asked the tea lady entering his bedroom and placing a cup on his bedside cabinet.

"Thank you," sighed Mentall.

She turned towards him and allowed her ample bosoms to come to a natural rest. Mentall was pleased he'd had the forethought to raise his knees.

"I expect you're looking forward to this afternoon," she said enthusiastically.

"What for?" he asked distinctly unenthusiastically.

"Your medical, it's at four p.m. All new residents have to have one. The doctor is a good man, he'll make sure you're fit and healthy and keep you going a good few years yet."

If his life was to be stuck in this place being kept 'going a good few years yet' was the last thing Mentall wanted. An incompetent bumbling doctor was more what he had in mind. Either way his new escape plan was taking shape.

*

Foster beckoned his wife away from the kitchen's fridges and directed her towards a screen displaying pictures from the security cameras. "You've got to see this."

"What *is* he doing now?" chuckled Ellie, peering at the grainy black and white images.

"Trying to get over the fence by building himself a staircase," replied her husband. "He's using the trestle tables from the shed."

"Doesn't he know he's on camera?" asked Ellie.

"I watched him recce the grounds. He thinks he's found a dead spot in the camera system. But he's missed the one at the back, high up on the chimney."

"I almost feel sorry for him," said Ellie.

"Good going for an eighty-three year old," said Foster.

"That's the trouble with the dementia cases," said Ellie, "strong as a bloody ox some of them. You should try dressing one of them when they've got it into their head you're trying to kill them." She then paused and added, "Why haven't you gone and stopped him?"

"What, and miss the entertainment? At least I know where he is."

"How's he going to get down the other side of the fence?" she asked.

"I don't think he's worked that one out yet."

"Go and stop him," said Ellie, "I don't want him crippling himself."

*

Mentall hauled himself onto the third trestle table up and steadied himself against the diamond lattice security fence. *Nearly there,* he thought. His heart sank with despair when, from the direction of the house, he heard Foster calling, "Mr Miles. Mr Miles."

He felt the pile of tables sway then start to tip beneath him. He made a grab for the top of the fence just as the tables fell away from under him. He clung to the wire for a second or so before he felt his hands lose their grip. He crashed to the ground, landing heavily.

He heard Foster approach then ask him if he was okay.

"No I'm not bloody okay," growled Mentall, sat on his backside.

"Why do you keep trying to escape?" asked Foster.

"Well, if you can remember as far back as yesterday, you might recall our conversation where I explained that I'm a judge who has been kidnapped. I don't suppose you've done anything about that."

"I've made a few enquiries," said Foster.

"Like hell you have," barked Mentall. "You think I'm just some old nutcase who thinks he's a judge. Well I *am* a judge. Oh for fuck's sake," he screamed as he saw Ellie marching across the lawn, accompanied by Madge with a rather large syringe.

"Grab him," yelled Ellie.

Mentall came around to a knocking at his bedroom door. His head felt groggy; this latest chemical cosh must have been quite a strong dose.

"It's ten to four," said a voice from the other side of the door. He recognised it as Madge's.

"What about ten to four?" he groaned.

"Your medical is at four p.m. Do you need a hand getting yourself down there?"

"No, I'll be fine," he replied. He waited until he heard Madge's footsteps depart along the landing before swinging himself off his bed.

He made his way downstairs and along the hall towards a sign, suspended from the ceiling, denoting the surgery. Mentall sat on an orange plastic chair and looked towards the varnished door with gold-coloured letters indicating 'Dr George Webber' resided within. Mentall could hear voices from behind the door.

"So, Mrs Somerbee, if you remove your undergarments we'll have a look at you."

Various rustling noises, accompanied by the strained tones of an ancient whalebone girdle giving up its quarry, emanated from the consulting room.

Mentall winced.

"And how long have you been having these abdominal pains?"

"Some two weeks now."

"Two weeks," replied Webber in high-pitched sarcasm.

There was a long pause. Mentall tapped his foot on the tiled floor of the corridor.

"When were you last with a man Mrs Somerbee?" asked Webber.

"Ohh, I spent the last evening playing whist with Squadron Leader Jenkins."

"No, Mrs Somerbee, when did you last have intercourse with a man?"

"Well the nice Squadron Leader was quite talkative."

"Oh God," Mentall sighed in a whisper.

"No, Mrs Somerbee," replied Webber in exasperated sarcasm, "I mean sexual intercourse not social intercourse." There was a pause then Webber added, "Come, come Mrs Somerbee, there's no need to be embarrassed. There's only you and me here and everything that goes on in this room is completely confidential."

"Did you know my Brian?" she asked.

"No."

"He died in nineteen eighty-three, it was then."

"Then that you last had sexual intercourse?"

"Yes."

"Well at least you had a love life right up to the end Mrs Somerbee," said Webber in a gentler humorous tone.

"That's probably what finished the old sod off," whispered Mentall.

"And how old were you when you first had sexual intercourse?" asked Webber.

Mentall wondered why a doctor would need to know that. In fact he was having grave doubts as to Webber's competence.

"Come now Mrs Somerbee, what age was it?" asked Webber.

"Thirteen," replied Mrs Somerbee.

"Thirteen!" replied Webber.

"Thirteen," said Mentall under his breath.

"Well I was saving myself," explained Mrs Somerbee, "most girls didn't, there was a war on you know."

There was another pause before Mentall heard Webber's voice again. "I'm just going to complete the examination, this may feel a little cold, metal always does."

There was another slight pause before Mrs Somerbee asked, "So what's wrong with me Doctor?"

"Well, I have to tell you that in a few months' time you'll be changing nappies."

"What, that can't be, me and Brian it's been so long. But, but surely not at my age."

"These things happen, Mrs Somerbee."

Mentall shook his head in slack-jawed amazement. *Another bloody idiot*, he thought.

*

Webber guided Mrs Somerbee to his consulting room door, took a quick swig from his hip flask and then beckoned his next client in.

"Take a seat now," said Webber, pointing towards an orange plastic chair. He consulted his notes. "Ah Mr Miles."

"I'm Mentall," blurted out Mentall.

"No, no Mr Miles, this is an H O M E, it doesn't mean you have lost it up top. You're here because your family is unable to support your needs at this stage in your life." In fact Webber thought the old sod had probably lost the plot but he always sought to humour his patients.

"No, you don't understand. I'm not mental. I'm Men-Tall. Judge Men-Tall in fact."

Webber had been warned, by Ellie Foster, that Miles had a fixation that he was a judge. He decided to ignore his claims. "So what can I do for you today?" he asked, settling himself into the sumptuous green leather of his swivel chair.

Miles appeared to relax. "I've been told I have to have a medical," he said in a resigned tone.

"Ah, of course, a new boy!"

After Mentall had been stripped and prodded Webber informed him he was in good health and in fact had the body of a man twenty years younger.

"Any trouble sleeping?" asked Webber.

"No, not too bad, could do with sleeping longer," Mentall replied, buttoning up his shirt.

"Ah some sleeping pills then?" asked Webber.

"Got any Mirtazapine?" asked Mentall.

Webber was pleased to justify his existence by dishing out some medicine. He took more care this time, the last time he had prescribed sleeping pills to an inmate he had made a mix up between valerian and Viagra. On being called out in the middle of the night he'd taken the poor old chap's pulse. At 179 beats per minute, and a face the colour of a beetroot, Webber summoned an ambulance. Only when the paramedics found something was hindering their attempts to roll him out of bed and onto a stretcher, did they uncover the problem. The subsequent article Webber penned for the Lancet, entitled 'The use of Viagra in preventing elderly men from rolling out of bed', was rejected.

20

Mentall sat down next to Mrs Somerbee and paddled a spoon through his breakfast porridge. "Just bloody typical," he muttered.

"What's that sonny?" croaked Mrs Somerbee.

"Oh nothing, I shouldn't be here."

"Well, it won't be long now – we'll all get out of here one day, one at a time in our coffins."

Mentall's spoon paused in its furrow and then he whispered, "Bingo! The way out's in a bloody coffin."

"Bingo, tonight?" replied Mrs Somerbee. "It's Thursday tonight, bingo is normally on Mondays. Oh, how exciting, bingo twice a week now."

"Well, no actually I was meaning–"

"Ohhh, do come as well, it will be so exciting and he's such a nice young man that runs it. A bit like that Les Dawson off the telly."

"Les Dawson's been dead for years," said Mentall.

"Well he was on the telly yesterday."

"Probably a repeat under the guise of some expression like classic, vintage or gold," said Mentall.

"Oh do come, we had cucumber sandwiches last time."

"Sounds delicious," sighed Mentall.

"Oh I can't wait. Two fat ladies, hee-hee."

Mentall had a tough job getting his mind off two fat ladies and back to the more pressing matter of an escape plan. "All I need do is play dead, old Webber will pronounce me mortis and I'll be out," he whispered.

"What's your name?" asked Mrs Somerbee.

Mentall's mind flipped back to the present. "My name," he paused and thought, "is Mr Miles," then added, "but I used to be a judge. And who are you?" he asked thinking that the likelihood of this wizened old crow remembering her name was about as remote as his morning tea lady going topless for him.

"I'm the pixie who brought you breakfast at the bus stop in 1977."

All day Mentall practised at playing dead, on his bed, in the dayroom and at the evening meal. Each time it failed, a tickle, an itch or not being able to hold his breath for long enough. Nothing appeared to substitute for actually being dead.

He returned to his room and laid on his bed then cast his memory back to boarding school, to the pranks and the tricks. Playing dead got one off lessons and Herbert Lawrence was a past master at feigning his own demise. Having stolen one of his grandmother's sleeping pills and, after performing a spectrograph in the chemistry lab and producing his own version, he'd managed to slide himself into a semi-coma and got himself sent home.

Mentall's eyes fell on the Mirtazapine Webber had given him. He wondered how many he would need to comatose himself. He got up from his bed, opened the packet and read the instructions. It stated to take no more than two if intending to drive the next day; the two the Pughes had forced on him had certainly made him drowsy. He read on. If more than four were swallowed medical advice was to be sought. Mentall pocketed eight, flushed the rest down the lavatory then passed the remainder of the evening in the dayroom, bemoaning the home and wishing he were dead.

21

"Mr Foster, Mr Foster," said Madge excitedly, entering her boss's office.

"What is it," Foster replied, looking up from his desk while tucking away the sports section of the morning paper.

"I'm afraid it's Mr Miles, he's passed away. His tea lady has just come and told me."

"Okay, I'll attend." Foster liked the word attend, it gave an air of importance and he had gleaned it from 'Casualty' on the TV.

*

Foster stood over Mentall and viewed the empty Mirtazapine blister packet. "Oh dear," he whispered. This could be awkward, questions might be asked. He slipped the packet into his pocket, returned to his office and called Doctor Webber.

"Yeah," replied Webber, sounding half asleep.

"Foster here, spot of bother I'm afraid."

"Who?"

"Foster."

"Foster who? I ain't bloody fostering anybody, clear off."

Webber's alcoholic state was never good before eleven a.m.

"Colin Foster at Smoking Chimneys. One of your few sources of income."

"Oh," Webber replied.

"Old Mr Miles has died in the night," said Foster.

"Oh double blast," replied Webber.

"Yes, I know."

"No, I've just knocked the bottle over. What did you say?"

"Old Mr Miles has died in the night," Foster repeated.

"Strange, looked bloody healthy to me when I saw him the other day. Still you can never tell, some people go on forever with every ailment and others just keel over at the first whiff of something."

"I need you to pop in and do a death certificate."

"Not my day Foster, I'm not in until next Wednesday, call a locum."

"Looks like he overdosed on sleeping pills."

"Oh."

"Sleeping pills you prescribed."

"Blast, thought I could trust the fellow."

"Yes, and I thought we agreed no self-administration."

"Bugger. I'll be right over," replied Webber.

*

Webber struggled in three hours later.

"Where is he then?"

"In his room. Can you just do the death certificate quickly?" A corpse on his hands and the threat of a post mortem, was making Foster impatient.

"Better take a little peek first, wouldn't want to be struck off for issuing a certificate for a non-existent corpse," said Webber.

Foster led Webber to Mentall's room where Mrs Syms, Mrs Somerbee and Squadron Leader Jenkins were all loitering at the door.

"Is he dead?" asked Mrs Somerbee.

"Never you mind," said Foster.

"Killed in the war was he?"

Foster brushed them aside. Webber followed him into the room and, after a brief examination announced, "I'll put it down as a massive myocardial infarction. It's usual in somebody of his age with acute angina."

"But he didn't have acute angina," said Foster.

"What was that?" asked Mrs Syms.

"Poor old Mr Miles has a cute vagina and died from a massive internal fart," replied Mrs Somerbee.

"Oh dear."

"Always thought there was something odd about that fellow," said Squadron Leader Jenkins.

"I still can't raise his family," said Ellie, interrupting the two men in Mentall's room.

"Can't raise him either. I best call old Fred then," Foster replied.

*

Fred, the Fosters undertaker of choice, known locally as 'Fred the dead', a thin forty-something pointy featured man with a cheap moustache, was delighted when Smoking Chimneys was converted into a retirement home. Prior to the Fosters taking over it had generated only two stiffs but now it was mustering at least one a month. With wintertime, and a handy influenza outbreak, the rate could rise to three or four a week.

That morning, and to save money on expensive fasteners, Fred had risen early to nail a client into his coffin: a light oak affair with green velvet interior sitting perched on trestle tables. He settled the lid onto the main coffin structure, then reached for his hammer and nails. With each blow he hummed his familiar tune.

You put the left leg in.
You put the left leg out.
In out, in out shake it all about.
Do the oak clad coffin and turn them out.
That's what it's all about.
Oh the oak clad coffin.
Oh the oak clad coffin.

Interrupted by his mobile phone, playing Chopin's funeral march, he laid the hammer to rest.

He pressed the accept call button and raised the phone to his ear. "Undertaker, how may I help?"

"Fred, another little job for you," said Foster.

"I'm a bit busy right now. Another one not like the cooking eh?" replied Fred.

"No, bit of a shock this one, thought I'd get another year or so out of this old boy. Still you never can tell and his family looked wealthy – you should get all the trimmings this time."

"I'll be right over."

"Okay. Oh and Fred, my ten percent commission. Not in front of Ellie again. Slip it to me casual like. I think she was suspicious last time that the money wasn't a win on the gee-gees."

"I thought she didn't mind your scams, she doesn't mind doubling up on the extras. How much do you charge for a blue rinse job now?"

"She comes over all self-righteous once they've snuffed it."

"I'll never understand women," sighed Fred. "Okay, see you in a bit."

The oak clad coffin song was reserved for the nailing down of the coffin lid. Figuring, if caught out he could explain the flippancy of the tune as a way of coping with the depressive nature of the profession, he saved his favourite ditty for the safety of the drive to pick up a corpse. As Fred pulled out onto main road he tapped his left foot and started to sing 'The Funeral Director's Ditty'. A song he had strung together while placing himself in an imaginary West Ham United supporters band called, 'The Stiffs'.

I'm forever collecting corpses,
Pretty corpses for their heirs,
They smell so high,
All littered with flies,
And fulfil my dreams,
Because my fees are so high.
Fortune's never hiding,
My cupboard's never bare,
For I'm forever collecting corpses,
Pretty corpses for their heirs.

Within a few hundred yards of Smoking Chimneys Fred slowed the hearse to a reverential speed and straightened himself for the immediate necessary professionalism. Foster was waiting for him at the open gates.

"Where is he?" asked Fred, leaning over to open the passenger door.

"First floor," Foster replied, sliding into the sumptuous leather seat.

"Those stairs again, I'll take the coffin to him. Last time the coroner asked too many questions about the bruising."

Fred pulled up at the front of the Smoking Chimneys. Foster and Fred then carried the coffin from the hearse to the back of the building and then negotiated the narrow rear staircase.

"He looks quite peaceful," said Foster, resting his end of the coffin on the bedroom floor.

"It's nice when they go quietly in their sleep. Much less fuss and–"

"My father did, in this room in fact," said Foster.

Fred looked at him.

"Before it was a home like."

"Oh, didn't realise you'd lived here before. My dad went peacefully in his sleep too, not a murmur from him and he was gone. Not like the pedestrians on the zebra crossing."

"Actually I grew up here," Foster replied.

"You must have known the Kipling sisters then?"

Foster nodded.

"Notorious they were by all accounts."

"Really?" asked Foster, raising his eyebrows.

"Oh yes, orgies back here in the sixties they say."

"Blimey, I never knew that."

"Apparently them Kipling sisters didn't need much persuasion. Tarts the lot of them."

"One of them was my mother," Foster replied.

"Oh, I didn't mean any offence like. Nice ladies by all accounts. Friendly I hear," replied Fred.

*

With the coffin in the back of the hearse, Foster and Fred in conversation, Mentall began to wake. Raising his right arm he smashed it into the lid. A stretch of his right foot confirmed where he was. *First phase complete*, he thought.

"That's the old boy loaded then," said Fred adjusting the position of the coffin in the back of the hearse.

"Usual place is it? I need to let the family know," Foster replied.

"Yep, Christian I presume?"

"C of E they put on the form."

"Always best to know. Families can get a bit tetchy if you get it wrong. Suddenly get all religious at these times. A nice burial the C of E. Quick service, a bit of the Lord is My Shepherd, a neat north to south hole, the Lord's Prayer, lowering of the coffin and back to some relatives house for a nice spread." Fred paused and Mentall heard the click of a cigarette lighter.

"Some of the other religions don't half pan it out. Take your Jew for example. I did one last month, had to ship in a quarry load of stone so the relatives could file past and each put a rock on the grave. And take your Muslims, they have to be buried facing Mecca. I did four last week then along came an ill-timed bible basher and ruined the entire flow."

Mentall was fully awake by now and waiting for the off. Not being claustrophobic was being tested to the full.

"Here's the standard ten percent," said Fred in a more business-like tone.

"Thanks," said Foster, "these notes are a bit of a mess. What's the extra pound coin for?"

"The cemetery's raised its burial cost by a tenner, so you get an extra quid. I gave them a bit of a talking to over it. Blamed the rise on the cost of living."

Foster laughed.

"Oh for Christ's sake," whispered Mentall, "he only gave you the extra quid so he could crack that joke."

"Okay then, give us a call when you make contact with the family," said Fred, getting into his hearse.

"Bye for now," called out Foster.

Purring off the drive the 4.2 litre vehicle didn't flinch at the additional weight. After the first bend Fred floored it.

"Go baby go," he yelled to the hearse's stereo blaring out Queen's, 'Another One Bites the Dust'.

Mentall's head took a battering as Fred threw the hearse into each corner.

"For fuck's sake," yelled Fred as the hearse braked, sharply, "bloody tractor drivers."

The coffin shot forward and Mentall gulped hard.

"And the same to you too," yelled Fred, accelerating the hearse away again. The coffin shunted back and forth.

It was hot, airless and he was starting to asphyxiate; all plans were reduced to smashing his fist on the inside of the coffin.

*

Fred turned up the music, the strange knocking from the back of the hearse would have to be checked at the next service. The only knocking he'd previously experienced from the rear was on a visit to the local dogging site.

Something bothered Fred but he couldn't identify it. The music whizzed around his head along with the events of the morning. Something was missing, something was odd, something was not quite right. Was the corpse a bit too warm when he handled it? Perhaps a bit too floppy? He turned the music down to think. It played on his mind for a couple more miles. He checked the rear view mirror as if he expected the coffin to have disappeared. Then there was that noise from the back again. Then it hit him and he slammed on the brakes, the hearse skidded to a halt and the coffin thumped into the back of his seat knocking Mentall clean out. There'd been no death fart.

He jumped out of the cab, opened up the back of the hearse, unscrewed the lid of the temporary coffin and dragged it around so the head was at the tailgate. As a young mortician the death fart had kept him amused. The manipulation of any stiff always resulted in the explosion of rectal gas. But now this was serious, Mentall hadn't farted when they lifted him into his coffin. Fred slid his hands under Mentall's armpits: he was still warm.

"Shit," hissed Fred, "the bastard's still with us and I've paid the ten percent."

Just to make sure he lifted Mentall up into a sitting position, his arms flopped forward, his head to one side and saliva dribbled from his mouth. Fred rocked him back and forth, no death fart came. Mentall let out a long sigh and Fred leapt back cracking his head on the tailgate. Hopping around in agony he slammed the lid back down, screwed it in place and was back in the driver's seat within seconds. Hurtling his way back to Smoking Chimneys there was no need for Queen to encourage excessive speed. At the gates he pressed the intercom.

"Yes," came the voice of Ellie Foster.

"Fred here," he barked, unable to hide his displeasure at not getting Foster to talk to. "Spot of bother let me in quick."

The gates slid back and Fred accelerated up the drive then braked to a sharp, gravel-tearing halt outside the front door. Ellie and Colin Foster were there to greet him.

"Fucker's not dead," yelled Fred, emerging from the driver's seat.

"What?" Foster replied.

"Got him back to the parlour, turned him out and he sat up. Slammed him down and brought him straight back. Thought you'd had him certified."

"We did. Let's get him to his room."

"Oh dear," said Ellie, "I've already had Madge clear it out, and I've contacted the Crosbys about their Aunt."

"Oh damn," said Foster, "they looked pretty loaded too. Could have got all the extras out of them. What about room thirty-seven?"

"We've promised that to the Parkers," said Ellie. "What shall I tell the Crosbys then? They're bringing her over today."

"Tell them it was a mistake," suggested Fred.

"Mistake!" exclaimed Foster. "Tell me it's a mistake, that shit-head Webber fellow should be darned well struck off. Normally when one of the codgers is on death's door he'll pull them through. Looks like this one clung onto the bleeding frame. Anyhow he's out of here, sacked."

"Calm yourself dear," said Ellie, "otherwise he'll be issuing you with a certificate. We really should get Mr Miles to his room."

*

Between the three of them they carried the coffin back to Mentall's room and, as they lowered it onto the bedroom floor, Fred began to undo the lid. Mentall was conscious enough to act dumb and let the others assume the blame. He didn't want them to suspect a purposeful escape attempt.

"Come on Mr Miles, did you enjoy the ride out?" asked Ellie, smiling gently.

"Yes."

"Let's get you into bed, then cook will bring you breakfast."

Mentall allowed them to lift him onto the bed and tell him he'd been having the kind of bad dream that he should not worry his daughter and son-in-law about.

*

"Ah Mrs Crosby, I'm glad I caught you," Foster purred into the phone. "There's been a slight hiccup with the room that's become available for your auntie. The previous occupant's family have made a rather strange request."

"Oh yes," replied Mrs Crosby from the other end of the line.

"It appears they don't feel comfortable relinquishing the room until after the funeral."

"As a mark of respect I presume," suggested Mrs Crosby.

"Ah yes that'll be it," agreed Foster gleefully. And for good measure he added, "And of course we will be forfeiting our fee for the period."

"Very admirable."

"Once they have buried the old bug… bu, b, chap I'll be back in touch and we can have your auntie in here in no time."

"Okay then, give us a call."

"Phew," exclaimed Foster, hanging up the phone.

22

"Here you go Mr Miles," said the cook, resting a breakfast tray on Mentall's bedside cabinet.

"Thank you," whispered Mentall from his bed. He still felt drowsy from the sleeping pills and the crack on the head he'd received in the coffin.

"Two fried eggs, bacon, beans, mushrooms and a tattie scone. Tea and toast too," said the cook before adding, "Hope this makes up for yer bad dream."

They're trying to make me believe it was just a bad dream, thought Mentall. He sat up and cast his eye over the tray. It looked amazing; this jock must have been told to rustle up the breakfast of his lifetime.

"Mrs Foster was telling me you danee mix with the other residents."

"I've better things to do with my time," Mentall scoffed, reaching for the cup of tea.

"Aye well, she's only concerned for yer welfare. Is there anything we can do for yee?"

Mentall thought for a moment. "Well could you take me shopping to Albridge?"

"Ah, Mrs Foster said yer not to leave the grounds. Have a think if there's anything you need."

Darn, thought Mentall as cook left the room.

He pulled the breakfast tray onto his knees and tucked in. *Not bad*, he thought. When he'd finished he returned the tray to the bedside cabinet, slid down the bed and drifted off to sleep. He did not wake again until mid-afternoon when Ellie Foster was tidying up the breakfast tray.

"How are you then Mr Miles?" she asked.

"I'm fine, thank you."

Ellie then went about patting pillows, moving objects and straightening the curtains.

"I know you're not one for socialising, but we're having a Daniel

O'Donnell evening tonight. Cook says he'll come and get you if you want to come."

"I'm perfectly capable of making my own way thank you."

"Ah good. Seven-thirty in the main dayroom," she replied, before picking up the tray and leaving the room.

"Bugger," whispered Mentall.

23

Mentall pushed open the door of the main dayroom. Ellie and Madge were guiding a few inmates to their seats, the Daniel O'Donnell impressionist was tapping a microphone while chanting, "One-Two. One-Two", and Mrs Syms was manoeuvring her wheelchair next to Mr Handcross.

Mrs Somerbee pointed towards Mentall and wailed, "A ghost, a ghost." Ellie and Madge took her by the arms and guided her to a chair. The Daniel O'Donnell impressionist, with all the gusto of a rock-star opening a concert, announced, "Good evening, Smoking Chimneys."

Madge knelt down and tucked a blanket around Mrs Somerbee's hips and explained, "It was all a mistake, Mr Miles isn't a ghost. He was only sleeping."

"What about the hearse and the man from the funeral home then?"

Madge glanced up at Ellie and then explained, "That was a mistake too."

"So many mistakes," croaked Mrs Somerbee. She then added, excitedly, "I'm with child you know." Madge stood up and gave Ellie an incredulous look.

The impressionist, who had began to sing 'Here I Am Lord', stepped back and forth, raised and lowered his arms in time to the music and directed a couple of bars at each resident.

Ginger Jenkins approached Mentall. "I can't quite put my finger on it but there's something a bit odd about that Daniel O'Donnell fellow."

"Well he's a Pakistani," Mentall replied.

"Ah that's it then," Jenkins replied and then added, "Didn't you die last night?"

Mentall made his excuses and sat down on a plastic coated chair. He was visited by both the Fosters, Madge and the cook. They all asked how he was feeling after his 'bad dream'. "It was definitely a nightmare," he replied to each.

As the impressionist began to sing 'Oh Danny Boy', Mentall felt his mood slump into one of frustrating despair. The escape had failed and it looked as if his life was now doomed to become a twenty-year sentence stuck in this place: his next departure as a real corpse. He felt a tear slip out of his left eye and roll down his cheek.

The singer sidled up to him and said, "It really gets you this one doesn't it," while smiling a smile of pity at him.

"Right, who's up for some karaoke? I'll sing the first bar with you and you can take it from there. Don't be shy now. What about you?" he asked, directing his microphone towards Ginger Jenkins.

"Not bloody likely," Jenkins replied.

"I saw you tapping your foot just now," said the singer.

"Keep my confounded foot out of this."

"How about you?" he asked old Handcross.

"I'm parked, thank you," he replied.

"Ooo, do you need a ticket?" asked Mrs Syms.

"Let's choose somebody," said Mrs Somerbee.

"That's a good idea," said Ellie, "how shall we do that?"

"Eeny, meeny, miny, moe," began Mrs Syms, "catch a–"

"Stop right there," yelled Ellie raising a hand. "I think it'll be best if we drop the karaoke. And as for you Mrs Syms I don't want to see you taking Mr Handcross's breathalyser tonight."

Mentall's despair turned to a plan. He went back to his room and jotted a note, 'My name is Judge Stephen Mentall and I am being held here against my will. Please help me.' He slipped the note into his trouser pocket and then returned to the dayroom.

As the evening drew to an end the impressionist brought his final rendition of 'She was my Tipperary girl' to a close. An ovation of bony hand clapping followed and Mentall took his cue. As the singer took his bows, he approached him with an outstretched arm. The singer gave his hand a firm shake, and Mentall watched his expression change as the he felt a piece of paper being pressed against his palm.

As Mentall left the room he eavesdropped on two elderly ladies. "Oh, such a lovely evening," said one.

"Oh yes," replied her friend, "we've not had so much fun since that nice Mister Uri Geller visited and ruined all the cutlery."

Christ get me out of here, thought Mentall.

24

Tadler sat at his office desk and flicked through his emails. He checked the time, it was just gone five p.m. He then read an email from Crimestoppers and let out a snort of laughter.

"What's that, Sarge?" asked admin assistant, Niky Smith, looking up from her desk.

"You got to read this!" explained Tadler. "Some fellow, calling himself Suresh Gurmani, says that he's a Daniel O'Donnell impressionist and claims Judge Stephen Mentall is being held against his will in an old people's home called Smoking Chimneys."

"Sounds a bit far-fetched," replied Niky.

"You're telling me. Where do they dig them up from? And it says the proprietor of the home is a one Colon Fister."

"Definitely a wind up. That's me finished for the day, see you tomorrow," said Niky, unhooking her jacket from the coat stand.

"Okay. Have a good evening."

"You too."

"I will now. This is a corker. Does he want a reward or something?"

Tadler deleted the email then grimaced as he clenched his buttocks to fend off a rather painful haemorrhoid; the burning and itching made every movement uncomfortable. Uncomfortable movements were playing a major role in Detective Sergeant DS1553 Peter Tadler's life. Bearing it no longer he stuck his head out of the office door and checked the corridor both ways. It was all clear so he slipped back into his office, took a tube of haemorrhoid cream from the top drawer of his desk and smothered his right index finger with the white ointment. He then loosened his belt, slipped his hand into his underpants and began to apply the cream. He then watched in utter disbelief as the handle turned on the office door and it opened to reveal DCI Marjorie Stainthwaite. "Detective Sergeant Tadler, what are you doing?" she bellowed.

"Erm."

"This is a disciplinary offence."

"No, no you don't understand."

"Don't understand. Don't understand. I, a defenceless woman, working late in the office have my dignity and peace of mind destroyed by a male colleague masturbating in front of me."

"I was not masturbating."

"Oh come off it Tadler," she boomed, "I'm a woman of the world. I know what I've seen and I know what a man looks like when he has been caught red handed with his trousers down."

This unfortunate turn of phrase did not fail to escape him. Although his hands had more of a white look about them and technically his trousers were still up.

"You *are* suspended. Warrant card and key fob please."

"Ah come on, Ma'am."

"Come on, do your trousers up, wash your hands and give me your warrant card and fob."

*

Sat in his BMW, realising his career could be in ruins, Tadler dropped his head into his hands. Marjorie Stainthwaite could make this stick, cases of sexual harassment were taken very seriously. "Bollocks," he uttered before leaning his head back to think through his options. If he could find that missing judge he'd be in the force's good books, and they'd probably scrub the charge against him. But he didn't have a clue where the judge was.

He thought about searching Stainthwaite's office to find something to pin on her. But she'd taken his key fob and there was no way into the building without it. "Bloody bureaucratic force," he whispered, rueing the rule which required everybody entering or leaving the building to use their own key fob: tailgating was banned.

He drove home, cracked open a beer and contemplated how easy it would be if he could arrest that judge: the door to the custody suite didn't require a key fob, instead the custody sergeant buzzed you through via a video phone.

He fantasised about touring the town looking for somebody to arrest. He picked up a fag packet and saw a name and number he'd written on it. "James Smethurst," he grumbled, "that bastard who woke me up with a wrong number."

Then he remembered that bloke, Lovering stealing his parking space and flicking the V sign. He was wearing a wedding ring, years in the force had taught him to note those little details. He fished his smartphone out of his trouser pocket and tapped the Facebook app. He then selected 'Friend Finder' and keyed in James Smethurst, Albridge. "Ha ha," he whispered as Smethurst's profile revealed him having a wife called Lizzy. *They're both married,* he thought.

His mind was hatching a plan to get the pair arrested but now his conscience told him to slow down. He tipped his head back and closed his eyes. They'd both been rude to him, Smethurst with his night-time wrong number and Lovering over the parking space. If he was going to do it he'd have to be full on, no hint of apology or sympathy. He tapped in Smethurst's number and his finger hovered over the Enter key. He recalled the wrong number, the lack of apology, the rudeness and the arrogance. He thought of losing his job and spending each day with just these four walls to look at. His finger lurched forward and pressed 'Enter'. It was answered after three rings.

"Yup," said Smethurst.

"Do you know your wife's having an affair with my sister's husband?"

"You what?"

"Your wife is having an affair with my sister's husband."

"Who is this?"

"The brother-in-law of the geezer your missus is shagging."

"Yeah, well I've kind of reckoned on that," replied Smethurst.

"I'd rather not give my name but I want it stopped. My sister is very upset."

"Well, yeah I can believe that. Can't say I'm too happy about this piece of news myself. How do I know you're telling the truth?"

"You are James Smethurst, married to Lizzy?"

"Yup."

"Well I've had a private detective on them. They're meeting tonight Brook Street, eight p.m. He'll be driving a blue Ford Focus."

"Oh God," said Smethurst, "really?"

"Yup."

"Okay, I'll put a stop to this."

"Thanks," said Tadler, "it'll be a great relief to my sister if you could."

Tadler then dialled Lovering, gave him the same story then settled back and sipped his beer.

25

Madge showed Jack and Sandra Pughes into Foster's office. Jack looked pensive as Foster shook their hands and invited them to each take a seat.

Ellie arrived with a tray of tea.

"What's this all about?" asked Sandra.

"It's your dad," said Ellie. "We don't feel he's settling."

"Oh," said Sandra. "I thought you said that the stability of the care home helps with dementia."

"Well," said Ellie, glancing towards her husband, "normally, yes. But your dad is convinced he is a judge. And, well there's the escape attempts too."

"Escape attempts!" said Jack.

"And we notice you haven't visited," said Ellie.

"We've been busy," said Sandra. "Dad took up so much time we've fallen behind with everything else."

"I do understand," said Ellie, "but an occasional visit does help."

"What about these escape attempts?" asked Jack, barely able to hide his horror.

"Well," said Foster, "he's tried to scale the fence twice and tried to fool us he was a laundry man by pressing the intercom button on the gates. He also convinced a couple visiting their uncle that he needed a lift to Albridge. The police had to bring him back on that occasion."

"Oh dear," said Sandra sounding shocked.

"And," continued Ellie, "more worryingly we're suspicious he overdosed on sleeping pills to feign his own death. We even had the undertaker come out that time."

Jack sat back in his chair with a stunned look on his face.

"What do you expect us to do?" asked Sandra.

"Madge has gone to fetch him," said Ellie, handing out the cups of tea, "She's settling him in the dayroom. Can you have a word?"

*

"All right, all right, I can manage," said Mentall, shaking off Madge's guiding hand and taking the seat he was directed to in the dayroom. He was not amused to hear that his 'daughter and son-in-law' were 'just having a chat with the Fosters' and would be along to see him directly.

Mr Handcross was sat in a chair opposite looking around him as if he was seeing the room for the first time. Mentall closed his eyes in despair. He had to get out. Even if he lost his career and status at least people would know he had once been somebody. In here he was treated like all the other idiots and that irked him more than anything.

He cast his mind back to his school days and the book he'd borrowed from the school library describing the heroic accounts of British prisoners of war escaping from Colditz Castle. Not knowing how long they'd be incarcerated for they took to culturing dry rot spores to eat through the stone walls. Mentall didn't intend to play that long a game but he took inspiration and decided to set a plan running to try and force his kidnappers into a mistake.

Sandra Pughes entered the dayroom with Jack trailing along behind her. "Hello Dad," she greeted him cheerily. The words sounded as odd to Mentall as they did to Sandra.

"Good afternoon," huffed Mentall.

"Can I leave you to it?" asked Madge.

"Yes, thanks," said Jack.

"They've been looking after you have they?" asked Sandra taking a seat next to him.

"Not bad."

"What's all this about you trying to escape?" asked Jack, taking the seat on the other side of Mentall. Sandra shot her husband a fierce glance.

"Given you've kidnapped me, what do you bloody well expect?" asked Mentall.

"Hush, keep your voice down," Sandra replied.

"I'm kidnapped, I'm kidnapped," yelled Mentall.

Madge came back into the day room. "Shall I get him a sedative?"

117

"No," said Mentall, "I've had enough of your needles in my backside, thank you."

"Then quieten down, you'll disturb the other guests."

Mentall looked around the room. He doubted anything would disturb this bunch of relics.

"Brought you some magazines," said Jack, passing over a carrier bag.

"Playing the good son-in-law?" asked Mentall.

"Something like that."

"Hmm, 'Take A Break', 'Chat' and 'Pick Me Up'. How did you know my taste?" he asked.

"Lucky guess," Jack replied.

"I don't suppose your newsagent stocks the 'The Law Society Gazette' does it?"

"I shouldn't have thought so. Bit pricey that one I should imagine."

"Well it won't be sixty-eight pence," said Mentall, glancing at the cover of 'Pick Me Up'.

"That's all right then," Jack replied, "I'll look out for it."

Mentall wondered how somebody so thick had managed to become part of a kidnap gang. He glanced them both over, taking in as much detail as he could. He doubted Jack was a stranger to 'Ferret Monthly' and, judging by Sandra's fake furs and cheap jewellery, the chances of a copy of 'The Lady' adorning her bedside table were about as plausible as the windup he intended to give them about the cook.

Mrs Somerbee shuffled into the room and headed to the seat next to them. "I'm going to have a baby," she announced.

Sandra looked on with raised eyebrows.

"Actually the doctor told her that," said Mentall. In a bizarre way he found himself enjoying their company.

"Surely not," said Jack.

"Blokes the biggest fool in this place."

Sandra looked furtively around her. "Right unless you stop these escape attempts we'll take you straight back to that room off the bathroom."

Mentall started to reply but was interrupted by Madge coming back into the dayroom carrying a pile of neatly folded sheets. She stopped by Mr Handcross and placed the sheets on the chair next to him. "Time to go to the toilet."

"I don't need to go," the old man protested.

"I know," she replied, "but if I wait until you're ready you'll have an old man's accident on the way."

Handcross grumbled as Madge got him to his feet.

"Have you been eating well Dad?" asked Sandra.

"Yes," Mentall replied. "The new cook's been dishing up some good food."

"Nice is she?" asked Jack.

"Well she's a he and a jock but takes the trouble to walk around and talk to us all. He thinks he recognises me though," lied Mentall, "but he can't remember where from." He then looked for a reaction from his so called daughter and son-in-law.

Mrs Somerbee fiddled with her glasses. "Did you know Brian?"

"Never heard of him," Jack replied, giving her the briefest of glances.

"Oh, that's a shame. You'd have liked him."

"That's was her husband," said Mentall.

Sandra nodded. "So you've made friends with this new cook then?" The words seemed to spring out of her mouth.

"He's offered to play cribbage with me one evening," he said adding to the lie.

"My glasses need repairing again," said Mrs Somerbee attempting to hand them to Jack.

"You need to take them to the optician's," he replied.

"Can't you fix them?" she asked.

"Play along with the poor old dear," hissed Sandra.

Jack took them. "She's loosened the left arm with her fidgeting. You haven't got that miniature toolkit in your bag have you?"

"I think so," said Sandra, "has she got a screw loose?"

Jack and Mentall glanced at each other.

"What's up with you two?" she asked.

"Two very naughty boys," replied Mrs Somerbee.

Mentall watched Sandra's stubby fingers root around her bag. Her flesh bulged around gold rings and her black painted nails curved like talons.

"I've got a hairpin," said Sandra.

"That's no good," Jack replied.

"Here it is," said Sandra and she handed Jack the miniature tool kit.

Sandra waited for Jack to tighten the glasses and hand them back. "So it's good you're making some friends then Dad."

"Yes," Mentall replied.

"And where does the cook recognise you from?" she asked.

"He was up before me in court a few years back."

Mentall looked at the shocked expressions on Jack and Sandra's faces. He was enjoying this.

*

Jack drove away from Smoking Chimneys.

"I don't like the sound of that cook one bit," said Sandra, checking her seatbelt.

"Probably nothing to worry about," said Jack, flicking at a fly that was buzzing near his left ear.

"Nothing to worry about?" asked Sandra, sliding her handbag into the passenger footwell.

"Well the cook can't remember where he recognises Mentall from."

"Mentall only has to remind him," snapped Sandra.

Jack took a sharp intake of breath.

"We need that cook out of there before Mentall spills the beans. We can't afford to take any risks."

"What's the problem if they do realise he's a judge?" asked Jack. "They'll just let him go and our problems will be solved."

Sandra sighed with irritation. "Jack," she hissed through pursed lips, "if it was that easy we'd have set him free beforehand. The whole point of putting him in Smoking Chimneys was to buy us some time. And what's more they think he's my father and have our

120

address." She paused for breath then added, "We need that cook out of there."

"How are we going to do that?" asked Jack, braking to let an overtaking car in.

"Let's go back and see the Fosters again."

"And what are we going to say?"

"I don't know, but we've got to get that cook out of there."

"But won't we be drawing attention to ourselves?" asked Jack, taking a sideways glance at his wife.

"Turn around, we're going to speak with the Fosters."

"Can't we wait?" asked Jack.

"No, we will do it now," stated Sandra curtly.

"Shouldn't we take a day to think about it?"

"Turnaround," Sandra replied.

"What shall we say?" he asked, after swinging round a roundabout.

"Leave it to me, Jack. How much money have you got on you?"

"Two grand," he replied.

"Two grand! Why so much?"

"Well most of it has never seen a bank account or a tax return. I always deal in cash."

"All right then, we'll have that up our sleeves as a bribe. And don't carry so much around in the future."

26

"Ah Mr and Mrs Pughes, please come in again," said Foster rising from his desk and eyeing them suspiciously: relatives leaving then returning a short while later had the habit of raising awkward issues.

"Thank you," said Sandra.

"Take a seat. How about a drink? Ellie has just gone to ask Cook for a pot of coffee, but perhaps you'd like something a bit stronger this time?"

"Yes, that'd be nice. A sherry for me," said Sandra.

"And a whisky for me," added Jack.

"It's a bit early for whisky isn't it?" hissed Sandra as Foster prepared the drinks.

"This is a difficult situation," whispered Jack, "I don't like it one bit. No way is he going to buy this story."

Foster hadn't been keen on his wife asking Mr Miles's family to visit. There was always the risk of losing a customer when the family weren't happy. He always had the drinks tray ready; a bit of buttering up went a long way.

Ellie entered the room. "Sorry I was awhile. Mr Sidebottom's colostomy bag was leaking."

"How did the chat go with your dad?" asked Foster, handing out the drinks.

"It appears the escape attempts are down to the food," said Sandra.

"The food!" exclaimed Colin and Ellie in unison.

Jack Pughes slugged back his whisky, which Ellie promptly topped up.

"Steady on, I've only got one mouth," said Jack.

"That's subject to some debate," snarled Sandra.

"You were saying about the food," said Foster cautiously.

"Well he thinks your cook is trying to poison him," replied Sandra.

"Better watch that coffee you've ordered," said Jack light-heartedly.

"I beg your pardon," said Ellie.

Sandra shot Jack a black look.

"This all sounds very strange," said Foster, "and what is the food doing to him? The cook is new, came with excellent references and the other guests appear to be very happy with him."

"Look," said Jack, "we will give you two grand to sack your cook."

Sandra glowered at her husband.

"Sack my cook," exclaimed Colin Foster, "sack my cook for two thousand pounds?"

A voice came from the open doorway. "Is that Mr Handcross in there?" All the occupants of the room turned to see Mrs Syms parked up in her wheelchair. "I've been looking for him everywhere."

Jack Pughes slugged back another whisky as Mrs Syms wheeled herself into the room and added, "I thought I heard Mr Handcross saying I have to pay a two thousand pound fine."

Ellie went to the corridor and called, "Madge, take Mrs Syms to the dayroom."

The door closed and Ellie, after topping up Jack's glass again, joined her husband behind the desk. Foster was gearing up to accept the two thousand pounds when his wife interjected, "This just doesn't add up."

"You see," started Sandra, "Dad was a prisoner in the Malayan Emergency," her voice was low and soft. "There was a cook, a Malayan National Liberation Army cook that tried to poison our boys. Dad has got it into his head your new cook is that man. That's why he keeps trying to escape."

"But Cook comes from Peebles," exclaimed Foster.

"There's no convincing him," offered Jack.

"I see," said Foster, "do you mean there's a Malayan fighter in my kitchen making coffee?"

"Did you want tea then?" asked Ellie.

"No," said Foster, "I mean, never mind."

"Why the money?" asked Ellie.

"Severance, we assumed you'd want to pay severance," said Sandra.

123

The room fell quiet. Jack relaxed into another whisky.

"We'll have to give this some thought," said Ellie. Foster shifted in his seat. Two grand was two grand, he was all for accepting it and kicking the cook out with zero severance, but he knew Ellie would protest about the extra workload for her and Madge.

"Okay," said Sandra, "it's just that Dad's so scared," she managed to tail her voice off to a gentle sob.

"Yes, yes," Foster replied, offering a paper tissue from a box on his desk.

"Colin and I will talk it over later," said Ellie.

"Thank you," Sandra replied.

"We doubt you *really* have a Malayan fighter in your kitchen," said Jack. His voice trailed off and he looked around the room awkwardly.

27

Jack drove away from Smoking Chimneys for the second time that day. He glanced across at his wife: her face was black with thunder. "Let's hope they take the bait and get rid of that cook," he said.

"You're a bloody idiot offering my two grand straight away," began Sandra, "what on earth did you think you were doing?"

Turning onto the main road he picked up speed and clicked on the air conditioning. He knew better than to argue about who owned the two grand. "I think I did–"

"You think you did what?" she scorned. "If they get rid of that cook it'll be no thanks to you Jack Pughes."

"Don't you *Jack Pughes* me."

"I'll darn well Jack Pughes whoever I bloody well want. Especially you Jack Pughes. You've cost me two grand you bloody idiot."

"I'd like to know how you'd have handled it without offering them money."

"I'd have given them the prisoner of war camp story like I did!"

"But you only thought of it *after* I'd offered the bribe, not before. If you're so fucking clever why didn't you say it *before* I offered the bribe?"

"Don't you fucking me."

"Don't worry about that, I won't be fucking you for a very long time."

"I wouldn't let you anyhow. And I always fake it."

Jack hammered the accelerator, the car obligingly hit eighty-five miles per hour before Jack broke hard to negotiate a roundabout.

Turning right onto a minor road he heard a siren and saw the flash of blue lights in his rear view mirror.

"Oh shit."

"Your own stupid fault," said Sandra with a tut.

"I've been drinking."

"Tell me something I don't know."

"Have you got any mints?"

"Oh we are going to try that well known remedy for covering up being pissed out of one's bloody mind are we?"

"I've got to try and get the smell of alcohol off my breath."

"Try and stop burping then."

"I'm not burping."

"You always burp."

"Since when," Jack protested.

"Since I've known you," said Sandra, glancing behind her to take a look at the police car.

"You've never mentioned it before."

"When it comes to your digestive system it's a case of choosing ones battles."

"Well thank you very much," blurted Jack.

"You're welcome."

"It's probably the dog farts you can smell at home," said Jack.

"The dog's been dead a twelve-month! I know they lingered but that's ridiculous."

"Quick, give me a mint I'm not feeling too grand."

"Too bloody right," Sandra replied, "you offered it to that Foster couple."

"Ha ha, very funny."

The police officer approached and Jack lowered the window.

"Name?" asked the officer.

"Jack Pughes."

"Occupation?"

"Well, erm…"

"What do you do?" asked the officer, raising his eyebrows.

"Whatever I bloody well tell him," chipped in Sandra.

The officer briefly glanced towards Sandra. "Very good madam." He then turned his attention back to Jack. "Do you have your licence on you, sir?"

"Er… yes," Jack replied, fumbling in his pocket.

Sandra huffed impatiently.

"And what is this?" enquired the police officer, looking at Jack's outstretched hand.

"A twenty pound note," said Jack, raising his eyebrows and nodding.

"Do I take it, sir that in some way you're offering me a gift?"

"Yes, yes. That's right. A gift," Jack replied.

"And you think I'd risk my house, salary and pension for a twenty pound note?"

"Well er… there's no risk."

"Tell me, sir, do you always attempt to bribe a police officer when you have been pulled over?"

"Well it's the best time to do it," Jack replied.

"Very droll, sir. Do you know why I've stopped you?"

"Er… no officer."

"I expect it's the number plate light," offered Sandra, smiling towards the police officer. "I have been on at him to get it fixed."

"Be quiet," hissed Jack.

"No madam," replied the police officer, taken aback at Jack's rudeness, "not the number plate light. And it's daylight madam, your husband didn't have his lights on."

"One of the brake lights then?" she enquired.

"Shut up woman," hissed Jack.

"No, the reason I have stopped you is the way your husband braked sharply at the roundabout."

"I told you to slow down," said Sandra.

"Be quiet will you," said Jack.

"Your approach to the roundabout was way too fast, sir. You failed to get your speed down in time. Fortunately for you, sir I was not tracking your speed and, as I didn't have the camera running, this is just a verbal warning this time."

"I'm always telling him off for his speeding officer."

"Just bloody be quiet will you," Jack exploded.

"Tell me," said the police officer lowering and directing his voice to the passenger compartment, "is your husband always this rude to you?"

"Only when he's been on the whisky, officer. He's okay with the gin."

The police officer turned his attention back to Jack. "Right, right you – out the car you get. Come with me."

Jack turned and glowered at his wife before getting out and following the police officer to the patrol car. His shoulders were hunched safe in the knowledge that certain arrest was pending and further wrath was due from Sandra. When directed he obligingly sat in the rear passenger side seat. He waited until the police officer had settled himself in the driver's seat. "I'm as sober as a judge," he protested.

"Your wife said differently, sir."

"My wife's mad."

"You shouldn't be so hard on yourself, sir."

Pughes dropped his head into his hands. "I need the car for my work," he said in a last ditched attempt.

"Do you think I care about that?"

"No. Sorry."

"That's okay, sir. An easy mistake to make."

"But my wife's over the limit too."

"She wasn't driving was she?"

The officer then took an Intoximeter from the glove box, fitted on a mouth piece and handed it to Jack. "Blow into this tube please, deep breath now."

Jack inhaled and then blew and the police officer smiled. He took a pair of handcuffs from his belt, snapped them on Jack's wrists and then read him his rights.

"Like taking candy from a baby," said the police officer. "I'll just have a word with your wife before we go."

"I've had several myself," Jack replied ruefully.

Jack watched Sandra half lower her window and speak to the police officer. He cringed and rehearsed conversations to be used later.

The police officer returned alone. "Believe me, sir I think a night in the cells is the safest place for you," he said before settling himself into the driver's seat. He then spoke into the radio attached to his lapel, "M2GW this is U3 bringing in a PBT."

"Roger that U3," came the reply.

"He's a double limiter too," said the police officer.

"You've not had one of those since New Year's Eve have you?" replied the radio.

"Nope and I can bang this one up. No letting *him* off the hook."

As they pulled away Sandra glared through the now wound up window.

"Why do you have to bang me up?" asked Jack. "Can't you let me off the hook like this fellow on New Year's Eve?"

"Well that fellow on New Year's Eve was the chief superintendent of traffic division and, for reasons of sudden career stagnation, I was obliged to forget all about it."

"I suppose you're in the same lodge or something?" asked Jack sounding piqued.

"What are you exactly accusing me of?" asked the police officer, with an accusatory tone in his own voice.

Jack thought for a while. "Nothing."

28

Just before eight p.m. Sergeant Tadler pulled into Brook Street, switched off the engine of his BMW and surveyed the scene. A row of shops backed onto the pavement: each with the obligatory overflowing blue waste bin. A squirrel leapt from a tree and ran along the top of a wall.

All was quiet until Lovering's blue Ford Focus turned into the street and slowly pulled up. Lovering got out, stretched and looked around. He was about six foot one, short dark hair, around thirty years of age, with a drawn worried look. He looked towards the BMW. "Not me you idiot," whispered Tadler.

A scruffy Honda Jazz arrived from the other end of the street and pulled up in front of the Ford Focus. Tadler surveyed Smethurst getting out of his car. About forty, five foot seven, balding, portly with a moon face. "Got me a paedophile," he whispered while considering the state of this guy's hard drive. When it came to the photo call section on any episode of Crimewatch UK, Tadler prided himself on guessing the offence from the photo-graph.

Tadler watched them eye each other up.

"You been seeing my wife?" asked Lovering.

"I was going to ask you the same," replied Smethurst.

"Where is she?"

"Where's who?"

"My wife?"

"Don't be a tosser," replied Smethurst, "I haven't got your wife. It's you that's been seeing my missus."

"No I haven't," replied Lovering, "and don't call me a tosser."

"I'll call whoever I want a tosser," replied Smethurst, squaring up to Lovering and throwing a punch.

Lovering dodged the blow then retaliated by pounding his fists into Smethurst's chest.

Tadler buckled forward with laughter as tears streamed down his face. Smethurst was getting the beating he duly deserved: if arresting

130

these two didn't lead to his suspension being revoked at least he'd had his entertainment.

The cries of 'Tosser' started up again and Tadler decided it was time for professional action. He leapt from his car and yelled, "Stop, police."

The two contenders froze for a moment before turning towards him. He smiled: they'd have run off if either had been in trouble with the law before.

"What's all this about then?" he asked.

"He's been having it away with my wife and calling me a tosser if you please," said Smethurst.

"It's you that's been sleeping with my wife!" replied Lovering.

"No, I bloody well have not."

Intent on dismissing all claims and counter claims Tadler cuffed them, stuck them in the back of his car and, ignoring all requests to see his warrant card and queries about an aged BMW being a police vehicle, he set off for the cells.

He parked around the back of the police station, unloaded his two prisoners and marched them to a door marked 'Custody Suite'. He pressed the button on a video intercom and sighed with relief when they were buzzed through: clearly news of his suspension had not yet got around.

A custody sergeant stood behind a desk which ran the entire length of the room. "What have we here then?"

Behind him was an office area with desks littered with computer screens, piles of paper and discarded coffee cups. A hatch in the far wall, where members of the public could make enquiries, framed a withered old man standing next to an equally withered old lady.

"Excuse me, excuse me," said the old man.

"Sorry, Pete," said the sergeant rolling his eyes. "I'm having to man the enquiry office *and* the custody suite tonight." He turned and addressed the old couple. "What can I do for you two?"

"My wife and I have come to visit your web site," said the man, clearly proud of his courage.

"You what?" replied the sergeant.

"On the local radio news this evening they said to visit the police web site for tips about crime prevention," explained the man.

The sergeant turned to face Tadler, raised his eyebrows then returned his attention to the elderly couple. "So you drove here to visit our web site did you?" he asked, just managing to suppress a laugh.

"No, we came on the bus. Our car was stolen last month."

"Have you found it yet?" asked the lady. "It was a Toyota Yaris."

"Probably not," replied the sergeant, drumming his fingers against his right hip, "if they don't show up in a couple of days they're gone for good. Some nasty gangs working out there. By now it'll either be a ringer, shipped abroad or broken for spares. Best you go through your insurance company."

"We have," said the old man, "but they won't pay up."

"These insurance companies are as bad as the crooks if you ask me," called out Tadler. He was keen to get his prisoners booked in and didn't want to get embroiled in another complaint about this particular sergeant's bedside manner. His last dealings with an elderly man had resulted in a stern email, to all staff, regarding the inappropriate use of the word 'Grandpa'.

"You need to get yourself on a computer to see our website," said the sergeant. "You don't come in here to see it."

"We don't have a computer," said the old man.

The sergeant shrugged his shoulders.

"Come on dear," he said, leading his wife away.

The sergeant turned his attention back to Tadler. "What have we here then?"

"Affray, caught them in Brook Street punching each other and repeatedly calling one another tosser."

"I see. Back street rendezvouses, fighting and calling each other names eh?" said the sergeant. "Look we get all types in from that Brook Street, you'd be surprised. Doctors, dentists even respectable people, like. I blame the internet, puts you poofters in contact with each other. Personally I don't care if you hammer one another's testicles to a table, or whatever you do, but the law is the law and we are here to administer it."

"Poofter!" exclaimed Lovering.

"I'd strongly advise you *not* to get personal," said the sergeant. "This can all be used in evidence against you."

"No, you don't understand," said Lovering, his voice cracking with anger. "This man has been seeing my wife and when I catch up with him he calls me a tosser and picks a fight."

"I like that," said Smethurst.

"He has the gall to admit it," replied Lovering.

Smethurst struck back, "It's you that's been seeing my wife."

"Wives or no wives doesn't wash with me for a cover story," replied the custody sergeant, drawing his voice out to indifference. "That Brook Street is notorious and you're both booked and spending a night in the cells. Name?"

"Lovering, Edward Lovering," replied Lovering.

"Love Ring," replied the sergeant, entering the name into the custody book.

"No, it's Lover ing."

"Spell it."

"L O V E R I N G."

"Love Ring," replied the sergeant hanging on each word.

Tadler fought back the tears and did not dare catch the sergeant's eye.

"And you?"

"James Smethurst."

"Smear Test and Love Ring. Quite a couple of likely lads you two knob gobblers are. Right, we've only got the one cell free at the moment so I want you both on your best behaviour. And," he continued, pointing to a monitor on the wall, "I can see your every movement so no more dustups."

29

"It smells a bit rank," said Edward Lovering breaking the ice and eyeing up the stainless steel toilet in the corner of the brick lined cell.

"Just airless," said Smethurst.

"I've never been in a cell before."

"Me neither, and I wouldn't be now if it wasn't for you," replied Smethurst.

"Look," said Lovering, "I've *not* been seeing your wife. I don't know you or your wife for that matter."

The key turned in the lock of the cell door. It swung open and came to rest under its own weight. The custody sergeant spoke. "I'm moving somebody in with you so we can free up a cell for a violent offender."

Jack Pughes was then hurried into the cell, and the door was shut and locked behind him. He took his seat and surveyed the other two. "What you been up to then?" he enquired.

"Nothing," they both replied.

"And nothing buys you a night in the cells?"

"It's all a mistake," said Lovering.

"It always is," said Pughes with a chuckle.

"Nah, it's all your fault," said Smethurst, pointing to Lovering.

"Keep your voice down, you'll get us chucked out," said Pughes with a laugh.

"You keep out of this," said Lovering.

"All the same to me," replied Pughes, shrugging his shoulders. "First time in the cooler?"

"Yes, it bloody well is," said Lovering.

"Me too," added Smethurst, glancing up to the bars at the top of the ancient, yellow door.

Pughes, turned and stretched out his legs on his concrete bench. "Ah, you'll get used to it. You'll get used to it. The first night's always the worst but after that they can throw most things at you and you can deal with it. I'll wager you at three a.m. you'll both be wanting your mothers but after that, well it's plain sailing."

"So you've done time before?" asked Lovering.

"Oh yes, many a time. Normally small stuff, never been able to lay the big ones on me. Never. Too shrewd I am, got to know the tricks. Got to know when to let a copper bust you for something minor so it keeps him off the scent of the big ones. I've even done time for stuff I've never committed, just to keep the boys in blue off the trail. That's the cunningness, that's the cunningness."

"That doesn't impress me," said Lovering, with an air of self-confidence.

"Oh, so I don't impress you eh? Made my life out of crime I have."

"There's no such thing as a *life* of crime. An existence maybe," replied Lovering.

"Oh there is, there is. I've masterminded more crimes than you've had hot prison dinners."

Lovering and Smethurst looked at each other in total incredulity. "We've never been to prison," said Smethurst.

"Look boys, you're just a pair of amateurs I know. Not in my league. Don't pretend you are. Gets you nowhere."

"What *big job* are you in here for today then?" asked Lovering.

"Well, a bit of drunk driving."

"Drink driving, that's hardly the hand of a mastermind," said Lovering.

"But that's the beauty. The law's got me for something, hides the big job."

"And the big job is?" asked Smethurst, his voice riddled with scorn.

"Well that'd be telling, never divulge. Never divulge."

"There's no *big job*," scorned Lovering. Smethurst smiled and nodded, "you've just got yourself done for drink driving and that's that."

"Hah, wouldn't you like to know." There was a defensiveness in Pughes's voice.

Lovering blew his cheeks out. "Yes. Okay we do want to know."

"Well then. Now you want to know. Have you read about that judge that's gone missing?"

Lovering and Smethurst nodded.

"Well, me and the missus have got him stitched up in an old folks' home. I was on my way back from a visit when a copper picked me up. We're just biding our time until we can extract the right fee. That copper didn't have a clue – thinks he's a clever dick for getting a drink driver. The real crime is just out of his reach."

"And you expect us to believe that?"

"Nope. You're too small time to bother with. This is the plan of a mastermind."

30

Tadler spent the night searching DCI Marjorie Stainthwaite's office. He went through each drawer of her wooden desk and metal filing cabinets. He inspected everything with meticulous detail and found nothing.

At eight a.m. he returned to the custody suite in the hope that Lovering and Smethurst would crack under interview and agree to plead guilty to a charge of affray. A double arrest, while suspended, would show him in a good light.

"Right you first," said Tadler, pointing at Lovering.

Lovering slunk out of the cell looking as if he was glad the night was over. Tadler showed him to a barren interview room and directed him to take a seat. He was offered no legal representation, no second officer as a witness, and there was no video or tape-recorder running. Having never been in trouble with the law before he was unaware of his rights.

"What have you got to say for yourself then?" asked Tadler.

"Not very much. I got a call yesterday from some bloke saying my wife has been seeing his brother-in-law and they'd be in Brook Street at eight p.m. I turn up, Smethurst is there, calls me a tosser and picks a fight."

"And you expect me to believe that?"

"Well, it's the truth."

"I'll be the judge of that," said Tadler, "I'll be the judge of that. Remember you're under arrest for causing an affray. The courts are clamping down on things like that."

"Look it's not my fault."

"But you were involved in a street fight."

"I was attacked," replied Lovering, raising his arms.

"But I saw you throw punches."

Lovering straightened himself. "I recognise your voice from somewhere."

"Ever been in trouble with the law before?" asked Tadler, deepening his voice.

137

"No, I've never been in trouble with the law and I've done nothing wrong this time either. Smethurst is the culprit and that other chap in our cell, Pughes or whatever his name is, claims to be going round kidnapping judges. Why don't you go after them?"

Tadler was silent and thought for a while. This was *very* interesting; a possible lead about the judge and from an unexpected chain of events.

"I'm sure I recognise your voice," said Lovering.

"Right you're free to go for now," said Tadler, realising that Lovering was getting suspicious.

"What?"

"You're free to go for now, out you go. We might be in touch with charges soon. We'll see."

Tadler showed him out into the foyer then, after watching him pause the other side of the glass entrance doors, and shake his head, turned back to the custody sergeant.

"Where's that Pughes fellow we're holding?"

"He's already been fetched for the magistrate's court."

"Shit," Tadler replied.

*

"Right," said Tadler sitting the other side of the desk to Smethurst in the interview room, "what's all this then about back street rendez-vouses, picking fights, calling people tosser then causing an affray in a public place?"

"I never have, least of all with that other guy."

"Least of all? So there have been others."

"No."

"You just said 'least of all'. Sounds like there are others to me."

"It was just a figure of speech. Anyhow this is ridiculous, where's the video camera and somebody else sitting in? And where's my legal representation?"

"Quite the lawyer aren't we," Tadler replied, raising his eyebrows.

"I know my rights."

"I'll be reading them to you in a minute. So how do you know so much about police work then?"

"If you must know I used to work in the Eastshire control room as a nine-nine-nine call taker."

Tadler paused, this was getting tricky. But he was already suspended so as tosses went this was worth giving.

"Okay, you're not under caution. You're free to leave when we're done, and I'll scratch any charges against you. However, tell me about that other guy in with you?"

"What, the self-confessed judge-napper?"

"Yes. Tell me all about him."

"There's nothing to tell really, other than he claims he's got him hidden away in a care home. That's all he said. Full of crap if you ask me."

"I wasn't asking you."

"You just said tell me about him," spluttered Smethurst.

"Which care home?" asked Tadler, ignoring Smethurst's nit-picking.

"He didn't say."

"No clues at all?" asked Tadler.

"Nope."

Tadler leaned back and scratched his head. "Why did you leave your job at Eastshire?"

"The force merger, I was made redundant. They moved the control room to Northshire and all us civvies got the push."

"What are you doing now?"

"Not much. Odd bits of work here and there," he replied, shrugging his shoulders.

"Ever thought of joining the police?"

"Ha. Why do you ask?"

"Oh, I just thought."

"Playing the nice cop now then?" replied Smethurst, giving him a stare.

"I might be," Tadler replied.

"I did apply and went for a selection day."

"What happened?"

Smethurst sighed and shook his head. "We had to write an essay on how we'd have handled a gang of youths running amok in a town centre. I knew the exact police procedure, but they claimed I'd been watching too much telly and gave me bottom marks. I stood my ground and when they realised I'd been a call handler they upped me to top marks."

"And you didn't get past the selection board?"

"No, they claimed I was too argumentative."

Tadler let out a snort of laughter. This boy was good. "Nothing going in the new control room?"

"I wouldn't go back. Not now. I thought they'd turn me down as a regular on account of my age, not on account of me knowing how the police work."

"A night in the cells put you off too?"

"You could say that. It stinks. Do you know what?"

"What?" asked Tadler.

"Whenever I took a nine-nine-nine call I might as well have asked, 'Does any senior police officer's career depend on us attending?' because that's what it amounted to."

"Is that so?" asked Tadler.

"Yes."

"Well it's different in Westshire," Tadler replied.

"How so?" replied Smethurst, fixing him with another stare.

"We use our initiative more."

"Oh yeah," replied Smethurst, "like arresting me last night for something I hadn't done."

"You were having a fight weren't you?"

"You said I would be free to go, no charges," replied Smethurst.

"Yeah all right, you can go," Tadler replied.

Tadler saw Smethurst out then, from the custody book, took a note of Pughes's address and car details.

31

Mentall grunted loud enough to invite whoever was knocking at his bedroom door to enter.

"Lovely cup of tea?" asked the wide-bottomed tea lady, stepping into his room and placing a cup on his bedside cabinet. She then crossed to the window and pulled back the curtains. Mentall yawned and blinked as the morning sunlight flooded into the room.

"Thanks," he said, eyeing up her ample frame. He figured as care home assistants went she was not bad, as massage parlour assistants went she was anything but. However, her body alleviated the boredom, and chatting her up past the time. "It must take you an age doing the rounds."

"Tell me about it," she sighed, turning towards him. "We used to only visit the residents that needed help getting dressed. Now it takes half the morning to get round everybody."

Mentall sat up and adjusted a pillow to support his back. "Why the change?"

"Well between these four walls one of the more able-bodied residents died in his sleep. Nobody noticed until the smell brought it to our attention."

"My goodness," Mentall replied, contemplating how rancid the corpse must have been to outdo the normal ambience of the place.

She folded a towel and hung it over the back of a chair. "Are you looking forward to this afternoon?"

"What for?" enquired Mentall suspiciously: there wasn't much to look forward to in this place.

"It's your bath day. There's a rota on your door."

After she had left Mentall inspected the rota and saw he was a category C resident marked as 'Mobile, some faculties remaining, bath once a fortnight in case patient is not dealing with own personal hygiene'. Recalling the amount of money Madam Suzie's House of Pleasure charged for a bath he decided he would get his money's worth.

He then stood at his window, gazed out and reviewed his plans to date. The Daniel O'Donnell impressionist didn't appear to have done anything: the real one would have sent a chauffeur driven Rolls Royce to collect him. Then there was the story he had told the Pughes about the cook having recognised him: nothing appeared to have come of that. He needed another opportunity, and perhaps this bath would be it.

*

Madge let herself into his room. "Bath time, Mr Miles," she called, making her way towards the en-suite. Mentall checked his watch, it was spot on three p.m.

He heard the gush of water thundering against the enamel as a cloud of steam obscured the view into the bathroom. As there was no sign of Madge returning to fetch him he made his own way in. *Not quite the pre-bath service at Madam Suzie's,* he thought.

"Get yourself undressed now," said Madge, opening the window slightly.

Mentall liked the tone of authority in her voice. *This is more like it,* he thought. He quickly stripped and got into the bath. Forgetting where he was for a moment he rolled onto his stomach, raised his backside into the air, and announced, "I've been a very naughty boy."

"I *beg* your pardon?" said Madge, spinning around.

Mentall, realising his mistake, righted himself and mumbled, "Land ahoy. I said, Land ahoy. I was playing battleships."

"Hmm," she replied suspiciously, thrusting her hands on her hips.

He then watched her wet a bar of soap and waited, in excited anticipation, as she soaped up a flannel. To his utter disappointment he found that where Madam Suzie's House of Pleasure concentrated, Madge was brief, and where Madam Suzie's House of Pleasure was brief Madge imposed full hygiene.

When finished she pulled out the plug and Mentall's fantasy, of her stripping and soaking with him, slipped away with the bathwater.

As she reached for a towel he stood and took his opportunity. He had to make it look convincing, look like an accident and leave her mortified. He lifted his right leg, leant back and allowed his left foot to slip on the wet floor of the bath. He landed heavily on his bottom, flopped backwards, dropped his chin onto his chest and then tilted his head to one side.

"My God, are you all right," said Madge, bending down to examine him. She shook him by the shoulders. "Mr Miles, Mr Miles, can you hear me?"

He did not respond.

"Don't peg out on me," she hissed. "Come on you old duffer, wake up."

She's in trouble, thought Mentall.

"Oh shit," she added, before leaning across the bath and pulling on the emergency alarm cord.

Within seconds he heard people running up the stairs and along the landing. "In here," called out Madge.

"What's happened?" asked Ellie Foster.

"He slipped in the bath," explained Madge, "he's out cold."

"I've never known an inmate involved in so many scrapes," said Colin Foster. "Any sign of bruising?"

"Why?"

"We don't want social services asking questions."

"I'll go and call an ambulance," said Ellie.

*

It was around twenty minutes later that Mentall heard somebody being shown into the bathroom.

"Here's the paramedic," said Ellie.

He knew he had to get this right for a ride in the ambulance.

"Mr Miles, Mr Miles," called the paramedic. It was a young woman's voice.

He felt his eyelids being opened to the touch of a latex glove. He rolled his eyes back and caught sight of her 'Student Paramedic' lapel badge. He then took a quick peek down her low collared, green uniform: she wore an amply filled black bra.

Don't you dare you bastard, he thought, tensing his groin muscles to try and contain himself.

He felt her fingers press lightly beneath his clavicle as he caught a gentle whiff of her deodorant. He felt a stirring in his loins.

"Oh my God," said Ellie, "he's got a hard on."

"I feel sick," said Foster.

"That's *not* one of the vital signs I was taught on the Glasgow Coma Scale," said the paramedic. "I'll try a knee reflex next."

Mentall felt a sharp rap below his left knee. His leg kicked up and his big toe buried itself in the orifice of the hot tap. A howling pain shot through his toe and he screamed out.

"Good, that's brought him back," said the paramedic.

"Where did they teach you that one?" asked Madge scornfully.

"The knee reflex is part of our standard training," she replied.

"Jesus buggering Christ," yelled Mentall, buckling forward and grasping his shin.

"How are we going to get his toe out of there?" asked Madge. "I doubt they taught you that one in training school."

"Do you have any lube?" asked the paramedic.

"Not the kind of thing I'm in the habit of carrying around," replied Madge.

"Colin, go and get some," said Ellie.

"Where from?" he asked in a whisper.

"The bedside cabinet," she hissed.

Mentall sank back, closed his eyes and waited until he felt the cold of the gel being smothered around his big toe.

"Is it working?" asked Foster.

"Not really," replied Madge.

"Try running the tap, the hot water will expand the metal," said the paramedic.

"And scald his toe," queried Ellie.

Mentall, figuring that a mangled toe might already be enough to get him a ride to hospital, yanked down. He cried out in pain as his toe obligingly extricated itself.

"Looks like a hospital job," said Madge.

"Not with his record of trying to escape," said Foster.

"Can you patch him up?" asked Ellie.

"Yes, it's only a bit of superficial damage," said the paramedic.

Mentall sank back in defeat.

32

Tadler, after having spent an evening in The Red Lion, returned to his bedsit and spooned a chicken vindaloo takeaway onto a plate. He then slumped into his armchair and began to munch his way through.

That afternoon he had attended an interview with a senior officer regarding the sexual harassment charge he was facing. When Stainthwaite's statement was read to him he had made it very clear what he thought of her. Tadler knew he hadn't played it very well; his body felt heavy with hopelessness.

As he swallowed the last mouthful of his takeaway he cast his eyes around his shabby bedsit. He needed to get reinstated to have any chance of getting out of this place. And catching that judge appeared to be his only hope. He picked up his mobile phone and dialled. It rang for half a minute before a female voice answered: he then asked to speak to Edward Lovering.

"I'll just get him," she replied.

It was another half a minute before Lovering came on the line. "Who is this?"

"DS Tadler."

"It's a bit late isn't it?" said Lovering testily, "It's nearly midnight."

"So it is," said Tadler, checking his watch. "Anyhow I was interested in what you said about your cellmate being the kidnapper of that judge."

"Hold on a minute," said Lovering. Tadler heard a door being closed then Lovering came back on the line. "Look, he was *not* my cellmate."

"Same cell wasn't he?" Tadler replied.

"Yes."

"Then he was your cellmate. Now go over again what Pughes said."

Lovering sighed heavily. "He claimed that he and his wife kidnapped that judge and hid him in a care home."

"Any idea which home?"

"No, but he said they'd just visited him."

"Okay, that's useful. I might have to call you again."

"Don't expect me to be too co-operative though, you're still threatening to prosecute me with street affray. Which I have to remind you was *not* my fault."

"I'll see what we can do about those charges," said Tadler, "if you can be co-operative over Pughes we might be able to let them slip off the book, if you see what I mean."

"Yes, I do see. How did you know my number though, I only gave the custody sergeant my mobile."

Tadler hung up.

News of suspensions travels fast. Tadler had to act fast. At first light he phoned the police officer that had arrested Pughes. It answered after one ring.

"Hi Pete," replied the voice from the other end of the line.

"That Pughes character you arrested for drunk driving, what was he like?"

"A bit shady, I ran a check on him, a few minor offences."

"Where did you pick him up?"

"Just off the roundabout on the Maston bypass. Why?"

"Oh just had my eye on him. Was he long into his journey?"

"Dunno. But he was so pissed I'd have been surprised if he'd travelled far."

"Okay, thanks," Tadler replied then hung up.

He searched through a pile of papers and magazines, littering his coffee table, until he located a copy of the Yellow Pages. He flicked through it until he found a list of private doctors: he needed an independent examination to prove he had haemorrhoids and a legitimate reason why he had his hand down his trousers when his boss, Stainthwaite, had walked in on him. He phoned around and managed to book an appointment for the following Monday, the day before his preliminary tribunal.

Tadler was about to cast the Yellow Pages aside when his eye was drawn to a list of 'Private Care Homes', above the list of 'Private Doctors'. He got out an ordnance survey map of the area, marked

Pughes's address, the position of where he was arrested and all the local care homes. As he circled Smoking Chimneys he realised it fitted the journey perfectly. "Oh shit," he whispered, recalling the Crimestoppers email from the unlikely sounding Daniel O'Donnell impressionist. He dropped his head into his hands – he could have wound this case up long ago and kept in Stainthwaite's good books.

Tadler took a ride over to Smoking Chimneys and parked half a mile down the road. He followed the high fence back to the entrance and peered through the railings of the tall metal gates. The drive was on a curve, obscuring the house from his vision. *Clever,* he thought.

He climbed a stile opposite and made his way up a path through a wooded area. Through the young growth he could just make out the chimneys, but not much else. He decided that if the tribunal did not get him reinstated he'd try and blag his way in to the care home and seek out the judge.

33

Tadler parallel parked his BMW alongside a rundown terrace of bay fronted Victorian houses. He double checked the doctor's address with the Yellow Pages advert. He got out of the car, slammed the door behind him and climbed the three crumbling stone steps to the front door. A small brass plate, screwed to the brickwork, announced that Dr George Webber, private physician, practised within. He pressed the doorbell.

He heard distant movement from deep within the house. A shadow then appeared behind the nineteen-sixty's glass panelled door: it squeaked on its hinges as it was opened. A whiff of stale air caught his nose. Before him stood a stocky, grey-haired, middle-aged man with a bulbous nose littered with red veins. *An alcoholic,* he thought.

"Tapler?" enquired Webber, fixing him with a stare.

"Tadler actually."

"Very well," replied Webber, beckoning him in.

A brown swirly patterned carpet stuck to his feet as he stepped into the lounge. A black leather sofa sat opposite a wall mounted television. In the bay window stood an examination table.

"I think I've got haemorrhoids," said Tadler.

"Ah the old asteroids," replied Webber.

"No, haemorrhoids, piles," said Tadler.

"That's right. Asteroids. Arse Turd Oids around Uranus. They can hurt like buggery," replied Webber.

"You are a registered doctor?" Tadler wondered if he'd have been better off holding out for an NHS appointment.

Webber ignored the question. "On the phone you mentioned something about a tribunal."

"I need you to appear for me regarding my haemorrhoids."

"Ah, an expert witness?"

"Of sorts," Tadler replied.

"Five hundred pounds sound fair?" asked Webber.

Not really, thought Tadler but he knew time was not on his side.

"Well pop your things down and lay sideways on the table and I'll give you a prodding."

"You mean a digital examination?" asked Tadler.

"I prefer the traditional methods," replied Webber, "too much of this digital stuff around these days if you ask me. Now tuck your knees up to your chest."

Tadler eyes bulged and he grimaced with indignity as the offending area was inspected. He made a mental note to check on Webber's zip fastener once the examination was complete. The slightest sign of adjustment and there'd be plenty more than a tribunal to worry about.

"Haven't I examined you before?"

"No," Tadler replied, thinking this guy wouldn't be much use on an identification parade if his recognition techniques depended on a rectal viewing.

"You've quite a few of the little bleeders," announced Webber before adding, "Right you can sit up now and put your things back on."

Tadler sighed with relief and pulled his underpants and trousers back up.

"Yes, you've got Arse Turd Oids around Uranus," said Webber.

"I'd prefer you didn't say that at my tribunal."

"Very well my boy, I know how embarrassing it can be."

34

At his preliminary tribunal, on the charge of masturbating in front of a female police officer, Tadler asked for Webber to be called to the stand. His heart lifted when he saw Webber was dressed in a smart two piece suit with a neat white shirt and a yellow silk tie.

"You examined me did you not?" asked Tadler.

"Indeed I did," replied Webber.

"And can you tell the tribunal whether I have haemorrhoids or not."

"I'm happy to say you do not, you're all clear." He gave Tadler a smile and a nod, he'd kept his word; he didn't want to embarrass the lad. Tadler dropped his head into his hands.

"I think we can safely strike that from the record then," said the chairman and head of Professional Standards, Chief Constable Robert Wytton.

"But I do have haemorrhoids," Tadler protested.

"It appears to me," he replied while directing his voice towards the other members of the tribunal, "Detective Sergeant Tadler's defence to the charge of masturbating in front of a female officer is he was applying cream to a particularly painful haemorrhoid. DS Tadler engaged the services of Doctor Webber who has just confirmed his patient is not suffering from any rectal anomaly. This matter is therefore closed. As this is your primary defence how say you now, Tadler?"

"This is a stitch up. The whole thing's a stich up. I got dumped with the Judge Mentall case because no senior officer wanted to taint their career with it. I'm stressed out, overworked, got piles and was just sorting myself out when in walked DCI Stainthwaite and claims she caught me having a wank."

"You were in *fact* entrusted with the Judge Mentall case," Wytton replied, "and I'd ask you to moderate your language."

Tadler got to his feet and yelled, "Webber's a fucking idiot."

"DS Tadler," bellowed the chair, "I will not have such language in *my* tribunal. Doctor Webber is a respected physician. Why you called him as a witness when he'd diagnosed you as haemorrhoid free beggars belief and perhaps is more of an indication on your fitness to continue in the force than the original charge the panel is considering this afternoon. You will kindly refrain from swearing."

"Oh fuck off," blurted out Tadler.

Wytton tore the glasses from his face and glowered at him. "DS Tadler, I find you a particularly offensive individual." He turned to his colleagues and continued, "It may interest the panel to hear that when interviewed, following his suspension, DS Tadler referred to DCI Marjorie Stainthwaite by the C word." Turning back to Tadler he added, "That wasn't clever was it?"

"No it was cunt, Sir," said Tadler, fed up with the entire proceedings.

Wytton took a sharp intake of breath. "I can't see we are getting anywhere with this. I'll move on to the next point of the hearing, your general performance and attitude as a police officer. You state you were on the Judge Mentall case but it appears you made no effort to find the judge and have singularly failed in your duty and, in so doing, have embarrassed Westshire."

A panel member leaned across and whispered to Wytton.

"I mean Shire Force," he clarified.

"Not so," said Tadler forcefully.

"Not so what?" asked Wytton.

"Not so I have failed in my duty."

"So you have found Judge Mentall then?" asked Wytton suspiciously.

"In a manner of speaking Sir, yes."

"And where is the judge? Do I see him in this hearing?" asked Wytton, turning his head from side to side.

"No, that's because I've been suspended."

"So where is he?" asked Wytton.

"He's in an old people's home."

"He's what? Oh come, come Tadler. You seriously can't expect me to believe this is credible."

"Think what you want," Tadler replied.

Wytton took another deep breath. "Which home, Tadler?"

"Smoking Chimneys."

"And you're telling me Judge Stephen Mentall is a resident in the Smoking Chimneys Rest Home?"

"Yup."

"But why?"

"Search me," said Tadler with no intention of explaining a Daniel O'Donnell impressionist with an unlikely sounding name, Pughes, Smethurst and Lovering.

Wytton sat back, stroked his chin and thought for a few moments. "I think we'll postpone this hearing. You'll remain suspended, Tadler."

35

Mentall laid in bed waiting for his morning cup of tea. It had been three days since he'd spun the Pughes the story about the cook having recognised him. He hoped this would've forced them in to some form of action, but nothing had happened.

He pondered how he could outwit the police should he manage to escape. He also wondered how he could get hold of some money: he hadn't seen his wallet since he left Madam Suzie's House of Pleasure and, in any event, Petronella had just relieved him of the majority of its contents. Clearing his name was one thing but clearing it while sleeping in hedgerows was an altogether different prospect.

There was a knock at the door. Moments later it opened.

"Morning Mr Miles," said the wide-bottomed tea lady, "lovely cup of tea?"

"I'll just have your usual," gruffed Mentall.

"Did you sleep well?" she asked, placing the cup on his bedside cabinet.

"Not bad."

She crossed to the window and pulled back the curtains. "And how is the toe this morning?" she asked.

"Much better," he replied.

"I expect you're looking forward to this afternoon," she said, turning towards him and allowing her ample bosoms to come to a natural rest.

As far as Mentall was concerned this was becoming a bit repetitious. First it was a medical, then it was a bath. Now knowledge of some other delight, unbeknown to him, was about to be imparted. And added to that he was starting to go off her sexually.

"The Maston Primary School Drama Club," she continued, "are visiting to perform Charlie and the Chocolate Factory. That'll be fun won't it?"

"Oh bloody hell," groaned Mentall.

"Oh dear, have you seen it before?"

"Yes, yes," Mentall replied, thinking faster than when he had got hoodwinked into attending the Daniel O'Donnell evening.

"Well perhaps you'd like to come along anyhow. They need all the support they can get."

Mentall wasn't surprised to hear that.

"And between these four walls half the clientele in here won't have a clue what's going on. An educated man like yourself will know when to applaud."

"Preferably when they've finished," said Mentall, taking a sip of his tea.

"Oh Mr Miles do you have to be so cynical? You were a little boy once in need of encouragement."

Mentall couldn't recall needing any encouragement when he was a little boy.

"It starts directly after lunch – one thirty in the dining room."

*

As he was right out of ideas for escape plans he decided to give it a go. Sitting in his room wasn't going to get him anywhere, and the play might give him inspiration or one of the teachers might be helpful. Though in the present circumstances he couldn't see how.

Mentall entered the dining room. The Fosters, and what appeared to be two teachers, were arranging chairs and directing school children as to where they should stand. A number of residents, including Ginger Jenkins, Mr Handcross, Mrs Syms and Mrs Somerbee, were sat in the area laid out for the audience.

On seeing Mentall, Jenkins got to his feet and called out, "Hello there, come to see the concert party?"

"Thought I'd give it a go."

"Come and join me and Handcross. We're the only chaps here. Though Johnny should be back soon."

"Who's Johnny?" asked Mentall, walking towards the seat that Jenkins was pointing out.

"You know, Johnny whatnot... just been scrambled – up there

giving the Hun what for. Be up there myself if my kite wasn't in for an overhaul."

Mentall sighed and surveyed the room.

Colin Foster stepped forward and cleared his throat. "Thank you all for attending. Let's start with a round of applause for the children of Maston Primary and their teachers, Mr Sutherland and Miss Wanless."

"He's not our teacher," shouted one boy but was drowned out by impressive clapping from Ginger Jenkins and Mrs Syms.

"Right," said Miss Wanless, "this is an audience participation production."

Mentall wondered where this was going. The last audience participation he'd been to was in Amsterdam.

"As you can see," continued Miss Wanless, "the production is a bit short on old people and as you'll no doubt recall Mrs Bucket, played by myself, has to look after Charlie's four aged grandparents. So who wants to be a grandparent?"

"Do we all have to be in the same bed?" asked Mrs Syms.

"Well yes, but it's just blankets and pillows on chairs arranged opposite one another. And you can stay in your wheelchair."

"Count me in," she replied.

Based on her reputation Mentall figured he might be about to see a repeat of what he'd witnessed in Amsterdam.

Mrs Syms was wheeled into position. Miss Wanless gesticulated to Mr Sutherland how she wanted the chairs arranged and then asked, "Who's going to be the other grandmother?"

"Me, me," said Mrs Somerbee, raising a bony hand.

Ellie Foster helped her to her feet and guided her to the chair next to Mrs Syms.

"Right," continued Miss Wanless, "now for the grandfathers."

"Not you, Mr Handcross," said Ellie, "I don't want you in the same bed as Mrs Syms even if it's chairs pushed together."

Mentall drew in his breath. With only three men present, and old Handcross now out of the selection procedure, he could see where this was heading.

Ellie guided Ginger Jenkins to the chair opposite Mrs Syms and returned for Mentall.

155

"Is this really necessary?" he asked.

"Now Stephen, let me help you," she said, lifting him by the arm and guiding him towards the makeshift bed.

"No need to fuss," gruffed Mentall, settling himself down.

"Just like when I was a little girl," said Mrs Somerbee. "Four in a bed."

Mentall hoped this was as far as she wanted to rekindle that particular memory.

"Right, we're ready then," began Miss Wanless. "Mr Sutherland will take some photos to post on the school's Facebook page while I set the scene. I'm waiting for Mr Bucket to return from his job at the toothpaste factory and my son, Charlie has just come home from school. Meanwhile I'm boiling cabbage, the only food we have left in the house."

"Soggy, boiled bloody cabbage is all we get in here," shouted out Handcross, "the place stinks of it."

Mentall was never too sure if the smell was the cabbage or the after effects.

Miss Wanless faced the audience and opened the play. "Oh Charlie we have no money," she wailed.

"Oh Mother I'm so sorry we are so poor," replied the boy playing Charlie.

"What will your Father say when he sees it's boiled cabbage again?"

"Don't cry mother."

"Oh Charlie."

"Oh Mother."

"Oh fucking hell," muttered Mentall.

36

"Thank you for attending, gentlemen," said Home Secretary, Toby Peers. "Item one on the agenda is the response to the press release regarding the misdemeanours of Judge Stephen Mentall." Peers, looked in turn at the three chief constables of the unified Shire Force. "I *said* item one on the agenda, the response to the press release."

"I heard you," said Nortly.

"Right, nothing else you want to talk about?" he asked nervously.

Nortly, Wytton and Edgeson shook their heads.

"Thank Christ for that," sighed Peers, remembering the previous meetings where the agenda had been hijacked by petty squabbles between the three chief constables.

A scrawny looking pigeon landed on the stone windowsill and cocked its head towards the room.

"The press have really taken the bait," continued Peers enthusiastically. "It's not been off the front pages all week. If he was abducted it's now a real possibility his captors will panic and release him."

"Or kill him," said Edgeson.

"Okay Item two," said Peers, ignoring the casual nature of Edgeson's remark. "Robert, how are you getting on trying to locate him?"

Wytton rested his elbows on the table. "It was a slow start–"

"I heard your detective got himself suspended," interrupted Nortly.

"He did," Wytton replied, "but I acted immediately and took over the investigation and I now know where Mentall is." Wytton looked around the room clearly hoping for some recognition of his abilities as a detective. With none forthcoming he added, "He's a resident in an old people's home."

"He's what?" exclaimed Peers, letting out a snort.

"What's the name of this old people's home?" asked Edgeson doubtfully.

Wytton smoothed down his bushy eyebrows. "Smoking Chimneys."

"Do you have it under observation?" asked Nortly.

"Yes, we've been regularly flying a drone over the building and beaming back real time images."

Peers took a sip of coffee. "Very impressive. And from this you've ascertained Mentall is a resident?"

"Well, not exactly. I got that from another source."

"What has the drone *actually* told you then?" asked Edgeson.

"Well, as you know drone technology is still in its infancy," Wytton explained. "It's only line of sight, and drones are susceptible to sudden gusts of wind."

"So *what* have you actually ascertained?" asked Edgeson with clear frustration in his voice.

"That he's not hiding on the roof," Wytton replied reluctantly.

Edgeson sat back in his chair triumphantly.

"But," continued Wytton, "we've planted an undercover officer in there. He's disguised as a visiting school teacher and I'm hoping he's going to send me a photo for confirmation." He then gesticulated towards his iPad.

The chimes of Big Ben striking two p.m. sounded through an open window.

"So are you saying the kidnapping theory is a red herring?" asked Peers.

"Yes, I reckon so," Wytton replied. "I think he's probably there of his own free will." His iPad then made a pinging sound. He tapped the screen. "What do you reckon?" he asked, handing it around.

"Four old people in a bed," said Edgeson, "I know these homes run on a shoestring but that's ridiculous."

"It's a production of Charlie and the Chocolate Factory," explained Wytton. "The old-folk are playing Charlie Bucket's grandparents. Either way is that our rogue judge, top right?"

"Looks like him," said Edgeson, "though he's shaved off the moustache and lost the hairdo."

"Definitely," said Hamilton-Smith, "concentrate on his nose and eyes."

"So do we plan a raid?" asked Nortly.

"I don't see what else we can do," Edgeson replied, shaking his head.

"You need to go careful with a raid," said Hamilton-Smith. "It'll be stuffed full of people with Alzheimer's, forgetful, talking nonsense all the time and unable to understand even the simplest instructions." He then looked around the room before gleefully adding, "There'll be the residents too."

"*Bertie...*" Peers pursed his lips and shook his head. "*Don't provoke them. Let's concentrate on how we're going to tackle this.*"

"As I cover crime I'll take responsibility for the raid," said Edgeson.

"Hang on a minute, I've done all the leg work to find him," said Wytton.

"And I'm operations," Nortly protested.

"What about you, Bertie?" asked Peers. "Do you want it?"

"You've just assigned the Brexit deportations to the NCA," Hamilton-Smith replied. "We've got our hands full."

"How are you getting on with that?" asked Peers, helping himself to a chocolate digestive.

"No problem, Home Secretary. Just about ten thousand EU nationals, who arrived after the deadline, to locate and expel."

"We'll chat about that after," said Peers, raising his hands to quieten any further protests. "Well that leaves me with the casting vote. Robert, as you have located him can Westshire run with this?"

Nortly sat up straight. "So you're putting the head of Professional Standards in charge of a raid!"

"Not as such," Peers replied. "Robert still has the resources of his force to do draw on."

"His force? I thought we were one big force now," said Edgeson.

"No cockups now Robert," said Peers, ignoring Edgeson, "take a few days to plan it."

*

Outside the Home Office Simon Nortly, the Chief Constable for Operations in the Shire Force, and former chief constable of

Northshire, made his excuses, walked half a mile down Marsham Street, snapped open his mobile and dialled the chief superintendent in charge of SOAP.

The phone answered after three rings. "Special Operations Armed Police Unit, Trevor Riseback speaking."

"Trevor, Nortly here."

"Oh, hello Sir."

"Trevor," continued Nortly, pressing a finger in his spare ear to cut out the drone of the London traffic, "it appears our wayward judge is hiding out in an old people's home called Smoking Chimneys. Know it?"

"Yes, but it's on Westshire's patch."

"No such thing anymore."

"Right," replied Riseback.

"I want him arrested, tonight."

"What? A raid at this short notice?"

"It's an old people's home. It's not going to be difficult," Nortly replied, turning his back to the traffic.

"It'll mean overtime for the lads."

"You've got it. I want it done tonight. Understand?"

"Yes."

"I don't want Westshire stealing the glory."

"But I thought you said Westshire doesn't exist anymore?" asked Trevor.

"Trevor, just do it."

"Right, Sir but if I may–"

"No, you may not. I'll call you at nine a.m. tomorrow morning for an update," and with that Simon Nortly hung up.

*

Chief Superintendent Trevor Riseback had a sinking feeling about this one. Nevertheless he phoned through to the sergeant in charge of SOAP and passed on the order.

37

Tadler took a beer from the fridge in his bedsit. He then slumped into his armchair, thumped his feet onto the coffee table and opened the can. He tipped his head forward and sucked up the froth before leaning back and taking a first swig.

He half rued divulging the judge's whereabouts at his tribunal. However, it had had the desired effect of buying him some more time. But something niggled him. He knew the force too well. After another swig of beer his mind became clearer. If they'd dismissed him he might have gone public about the judge's whereabouts. Suspended and he'd keep schtum in the hope of reinstatement. But now it struck him, like a cricket bat to the head, that Wytton would probably organise Mentall's rescue, take all the credit and then dismiss him without a word of thanks.

For any chance of reinstatement he had to get hold of Mentall and arrest Pughes at the same time – if Pughes got away Wytton would use that as another excuse to get rid of him.

Having never met Pughes he needed somebody who could actually identify him. He pulled his mobile from his trouser pocket and dialled Lovering's number. The phone was answered on the third ring and, following some stilted pleasantries, Tadler asked, "Are you doing anything tomorrow morning?"

"Why?" asked Lovering.

"Got a little job, if you co-operate all charges go in the bin."

"Is this how the police *really* work?"

"No, not always. But sometimes we are prepared to negotiate. Sometimes we need a bit of help with our enquiries and that allows us to be lenient elsewhere."

"But what kind of help do you need?" asked Lovering cautiously.

"Well you claimed the guy in your cell," Tadler decided not to use the term 'cellmate' this time, "said he'd hidden that judge in an old people's home. Now I think I've traced the home in question, and I'm planning to visit tomorrow. I need you to come along to identify Pughes as the man who claimed to have kidnapped the judge. Without you Pughes could claim he had nothing to do with it."

"What's the chances of Pughes being there when we visit?" asked Lovering sceptically.

"When we get there I'll ask the owners to phone him and say he needs to visit urgently. I'll be in uniform, people are normally cooperative."

"And the charges against me go in the bin?" asked Lovering.

"Yes," Tadler replied.

"I'll take the day off work," he said with a sigh.

"Good. I'll pick you up from your place tomorrow, eight a.m. sharp."

38

The door to SOAP's briefing room swung open and the sergeant in charge of the squad stepped in. He was a slightly overweight, middle-aged man with a light grey beard. He carried two black holdalls which he dropped on the floor before raising a hand to quieten the room. Charts from previous raids were pinned to the walls and various trophies, including an array of plastic sex toys, sat on top of grey filing cabinets.

"Thank you for coming in at such short notice," he began, while glancing around at the twenty or so assembled members of SOAP. "I'm sure you're all aware of the disappearance of Judge Stephen Mentall–"

"Wasn't he the judge at Teddy Sawman's trial?" asked PC Newman, who was known for his ginger hair and forthright views.

"Yes, that's right," said the sergeant.

"Bastard, I'd love to get my hands on him."

"Well, you'll have your chance in the early hours of tomorrow morning. However, you'll be disappointed to learn that our orders are to merely arrest him. Though *reasonable* force might be required if you get my drift. But *don't* quote me as having said that."

"I was there when you didn't say it," said Philip Coleman, an older officer known for his dry humour and momentous gut.

"Right. Now before I forget," continued the sergeant, "I must introduce the first female officer to join SOAP – Jackie Hooper from C Division."

Jackie nodded and smiled as all eyes turned towards her. She was petite and attractive but looked very capable of looking after herself.

"This will be Jackie's first operational duty as an armed officer," continued the sergeant, "so make sure you show her the ropes. Now I've been told we've got to move quickly on this one. This is our chance to show Northshire is still a force to be reckoned with–"

"I thought we were one big happy force now," said Coleman.

"Something like that," said the sergeant, before clearing his throat and continuing: "It appears our wayward judge is hiding out in the rest home known as Smoking Chimneys. Our brief is to arrest him. However, there'll be other residents to consider. So the utmost tact is required. Okay?"

"Utmost tact, my arse," said Newman, "he stitched up Teddy then did a runner."

"To be fair," continued the sergeant, "it was actually the prosecution who determined which bullet killed that bank robber."

"You mean the one they found lodged in his brain, Sarge," said Coleman dryly.

"Bit of bad luck they pinned it on the one from Teddy's gun," said SOAP's dog handler, PC Johnny Jones. Jones was a short, dark-haired man with a reputation for being as strong as an ox.

"What are the risks?" asked PC Andy Bloc.

"Somebody might yell, 'Armed Police, hands up'," said Coleman wryly.

As the rest of the room descended into roars of laughter Bloc's face turned a bright shade of crimson. The bank job, leading to Teddy Sawman's conviction, had been his first operational duty with SOAP and, in the run-up, he'd spent most of the time sat in a toilet cubicle with stomach cramps. So keen had he been to follow every order, and stay alive, he'd taken the command, 'Armed Police, hands up' rather literally: his newfound nickname of 'Andy Hoc' had stuck.

"Apparently," began the sergeant in reply to Bloc's question about the risks, "they've had the home under surveillance. The place is wall to wall with coffin dodgers, and your worst fear is putting a foot in an ill-placed Edgar Allan. Whatever is going on in there isn't going to take the bravery of twenty highly trained members of SOAP to deal with. However, to ensure the welfare of the oldies we're taking a doctor along with us."

"We've got a warrant haven't we?" asked Andy Hoc.

"I'm sure that's all taken care of," replied the sergeant dismissively. "We are going in the early hours, that's the brief. Right, now we need a name for this operation. What Sherlock Holmes characters haven't we used yet?"

"Baskerville," suggested Johnny Jones.

"We used that for the raid on the strip joints," said the sergeant, nodding towards the sex toys on top of the filing cabinets. "Any other suggestions?"

"How about Watson?" asked Newman.

"Used it," said the sergeant. "Perhaps, as Jackie is joining us for the first time, it'd be a nice touch to call it after a female character."

"How about Mrs Hudson?" asked Andy Hoc.

The sergeant smiled with relief. "Operation Hudson it is then."

"And what did Mrs Hudson do?" asked Coleman gleefully.

"She was the housekeeper," Jackie replied with a sigh and a shake of her head. A mischievous smile spread across Coleman's face.

"What's in the holdalls, Sarge?" asked Jones, casting his eyes to the bags by the sergeant's feet.

"We've got new uniforms. Army surplus, full camouflage. Come and take one each."

Jones was first up and pulled one out of the nearest holdall. He turned it over to examine it then exclaimed, "Sarge, I can't wear this!"

"Why not?"

"It's got TWAT printed on the back."

"Yeah, they were made special during the Blair years. One of his big ideas. It means 'The War Against Terrorism'. Funnily enough they've never been used and are now surplus."

"Why does that not surprise me?" asked Jones.

"There's not going to be one for me is there, Sarge?" asked Jackie Hooper, raising her eyebrows.

"Can't you try one of the smaller ones?"

"They won't be my shape, Sarge."

"Look we can't wear these," said Jones, "it was bad enough when we were first formed and called the Fast Armed Response Team. We managed to nip that one in the bud a bit sharpish. SOAP isn't brilliant but at least it ain't too bad. We can't go blazing into an old people's home dressed as a bunch of twats can we?"

"All right, all right. We'll go in standard riot gear and stab proof vests but do try and apprehend this judge before he sees we are SOAP." The sergeant then looked around the room at his team. He began to have an unsettling feeling that this operation was not going to be altogether successful. "I'd better do a check on the weaponry," he continued. "All got your guns?" In turn each SOAP officer produced their standard issue handgun.

"Okay lads," continued the sergeant after casting his eyes over the guns, "I've got to go through the list to make sure none of you is carrying anything illegal. Any knives or anything that could be deemed an offensive weapon?"

There followed a general shaking of heads.

"Any alcohol?"

"No, Sarge," piped up one of the newest recruits to SOAP.

"Don't worry lad," said Coleman, "you can have a swig of mine before we go in."

"Philip!" said the sergeant.

"Sorry, Sarge," replied Coleman with mock chastisement.

"Right are you all ready?" asked the sergeant.

"Yes," came a cry.

"And what are we going to do?"

"Succeed," the men yelled back.

"And why are we going to succeed?"

"Because we are Northshire. We are Northshire. We are Northshire," the men chanted back.

Jackie Hooper looked on in disbelief.

39

Ellie Foster lay awake listening to the rasping and grunting of her husband's breathing. Ever since Mr Miles's remark about inbreeds she had struggled with intimacy. Her head was now full of plans.

She glanced at her bedside clock: it glowed 03:59 in bright green LEDs. She contemplated getting up to make a cup of tea just as a flash of light skipped across a curtainless window. Her body tensed, her heart quickened and her ears tuned to the noise of footsteps cutting through the gravel.

"There's a prowler outside," she said, nudging her husband.

"What?" groaned Foster.

"A prowler."

"No, there is *not*," Foster replied, sounding in no mood to raise himself from the bed.

"Listen."

"Listen to what?"

"That noise in the garden, sounds like somebody moving around."

"It's probably just an animal."

"I'm sure I saw a light."

"Sssh woman, it's not a prowler. If it was the dog would have woken us up."

A few moments passed before she heard the crunch of gravel again. "There's a prowler I tell you."

"It's probably that Syms woman and that fellow Handcross up to their breathalyser antics again," moaned Foster.

"It's outside," Ellie replied.

"We've got a new dog, it would have woken us by now."

"Please go and check," she pleaded.

*

Despite his protest, Colin Foster knew there was to be no peace until he investigated. The sooner he could convince his wife there was no prowler the sooner he could get back into bed.

He emerged naked from the covers and shivered in the chill air. He hunted around for his clothes but opted for the convenience of his wife's frilly, pink nightdress. It normally covered her upper legs but only half covered his backside.

He stepped from the bedroom to the landing and then made his way to the top of the stairs. He steadied himself against the bannister rail as he took each step in turn. He stopped when his bare feet touched the cold stone floor of the hall. He figured that three to four minutes poking around would be enough to convince his wife that there was no prowler.

The door to the kitchen was half open and the hall was lit by the eerie glow of a cooker's digital clock. He stepped towards his office just as a moment of torchlight picked out the half-moon of glass above the front door. With his heart racing he crept forward and bent down to prise open the cast-iron letterbox. His naked buttocks felt cold as his wife's nightdress rode up his back. He peered through the letterbox: a draught of cool air caught his eyes. He blinked twice then made out the gravel driveway before he focussed on the outline of a man's legs standing no more than a few feet away from the door.

Ellie called from the landing. "Are you okay, love?"

"Sssh woman, it's a prowler," he replied.

*

Fang, a retired police dog, recently bought by Foster as additional security for the home, stirred from his slumber in the kitchen doorway. He eyed the bald headed beast at the door; six years in the force had taught him to be resourceful and he decided to handle this one alone. He bore his teeth, leapt and sank his teeth in.

The bald headed beast let out an ear piercing scream. Fang froze as he considered the situation. *How could it make such a racket with his jaw clamped onto its hairy chin?*

He released his grip and watched it sink to the floor, roll over and writhe in agony as it clutched what he now identified as testicles. Only then did he catch sight of his new master's face. He bowed his head and then slunk off into the shadows to await his fate.

*

Hearing blood-curdling screams of agony PC Andy Hoc, the officer who had been standing outside the front door, jumped back and beat a hasty retreat. Foster's shrieks also alerted most of the rest of the home.

"Bandits," yelled Ginger Jenkins, crashing out of his bed in search of his flying suit.

Mrs Syms, who moments before was fast asleep in her wheel-chair, engaged forward traction, yanked open her door and headed down the hall towards Foster. Peering into his crotch she announced, "Well I'm not blowing into that."

SOAP crashed through the door sending splinters of wood and glass showering into the hall: the remains of the door clocked Foster on the head. The overweight PC Coleman, nursing the shoulder he'd just put into the door, and three other constables, all desperate to be the arresting officer, made the initial entrance. Fang's former master, PC 1847 Johnny Jones and his new police dog Polio, followed them in.

Fang, aware that the small matter of the mangled equipment was still to be discussed, decided, as masters went, Jones was the better bet. He launched himself forwards and, with paws to shoulders, Jones fell backwards onto the floor. Only when Fang began to lick his face did Jones recognise his former dog.

Andy Hoc drew his staff and struck a sharp blow to Fang's head. The doting dog collapsed and spent his last few moments smothering his former master with the embers of his life's affection. Jones manoeuvred himself from below Fang's carcass and stood up to PC Andy Hoc.

"What did you do that for?"

"The bastard was attacking you," he replied, gesticulating towards Fang who was just getting the final twitch in.

169

"That's Fang the best police dog I ever had."

Andy Hoc knew there was to be no hint of mitigating circumstances. Johnny Jones held too much weight: his shaky career in SOAP was now all but over.

Polio, who by this point was receiving no coherent instruction from his master, decided it was time to act. He surveyed the scene and identified the man on the floor as the enemy. He sprung forward, sank his teeth into Foster's leg and held on.

Foster let out another scream of agony. "Pull him off, pull him off," he yelled.

"What will that do?" asked Andy Hoc incredulously.

"No, you jerk. I mean get him off my leg."

Andy Hoc, not wishing to go anywhere near Polio's mouth, kicked the dog up the rear. This, in turn, caused him to do nothing more than sink his teeth deeper into Foster's leg. The resultant scream was so high pitched that the dog mistook it for a whistle and unclamped his jaw.

More SOAP officers piled through the front door followed by a rather sheepish looking Doctor George Webber. Being strapped for cash he'd been delighted when asked to accompany a police job. It was only when he got out the police van did he realise the target of the operation was his other employer.

"You," grimaced Foster. "What in the feck are you doing here?"

"I'm a doctor."

"Doctor, doctor! You should bloody well be struck off."

Refraining from declaring that indeed he was already struck off Webber bent down to attend. Foster, realising the possibility of continuing his short love life with Ellie was a bit slim, allowed Webber to make an examination.

"Where are you bleeding from?" asked Webber.

"I bloody well live here, you twat."

"No, no the blood. Where's it from?"

"Me fecking knackers. That bastard dog," said Foster, pointing towards Fang's corpse, "sunk his choppers into them. And this other bastard," he added, pointing towards Polio, "attacked my leg."

"That other 'bastard' you refer to," said Jones, bending and grieving over the body of Fang, "happens to be a highly trained police dog called Polio."

"Don't you come it with me, one of your so called highly trained police dogs has sunk his choppers into my nuts and the other my leg," croaked Foster.

"Polio's a strange name for a dog isn't it?" asked Webber.

"Aye, well it's just his nickname."

P.C. Andy Hoc, having a sudden need for allies, explained, "We know him as Polio back at the nick because he'll have your legs in no time."

"Look Hoc," snarled Jones, "you've done enough damage for one day. Just piss off back to putting parking tickets on old ladies' cars. You're about as useful as a one legged bloke in an arse kicking contest."

While Jones and Hoc were having their spat Webber continued to examine Foster. "Can you roll over for me?"

Foster rolled over.

"That's better," said Webber.

"Why?" asked Foster in an agonised voice.

"Those testicles of yours were bothering me. They look like a couple of vacuum packed Tesco beetroot."

"Well they are bleeding well bothering me too."

In a fit of remembering what a good doctor should do Webber rolled him back over and examined his groin.

"My God, he's had your penis too."

At this Johnny Jones glanced down – this was not to be missed. In panic Foster raised his head and looked towards his groin.

"I don't think so," said Foster.

Webber peered closer, "What you mean that's–"

"It looks like an acorn in a hedge," interrupted Jones.

Another wave of SOAP officers, accompanied by the sergeant in charge, exploded into Smoking Chimneys knocking Johnny Jones unconscious and trampling over Foster.

From the top of the stairs Ginger Jenkins surveyed the additional officers piling into the hall. "Bandits, bandits at three o'clock."

"Bandits yes," a frail voice called back.

"Bandits where? Oh," said Mrs Somerbee, "I wonder if they knew Brian."

"We're under attack," yelled back Jenkins.

"Where's Mr Handcross?" shouted Mrs Syms.

Andy Hoc bent down to attend to the confused looking Johnny Jones. "How many fingers am I holding up?"

Jones, with his head swimming in a haze, tried to focus on Hoc's hand.

"What's your name?" asked Hoc.

"You prick," replied Jones.

The sergeant returned to the front door and looked at Jones. "What's up with him?"

"He's been knocked out, Sarge," replied Hoc.

"Is he bad? Can you get him active again? I need all the man-power I can get."

"Doesn't even know his name."

"Well, tell him he's RoboCop and send him in," replied the sergeant, gesticulating to the mayhem ahead of him.

"And him," added the sergeant, pointing at Foster. "What's the matter with him?"

"He's taken one in the knackers, Sarge."

*

Mentall was woken by the cacophony of noise. With his heart racing he stepped out onto the landing and watched Ellie Foster smile and nod wryly as she surveyed the scene in the hall below her. He followed her gaze to the men in riot outfits battling against a tide of old people.

Deftly avoiding a bewildered Jenkins, Mentall slipped back to his room and changed into his day clothes. He knew what this was about: either somebody had squealed on the kidnappers, they'd got bored and tipped off the police themselves or that Daniel O'Donnell impressionist had claimed some form of reward. But he knew from the newspaper reports that this would be no rescue: he was certain to be detained. Money or no money he needed to get away to clear his name.

Jenkins appeared at his door. "Going out in civvies?"

"What?"

"Escaping."

"Never you mind," Mentall replied wondering how this old duffer was on to him.

"Got many going with you?"

"Sorry?"

"Your escape party. Tunnel is it?"

"No, I'm going it alone," Mentall replied.

"I don't blame you. Going back to Blighty to have another crack at Jerry eh?"

Mentall looked bewildered.

"Tried three times myself, caught each time. What's your route?"

"Out through the front gates and across the fields," Mentall replied.

"Open country, at your most vulnerable."

"Well it *is* dark."

"I'll show you a better way, follow me."

Mentall followed Jenkins as he hobbled across the landing then down the back stairs. In the passageway, leading to the back door, Jenkins stopped and opened a door revealing a set of stone steps descending into darkness. "The back door's always locked at night, this is the best way."

Mentall followed him down the steps.

Jenkins fumbled around. "The light switch is here somewhere." There was a click and a light came on revealing a cellar. "Give me a hand with this," he added, pointing to a lump of cast-iron in the middle of the room.

"What is it?" asked Mentall.

"The old stove, this was the kitchen before they converted it into a prison camp."

"What's under it?"

"The tunnel, they've been working on it for months. You can hear them at night. They thought I wasn't on to them."

Mentall looked at the rusted bolts holding the stove to the floor. "Those bolts haven't been turned in half a century."

"Really. Oh. I could have sworn it was here."

"It's okay, I'll make my own way," said Mentall retreating up the stairs.

"Suit yourself," said Jenkins. He then shook his head and added, "I could have sworn this was their tunnel."

At the top of the cellar steps Mentall turned his attention to the back door. He tried the round brass handle only to find that it was locked.

Jenkins reappeared and pointed to the fanlight above the door. "Your only chance is through that window."

Mentall's eyes followed Jenkins's outstretched arm. "How am I going to get up there?"

"Wondered that myself," Jenkins replied.

"Give me a leg up," said Mentall.

"Righto," said Jenkins, turning his back to the door and interleaving his fingers and cupping his hands.

Mentall plonked his right foot into the offered palms, pressed down and made a grab for the top of the door frame. Jenkins's hands instantly gave way and, as he toppled forward, his right knee crashed into the old man's crotch. Jenkins gasped and bent double as his face turned a shade of beetroot red.

Mentall re-parked his foot on his backside and made another grab for the top of the door frame. With his legs swinging from side to side he managed to flip open the fanlight and haul himself halfway through the gap.

The night air felt cool against his face as his eyes took a couple of moments to adjust to the darkness. When things came into focus he surveyed the back garden. The lawns stretched to a far corner that was eerily lit by the blue echoes of a flashing police light. A bat darted by and an owl hooted in the distance.

He wriggled himself forward and dropped down onto the ground and made a dash for the far hedge. He followed the perimeter to the unguarded entrance and passed through the open gates. He crossed the stile opposite, made his way through the woods then across open fields until he reached the village railway station of Maston.

Back in the house the sergeant shuddered at the complete lack of planning; the operation was turning into a total disaster. His officers were chasing around the house looking for the judge: distressed old folk were being disbursed in all directions.

PC Andy Hoc, desperate to gain favour with his colleagues, grabbed an old man and dragged him to the ground. "Got him," he yelled.

"Okay lads, here he is," bellowed the sergeant.

"Are you sure?" came a reply.

Andy Hoc looked at the old man and asked, "Are you Mentall?"

"I'm old you know," replied Handcross.

At this point Mrs Syms, from her wheelchair, began to bash Andy Hoc with a walking cane. "You leave him alone. He may be mental but he's my best friend."

"Positive identification, Sarge," yelled Andy Hoc.

"Okay, drag him out."

Mrs Syms cried, "You can't take him from me, you can't take him."

"Madam, he's a wanted criminal."

"No, no it's me you want. It's me that owes all the parking fines."

The sergeant exchanged a glance with Andy Hoc and left Jackie Hooper to calm Mrs Syms's distress.

The rest of the SOAP officers continued flying from room to room still in search of Mentall. The sergeant stepped into the kitchen and watched PC Newman and PC Coleman wrestling with an old gentleman who was cowering between an oven and a sink. Unable to drag him out they wrenched the cooker away from the wall and grabbed hold of him.

"Got him Sarge."

"Who?"

"Mentall."

"But we've already got him," said the sergeant.

Ellie Foster, hot on their tail, said, "That's Mr Sidebottom."

"Are you Mr Sidebottom?" yelled the sergeant.

"Yes," he replied with a feeble voice.

"Let him go, let him go we've got Mentall," said the sergeant. He then paused with a worried look on his face. "Can you smell gas?"

"It's probably Mr Sidebottom's colostomy," said Ellie. "Oh my God no, shit, you've wrenched the oven from the wall, and the gas pipe's come away. It must be pouring out."

"Everybody out, everybody out," yelled the sergeant.

*

Mr Handcross was dragged out to a waiting police car and, while being roughed up for being Teddy Sawman's judge, was driven off at high speed.

At Albridge Police Station it soon became obvious to the custody sergeant that the old man they had brought in was indeed a Mr Handcross: he was released onto the streets confused and distraught. Three hours later he was arrested for exposing himself to an elderly female driver who had just double parked.

A rather trampled Colin Foster clutched his testicles and dragged himself into his office. Feeling a gripping pain in his chest he gasped, yelped, steadied himself against the desk and promptly dropped dead.

Ellie Foster called the Fire Brigade who were on strike. Instead an army crew were dispatched in an ancient military 'Green Goddess' fire engine which had been borrowed from the Museum of RAF Firefighting. Boasting speeds of up to thirty miles per hour it took the army crew forty-five minutes to arrive.

The army captain surveyed the scene: residents, clad in no more than their nightwear and looking rather bewildered, were wandering aimlessly around the building and grounds. Concerned that half of them were probably on their way to becoming hypothermic he dialled 999 and got the ambulance service to attend.

Meanwhile the army crew, searching the building and looking for the main valve to isolate the gas supply, came across the mangled body of Colin Foster. With badly bitten testicles, and clad only in a frilly nightdress, they unanimously concluded he was beyond mouth-to-mouth resuscitation.

176

Ginger Jenkins, found to have severe testicular bruising and suspected slipped disks, was rushed to Albridge General Hospital. After four hours queueing in the A&E department a porter, pushing a wheelchair, approached him and said, "Hello Mr Jenkins, I'm Jerry."

Jenkins promptly whacked him over the head with a walking stick while shouting, "Got you, you bastard Hun."

Mrs Somerbee was taken to the same hospital with severe abdominal pain. On announcing that she was an expectant mother a doctor was immediately called who, after examining her, suspected that she was likely suffering from bowel cancer.

"But Doctor Webber told me I'd soon be changing nappies," she protested. The doctor raised his eyebrows at the prophetic nature of Webber's diagnosis.

All the other residents were evacuated to nursing homes in the area. Anywhere there was a bed a confused pensioner was housed.

40

Mentall glanced up at the station's arrivals board for what felt like the one hundredth time. It was over an hour since he'd parked himself in Maston Railway Station's dilapidated waiting shelter. A discarded coke can, with a lump of chewing gum pressed into the aperture, sat below an overflowing litter bin.

Below the arrivals board stood an automatic ticket machine. He read the notice on its screensaver for one last time: 'It is an offence to board, or attempt to board, a train without a valid ticket'.

The public address system burst into life, confirming the train was about to arrive. Mentall stood as it pulled to a halt. The automatic doors slid open and, along with a handful of commuters, he boarded.

Mentall knew if he was caught running away it would not look good for him: he'd have directed any jury to convict. He had to escape the police to be able to have any chance of clearing his name, but he had, for the moment, the more immediate problem of no ticket and no money.

Mentall peered through the glass door that separated the first class carriages from the vestibule. It took him a moment to realise that the ghostly, dishevelled figure, that appeared to be staring back at him, was in fact his own reflection. He turned through one hundred and eighty degrees and surveyed the standard class carriages – a ticket examiner, moving from seat to seat, was heading in his direction.

Knowing he was stuck between a rock and a hard place, he cast his eyes around the vestibule looking for inspiration. His eyes settled on a bin which was tucked into a narrow alcove. It had a plastic liner which he freed from its flip top lid. He then emptied the rubbish back into the now bag-less bin, wiped the remnants of a sticky drink from his arm and proceeded into the first class carriages.

He took his time collecting crisp packets, abandoned newspapers and discarded aluminium cans. Towards the end of the carriage, while sweeping an apple core and a Styrofoam cup into his bin liner, he found himself face to face with top lawyer Rupert Hoxborough from the firm of Hoxborough, Barker and Smith. Mentall paused.

"Yes, and what can I do for you?" asked Hoxborough, returning Mentall's gaze.

"I'm Mentall," he replied, straightening himself up.

Hoxborough's furrowed his brow. "I can see that."

"Judge Mentall," he said.

"Don't you call me judgemental, I'll be having a word with your boss next. I've watched you all the way up this carriage and you're a layabout man, no wonder the railways are in such a state employing people like you."

Other passengers began to look on and Mentall, wishing to avoid a scene, retreated in the direction of the standard class carriages. He dumped the bag of rubbish in the vestibule area, waited for the automatic door to open, and then made his way forwards. He managed to find an aisle seat before he reached the ticket examiner. He sat down and stretched his legs out into the corridor and waited for the inevitable confrontation about his lack of ticket.

His seat was in a block of four. To his right sat a middle-aged man with medium length silver hair, a lined face and gold rimmed glasses. He was looking out the window and making notes in an exercise book. *Just my bloody luck, a train spotter*, thought Mentall.

Directly opposite him sat a slim, young woman wearing a medical neck brace. She was deeply engrossed in a 'Parkers Car Price Guide'. *On a train, possibly with whiplash injuries and looking for a new car,* thought Mentall, *she's clearly been in a crash.*

To her left sat a bullish looking man. He had a shock of thick black hair and a mobile phone pressed to his right ear. He spoke loudly into its mouthpiece: "What? YOU broke up. I'm on the train." He then listened intently before adding, "Nah, nah at least five hundred thousand."

The woman with the neck brace raised her eyebrows.

"You *are* pulling my plonker," continued the man on the mobile phone.

"Interesting timings today," uttered the train spotter above the din of the phone conversation.

"Oh?" Mentall replied, while noting the ticket examiner was getting dangerously close.

"They keep these timings quiet you know," he replied in a voice that sounded as if he was sharing a state secret.

"You *are* pulling my plonker," the man on the mobile phone repeated.

Mentall, noting that the ticket examiner was now only one block of seats away, felt palpitations in his chest.

"You *are* pulling my plonker."

The train spotter looked up and cast his eyes over the caller. "Do you mind?"

The man covered the mouthpiece and glared. "Do I mind what?"

"Not being so noisy, people are trying to have some peace, we don't want to listen to your conversation."

Mentall stiffened with unease, he did not want to get involved in some scene. However, the altercation had successfully stopped the ticket examiner in his tracks. The other end of the phone could be heard from the exposed earpiece.

The man briefly returned the phone to his mouth, "Hold on a second Rog, somebody's complaining about me using my phone, if you'd please."

He lowered the phone and addressed the train spotter again, "I *am* trying to have a private conversation here. Why don't you mind your own *bleeding* business?"

"You can hardly call that private," the train spotter scoffed.

The woman with the neck brace raised her eyebrows again and caught Mentall's eye. He returned her smile and began to consider the possibilities of giving her the benefit of his legal expertise for whatever accident she had been involved in. However, in that moment the train braked heavily and his thought, like the train, came to a shuddering halt. Mentall crashed to the floor, other people shot forward or backwards into their seats. Coffee slopped like miniature tidal waves.

"What the Jesus buggering fuck was that?" somebody yelled from further down the carriage.

"This is excellent, never been involved in a train crash before," said the train spotter.

"Probably hit a leaf or something," said a voice from somewhere behind Mentall, "no doubt one of those vicious little bastards with a piece of twig still attached to it."

A man entered the carriage from the vestibule area and announced, "Don't know what's happening but the line's crawling with pigs."

That was enough for Mentall. Avoiding the slopped coffee and disturbed baggage he dodged the confused looking ticket examiner and hurried down the carriages, only stopping when he reached the last vestibule.

He tugged at the double doors that allowed passengers to board and leave the train. "Blast," he said, noticing it was electronically controlled. To the right was a glass panel covering an emergency door release lever. He struck his elbow against it, cursed at the pain, then cleared away the broken glass and pulled on the lever. The doors slid open, and he lowered himself down onto the line and looked towards the front of the train.

Two small, pink pigs squealed excitedly and ran towards him. "What the heck," he began as they grunted and snorted around his feet. *Not the police then*, he thought with relief.

He turned back towards the train but the doors had closed, and locked, behind him. *Blast.* Feeling agitated he used the sleepers as stepping stones and walked towards the front of the train.

As he approached the driver's cab its door swung open and a grey-haired man, in his early fifties, dropped down onto the line. He stared with some surprise at Mentall before giving him a precise instruction to, "Get off the fucking railway line."

"I'm a passenger," Mentall protested.

"Well get back on then," replied the driver, rather obviously pointing towards the train.

"I can't. I thought we'd crashed so I got out but the doors closed behind me." He then added, "This is no way to treat a fare paying passenger. Can't you open the doors for me?"

The driver looked him up and down, shook his head then pointed at the ladder to his cab. "Climb up there, but don't touch anything."

181

Mentall climbed aboard and surveyed the array of switches, levers and dials that made up the train's control panel. Through the cab's front window he saw a farmer wrestling with a squealing sow: the shuddering rails and screech of the braking wheels had done nothing for the pig's nerves. Thinking her immediate fate was to be eaten by this enormous metal object, which had borne down on them, she lost all her sense of humour and sunk her teeth into the farmer's arm.

The farmer yelped in pain and let go of the pig. Sensing this was her only chance of freedom, she shot past both the driver and the cab's door then ran squealing along the track.

"Get them pigs off the railway line," said the driver, addressing the farmer. "You bleeding farmers think you own the countryside."

"We doz," shouted the farmer while clutching his arm and grimacing. "And my pigs got on the line through yer rotten railways fence."

"I don't care where they came from. Get 'em off the line. And what you got a gun for?"

"I always carries e with me," replied the farmer, widening his eyes.

"And what's that may I ask?" asked the driver pointing to a black and white lump lying between the rails.

"That be a badger," said the farmer, "been hit by one of yer trains I suspects."

"If it'd been hit by a train it'd hardly be intact like that."

"I don't knows about dat," said the farmer.

"That badger's been shot between the eyes."

"No e hasn't."

"Just get off the line," said the driver, waving his arms.

With that the farmer slid down the bank towards a gap in the fence. He then turned back towards the driver and yelled, "I'll be claiming compensation, you'll be hearing from my solicitor."

The driver returned to his cab, climbed aboard and closed the door behind him. "Bloody farmers," he hissed before directing Mentall towards a second seat. The cab's radio then crackled into life. "What's the situation now?" asked a voice.

"The farmer's off the line, but there're still a few pigs milling around."

"Proceed at five miles per hour until you are clear of the scene," replied the radio.

The driver turned a handle and the train pulled forward. Mentall began to cast his eyes over the controls. He focussed on a yellow, illuminated button marked, 'DOOR RELEASE'. "I thought you said you couldn't open the doors?"

"Hmm," said the driver, following Mentall's line of sight, "if I press that the entire network will grind to a halt with a guard's strike. Union rules – the guard has to open the doors from within the train."

The train, after much starting and stopping, took over an hour to reach the station at Albridge. The driver opened the door and gesticulated that Mentall should alight.

He hauled himself out and dropped onto the platform. Dishevelled and despondent he headed towards the automatic barriers and told the attendant he'd forgotten his season ticket.

"Go and have a word at the excess fare booth," he replied.

Standing second in the queue he glanced up and read the sign above the excess fares window. 'Our staff are entitled to work in a safe environment. We will prosecute ALL cases of verbal and physical abuse.'

When his turn came he repeated his claim of a forgotten season ticket.

"Where did you get on?" asked the ticket seller.

"Maston."

"Why didn't you buy a ticket at the station?"

"There's no ticket office there."

"Why didn't you buy a ticket on the train then?"

"He never got to me."

"Five pounds thirty," replied the ticket seller, adjusting his peaked cap and raising his shoulders.

"I've forgotten my wallet, it had my season ticket in it," Mentall replied.

"No money on you at all?"

"No."

"Well move along then."

Mentall knew the type; state educated, a chip on each shoulder and a position with a little bit of power.

"I'm not going to be able to get through the barriers without a ticket."

"Go and ask in one of the shops then. They might be able to lend you the money."

"You can't be serious," Mentall replied, imagining explaining his predicament to one of the oafish shop workers.

"Look, if you haven't got the money I can't help you."

"Balderdash," Mentall replied.

"*What* did you say?" asked the ticket seller.

A British Transport Police officer appeared at Mentall's side. "What is the problem?"

Mentall flinched.

"This passenger boarded without a ticket, expects a free passage and is being offensive," explained the ticket seller.

"No, I wasn't," Mentall protested.

"Do you have a ticket or the means by which to purchase a ticket?" asked the police officer.

"No."

"Right, name then," said the police officer, taking a notebook from his breast pocket and flicking it open.

Mentall was silent.

"Haven't I spoken to you before?" asked the police officer.

"I very much doubt that," Mentall replied.

"You do look familiar. Name then?"

Mentall was silent.

"Name, sir?" the police officer repeated, drawing out his words.

"I think I might be a missing person," Mentall replied.

"You're not about to tell me you fell out of your canoe are you?"

"No."

"And what missing person might you be then?"

"Stephen."

"Stephen who?"

He shut his eyes and weakly whispered, "Mentall."

41

Lovering clipped on the passenger seatbelt of Tadler's car. "Are you sure about this?" he asked quizzically.

"Yeah, it's fine," Tadler replied casually. "I just need you to identify that Jack Pughes character when he visits the judge. You can leave the rest to me."

Lovering shuffled uneasily in his seat.

"What's your problem?" asked Tadler.

"Well this old banger of a car for a start. It's the same one you picked me and Smethurst up in. It's hardly a police vehicle is it? And shouldn't there be more than one police officer present?"

Tadler slipped the car into drive and pulled out into the traffic. "Do you want the charges against you to go in the bin or not?"

"What, me being attacked by that Smethurst fellow and the only witness is a copper? I've Googled it and unless Smethurst makes a complaint there's nothing you can do."

A blue Honda Jazz cut in front of Tadler's BMW. "Stupid idiot," he shouted, holding the horn button down for a full five seconds. He then turned his attention back to Lovering. "I can charge you with affray and possible grounds of contravening the Sexual Offences Act 2003."

"Why?" asked Lovering incredulously.

"Making a homosexual rendezvous."

"Making a homosexual rendezvous! Is this bloody Life on Mars or something?" asked Lovering.

"Well, whether it was a homosexual or heterosexual rendezvous, it's still an offence if done in a public place."

"Look, I wasn't making a homosexual rendezvous. I'm thro..."

"You're what?" asked Tadler, checking his rear-view mirror.

"Nothing," said Lovering.

"You were going to say you're through with all that business weren't you?" Tadler smiled, pleased that he could still spot a whooper a mile off.

"Just lay off me will you," snapped Lovering. "I'm having a few marital difficulties at the moment."

This did not entirely surprise Tadler. He decided to let the conversation go, and they remained silent until Tadler swung his car onto the driveway of Smoking Chimneys.

"That was handy," said Tadler.

"What?"

"The gates were open," he replied. "And hello, what's that doing here?" he added, pulling up behind the Green Goddess fire engine.

"This place looks like some form of an abandoned retreat," said Lovering.

"Retreat? It looks like a complete surrender if you ask me," Tadler replied, killing the engine. He then opened the driver's door and stepped onto the driveway. "You coming?" he asked, before closing the door.

"I suppose so," said Lovering reluctantly.

The front door to Smoking Chimneys was open and Tadler led them in.

"Good job we're not health inspectors," said Lovering, pointing at Fang's corpse. "What's that strange smell?"

"Not sure, but it's not dead dog," said Tadler, turning up his nose.

"It's not gas is it?"

"Nah. Believe me this's nothing compared with the pong of a typical care home," Tadler replied taking another step forward. "It's pretty cold in here, you could catch your death."

"It is an old people's home after all," replied Lovering, sounding like a school teacher correcting a pupil.

"Yeah, I know. I was just making another joke. Never mind," Tadler replied, casting his eyes around the hall. "All the doors appear to be open. But I think it's fairer to say this place *was* an old people's home. Something's happened here, and last night if I'm not mistaken."

"Why do you say that?" asked Lovering.

"Well it's deserted but everything looks up together. Apart from a few upset things. And the dead dog."

The army captain appeared at the door between the hall and the kitchen. Raising an arm towards Tadler and Lovering he shouted,

"You two, get out of here! The place is full of gas!" He then turned towards the kitchen and barked, "Platoon, let's all take a break – we've been riding our luck for too long."

On the order to take a break Sapper Wayne Pughes, still searching for the gas stopcock, withdrew his silver plated lighter from his breast pocket and lit his first and last fag of the day. Tadler and Lovering froze in shocked disbelief as the force of the explosion threw the captain past them. He landed in a heap on the driveway just in front of the Green Goddess fire engine.

As a stream of soldiers coughed and spluttered by, Tadler made a dash for the door. Forgetting the remains of Fang, he caught his foot on the carcass and fell against the wall. His hand smacked against the light switch triggering a second explosion causing the building's walls, doors and windows to blow out and spew zimmer frames, incontinence pads and commodes onto the drive.

The army captain staggered back to his feet just as Fangs body, which had lain for the past few hours across the gas stopcock, was propelled out of the building. It smashed into his chest causing him to fall backwards and clout his head on a wheel nut of the Green Goddess. He dutifully passed out.

A long lost cupboard, boarded up since the Kipling sisters' orgies of the nineteen-sixties, blew open spewing its contents skyward. As one soldier, in wide mouthed horror, followed the trajectories of the various objects another radioed, with considerable alarm, that they were now being shelled by dildos.

Tadler and Lovering landed on the drive and covered their heads just as bricks, dust, four sets of handcuffs, numerous leather blindfolds and various other paraphernalia descended around them.

"I hope you're wearing clean underwear," said Tadler.

"Not anymore, but I'm not putting one of those things on if that's what you mean," said Lovering, pointing towards an aged hardened leather thong.

"I think that's the worst of it over," said Tadler, getting to his feet.

"Your car looks a bit wrecked."

"Yep, but let's give it a go," Tadler replied, sprinting towards the BMW's driver's door.

"What!" said Lovering, staggering back to his feet.

Tadler got into his car. "Let's get the bloody well out of here."

"But ain't we on legitimate police business?"

"Get in the car," said Tadler, leaning across and opening the passenger door. "The army are involved and we need to scoot."

Lovering got in and slammed the door shut. Tadler started the engine and began to negotiate his dented car out of the mass of fallen bricks, tiles and roof lines that any fly-by-night builder would have been proud of.

"You'd better tell me everything," said Lovering, just as one of the chimneys, which had teetered for a few moments on the remains of an end gable, crashed in front of them.

"I just need to get this thing out of here," said Tadler, slamming the car into reverse and grounding the rear differential on the remains of a roof balustrade.

"If I'm facing charges, for that so called street affray, I want to know what's been going on," he demanded.

"If I don't get this fucker out of here you'll be facing a few more charges than that," said Tadler. "Now get out and push me off this."

Lovering got out and inspected the airborne rear wheels which, at every dab of the throttle, span inanely.

"You've grounded it," he yelled back to Tadler.

"Chuck some bricks under the wheels."

"Where am I going to get bricks from?"

"Use your loaf – they're hardly in short supply," shouted Tadler.

Lovering took a quick look at the soldiers staggering out of the building and rapidly began to gather bricks. "Stop revving," he yelled, "I need to chock the rear wheels."

No sooner had he finished Tadler hit the accelerator causing the rear tyres to lathe their way through the soft Victorian bricks.

"How's it looking?" asked Tadler watching the bellowing cloud of red dust from his rear view mirror.

"I can't see," shouted Lovering.

"Jump on the boot," yelled Tadler.

With Lovering's groin flopped over the edge of the rear wing and his fingertips pressed into the gap between the boot lid and the car's main body, Tadler gave the accelerator a mighty blast and the car lurched backwards and clear of the rubble. Still with the pedal to the floor Tadler pointed the ancient beast down the driveway.

"Stop you bastard," yelled Lovering, clinging to the boot lid.

The automatic gearbox, having not had this much fun in quarter of a century, dutifully went through the gears. Tadler hit the side road at sixty-five miles per hour. Fortunately the brakes were far from being up to standard so the ensuing emergency stop had Lovering no more than sliding to the ground.

Tadler leaned across and opened the passenger door, Lovering piled in and repeated his question as to his parent's marital status on the day he was born.

"Calm down," said Tadler joining the main road, "I wasn't going to leave you behind."

"As I said you'd better tell me everything," said Lovering, "if I'm facing charges for that so called street affray I want to know what's been going on."

"Don't worry yourself about that, there'll be no charges."

"Are you sure?" asked Lovering, pulling the door closed and clipping on his seatbelt.

"Course I'm bloody sure. It'd be up to me to press them."

"You only involved me on the pretext I owed you a favour, didn't you?"

"Civilian witnesses stand up better in court."

"Is that because all you coppers have flat feet?"

"Ha bloody ha," Tadler replied, shaking his head sarcastically.

"You are a copper aren't you?" asked Lovering, turning towards Tadler.

"You saw me at the nick the other day."

"Yeah but you never showed me a warrant card."

The last thing Tadler wanted was another complaint against him. He thought for a moment then replied, "Look I *am* a police officer and I'm dropping the charges against you. Let's leave it at that, and today hasn't happened as far as you're concerned."

"I should dob you in."

"And face charges for street affray?" asked Tadler.

Lovering remained silent until Tadler pulled the wrecked BMW to a halt outside his house. A passer-by stopped and stared.

"Show me your warrant card and you've got yourself a deal," sighed Lovering.

Tadler was silent.

"You have got a warrant card haven't you?"

"Look, I'll level with you. I'm in a spot of bother at work and I just wanted to find that judge to get back in the good books."

"You're a bloody con-artist. I really should report this."

"Well *one* way of getting back in the force's good books is for me to press charges for street affray. That'll get the solved crime statistics up."

"What sort of bother are you in?"

Tadler took a deep breath. "My bloody woman boss thought I was having one off the wrist in the office."

"And were you?"

"Course I bleeding wasn't."

"So you've got to face some false charges then?"

"Yes."

"Now you know what it feels like," said Lovering, "and whether you were having one off the wrist or not you know what you are?"

"What?" asked Tadler.

"You're a tosser."

Tadler smiled. The boy was learning.

"So we got a deal then?" asked Tadler.

"Deal," said Lovering with a sick smile.

42

As cockups went, Chief Superintendent Trevor Riseback, in overall charge of the SOAP raid on Smoking Chimneys, knew this was a big one. The home was all but destroyed, residents were all over the place and they'd failed to arrest the judge.

He sat at his office desk, in the new headquarters building, staring at the rain blowing against a fourth floor window. He was waiting for the dreaded phone call from Chief Constable Simon Nortly; the very man that had instigated the raid. He had an unsettling feeling this gloomy day was about to get even gloomier.

He hated the controlling way that Nortly always made him wait for a phone call. He checked his watch again: it was ten a.m. – a full hour late.

When eventually the phone emitted an ear-piercing shrill he glanced down at its caller display: it was flashing Nortly's name. He felt his heart slamming against his ribs and hot needles of stress in his stomach. He lifted the receiver to his ear and spoke into the mouthpiece. "Sir."

"The grapevine is telling me things have not gone to plan," said Nortly.

You could say that, thought Riseback leaning forward on his office chair.

"I'm hearing *you* wrecked the house and Judge Mentall escaped."

"Well you didn't give us much time to plan it," Riseback protested.

"You can count yourself very lucky," continued Nortly, ignoring any claims of mitigating circumstances, "that Judge Mentall was picked up in Albridge."

"I hadn't heard that, Sir," replied Riseback sounding surprised.

"Well, and no thanks to you, he was captured by an eagle eyed British Transport Police Officer. That's another embarrassment I'm going to have to deal with. You know how BTP like to get one up on us."

Riseback took a deep breath. Nortly was going to lay the blame on him and there wasn't much he could do about it. However, he

191

felt compelled to stand his ground. "As I said, you didn't give us much time to plan it."

"Who knows you were at Smoking Chimneys?" asked Nortly sharply.

"Well, all the lads, the proprietors of the home, half the inmates, though I wouldn't worry too much about them, plus a doctor that accompanied the raid."

"You might just get away with it," said Nortly.

"And the British Army," said Riseback.

"You idiots!" blared Nortly.

Riseback took another deep breath. "Sir, what did you mean by 'you might just get away with it'?"

"Your botched attempt to arrest the judge."

"Under your orders, Sir," Riseback protested, thinking for a moment that this might give him the upper hand.

"Where did you get that idea from, Trevor?"

"The phone call you made yesterday instructing me to mount the raid!"

"I think you're very much mistaken there, Trevor."

"What?" Riseback replied in a high-pitched shrill.

"I only asked you for a feasibility study, not to go blundering in at the first opportunity."

"Oh come on, Sir," barked Riseback.

"Where's the paperwork requesting the raid?" asked Nortly.

"But–"

"And the completed risk assessment?"

"But, Sir," replied Riseback, barely able to control his anger.

"And the warrant?"

"Oh come on…"

And with that Nortly hung-up.

Riseback knew the force's rank structure prevented him from defending himself against a senior officer; Nortly was more than capable of making him take the wrap for this.

He pressed the end call button and then dialled the office number of the sergeant in charge of the SOAP raid. It rang three times before it was answered. "Sir," replied the sergeant.

"Last night's raid, anything logged on the computer yet?" asked Riseback.

"Not yet Sir, the lads are just having a cuppa and a bit of a debrief."

"Good, then last night's raid didn't happen."

"What?" asked the sergeant sounding confused.

"It didn't happen. It's scrubbed."

"But everybody saw us, the owners, the army."

"Destroy any proof you were there."

"That's going to be a bit bloody tricky," the sergeant replied.

"Just do it," said Riseback curtly while checking on the progress of the rain hitting the window.

"But Sir."

"Are you questioning my authority?"

"No, *just* your judgement."

Riseback took a sharp breath. "Sergeant, I'll overlook your insubordination on this occasion."

"You haven't got much choice if you want a cover up."

"It's *not* a cover up, Sergeant," Riseback replied patronisingly.

"*What* would you call it then?"

"It's manoeuvres to protect the force's reputation."

"And your career by the sounds of it."

Riseback leaned back in his chair. "I could have you on a charge for that."

"Yeah and then I'd tell the whole story."

Riseback knew the sergeant wasn't calling his bluff. In a strange way he admired him for having the guts to stand his ground. He was one of those types that wasn't interested in his career; he'd never applied for promotion above the rank of sergeant. And that allowed him to speak his mind.

"Look guv, what about the lad's overtime now?"

"They'll have to go without."

Riseback heard a sigh from the other end of the phone. "That's going to be a bit tricky."

"I've got the reputation of the force to think about. Give them time off or something."

"Oh come on sir this sounds a bit off."

"Sergeant, do you want Northshire to be the laughing stock of Eastshire and Westshire?"

"No."

"Good," and with that Riseback hung up.

He didn't like having to do this but he had an ex-wife, a new girlfriend, one daughter doing an internship and two others at university. A chief superintendent's pay was not to be sniffed at, but every penny was committed and he couldn't risk his income and pension.

43

Sandra Pughes blustered her way into the high ceilinged atrium of the Albridge General Hospital and made her way to a crescent shaped reception desk. "I've come to see my son," she announced to a middle-aged woman sat behind a computer screen.

"What's his name?" asked the receptionist, glancing up.

"Sapper Wayne Pughes," Sandra replied in a manner that sounded as if the receptionist should have already known this.

She looked down at her computer screen and began to type on a keyboard. "Let me just check for you."

Sandra tutted and fidgeted and watched her husband, through a plate glass window, take a drag on a cigarette.

"Nobody here of that name," she replied, shaking her head.

Sandra turned her attention back to the receptionist: her roots were showing beneath a head of dyed brown hair. "Look lady, some fellow calling himself an army family liaison officer has just phoned to tell me that my son has been admitted here following some kind of explosion."

"I'm sorry Mrs Wayne-Pughes," but he isn't registered here.

"What's with the 'Mrs Wayne Pughes'? I'm his *mother* not his *wife*."

"I know you said," replied the receptionist with her eyes still fixed on her computer screen.

"So why did you call me 'Mrs Wayne Pughes' then?"

"Well, I assumed Wayne-Pughes was the family name."

"No, it's Pughes. Wayne is his first name."

"I thought you said that was Sapper?"

"God give me strength," huffed Sandra. "Look lady his name is Wayne Pughes, Sapper is his rank. If he was called Sapper Wayne-Pughes he'd be some fictitious character in a novel a lily-livered author had invented to stop himself getting sued for libel."

"Quite, let me check again," said the receptionist, turning her attention back to the computer screen. "We've got a Wayne Pughes on the Dickens ward. That's on the third floor–"

195

"Don't worry I'll find it," Sandra replied and marched off towards the lifts.

Jack Pughes stamped out his Marlboro Light, pushed open the entrance door and followed his wife. He caught up with her at the lift doors. "You found him then?"

"In the end," Sandra replied. "But you needn't come."

"He's my son too."

"Stepson Jack Pughes, stepson."

*

Outside the ward Sandra repeatedly pressed the buzzer.

"It's been at least fifteen minutes," said Jack, "I don't think anybody's going to let us in."

"Shut it," Sandra replied.

"I was only being empathetic."

"Just shut up will you. Right now, with my son critically injured and a judge in a rest home to worry about, I'd readily take any opportunity to become a widow."

"Over my dead body," Jack huffed.

Sandra raised her eyebrows and sucked through her teeth. "Will you never cease to embarrass yourself?"

The door opened and Sandra eyed a short, middle-aged Indian woman wearing a green plastic disposable apron and holding a broom and pan. "You took your bloody time," she bellowed. "We've been pressing that buzzer for at least half an hour."

"Sorry buzzer not working."

"I don't know what we pay our taxes for," Sandra replied, brushing past her and marching to the ward desk.

The ward sister, sat behind a curved nursing station, informed them Wayne Pughes was in bay seven. Sandra marched off. Jack tagged on behind: his rubber soled shoes squeaking on the highly polished floor.

At bay seven Sandra stopped and took stock of her son. His head was heavily bandaged and his left arm was supported by steel wires from the ceiling. He was still wearing a surgical gown and his legs were covered by a pristine, white cellular blanket.

"What have they done to you?" she exclaimed.

"Hello Mum."

"What *ever* has happened?" she asked, taking the only seat. Jack stood at the end of the bed and gripped the top rail of the footboard.

"It was a gas explosion," replied Wayne.

"A gas explosion!"

"New type of weapon?" asked Jack.

"No, I was on fire duty, what with the strike."

"We'll see about this," said Sandra, "who caused this gas explosion?"

"I did, Mum."

"What!"

"I lit a fag and the whole place blew up."

"What *whole place*?"

"The place we were called to. Smoking Chimneys or something, it's an old folk's home and I wrecked it," said Wayne, his voice cracking with emotion.

"Holy shit," exclaimed Sandra, while trying to take in this sudden and unexpected turn of events.

"I'm sorry Mum. We were looking for the gas stopcock, the captain called a break and I lit up."

"There, there, don't worry yourself, my little petal," said Sandra, softening her voice while thinking at this precise moment she'd readily swap places with her son.

"You're not angry with me then Mum?"

"No, no, why should I be?"

"Well I thought you'd be really cross. I was dreading you coming."

"There, there my brave soldier, don't upset yourself."

"Many killed?" asked Jack.

"Jack! Don't upset the boy," said Sandra, before adding, "well was there any, Wayne?"

"I've heard one died of a heart attack. Our captain is being treated for concussion and one of our boys got hit in the throat by some airborne debris. He's having a tonsillectomy. But they'd pretty much evacuated the place."

"And you lit a fag?" asked Sandra with a wonderment that Jack and Wayne were not actually father and son.

"I know Mum. I didn't think."

"Don't fret yourself. I'm sure it can all be sorted out."

"This one that died of a heart attack," said Jack, "one of the inmates was he?"

"No, I heard it was one of the staff," replied Wayne.

"Pity," said Sandra.

*

Back in the car Jack turned on his mobile and brought up the BBC news web page. "Disgraced Judge arrested. Care home destroyed in gas explosion. One man dead."

"I don't know what's happened but either we're jolly lucky or we can expect a knock at the door," Sandra replied.

44

Fred yawned and opened his eyes. He'd been snoozing in a chair with his feet perched on a cellophane wrapped coffin. His mobile was vibrating in his back pocket as it played Chopin's funeral march. He staggered to his feet, retrieved his phone and glanced down at the display. It read 'Colin Foster'.

He pressed the accept call button and raised it to his ear. "Another ten percenter eh, Colin?"

"And just what *is* a ten percenter may I ask?" replied Ellie Foster.

"Oh, erm nothing. How are you Mrs Foster?" asked Fred straightening himself up.

"Having a trying day."

"Sorry to hear that. What can I do you for, I mean do for you?"

"Another job."

"Somebody else not like the cooking?"

"I think I'm getting a distinct impression of how you and my husband conducted business. Don't think I didn't know about these ten percent back handers."

"Oh," was all Fred could think to say.

"Anyhow, I need some prices to let the family know."

"What do they want?"

"I'm not sure yet. What's the most basic deal you do?"

"You mean straight to the crem?"

"Yes."

"About a grand."

"And the full works?"

"What posh church, horses and carriage and all in top hats?" asked Fred, thinking where the hell he was going to be able to lay his hands on a carriage.

"Yes."

"I suppose about ten grand all in."

"Okay, I'll let the family know. We're already at the mortuary, can you get here as soon as possible and bring the ten percent?"

"You at it as well?"

"I'm acting for my husband."

"Right you are."

*

Ellie, who had earlier got a taxi to the mortuary, waited on the tarmacked area reserved for the hearses. She smoothed down her borrowed clothes and then checked her watch: it'd had been half an hour since she'd phoned Fred. She paced up and down impatiently; she wanted this wrapped up as soon as possible. It was typical of Fred to be late. She never liked the man but she had to leave some aspects of the business to her now late husband.

After a further five minutes she heard the low rumble of a hearse's powerful engine. She sighed with relief when she saw it was Fred.

He pulled up smoothly alongside her and lowered the driver's window.

"The family have gone for the full works," said Ellie.

"That's good, it's been a bit thin on the old stiffs lately."

Ellie glared as him.

"I mean the departed," said Fred.

"That's better," said Ellie, raising her eyebrows and shaking her head. If Fred was going to work for her she was determined to knock him into shape.

Fred pulled a brown envelope from his inside jacket pocket. "Right here's a grand – that'll cover your ten percent."

"Thanks," said Ellie, taking the envelope.

Fred then opened the driver's door, stepped out of the hearse and asked, "Are the family in there?"

"His wife will be."

He walked round to the back of the hearse, lifted the tailgate and pointed to a coffin. "This is just the basic one, they'll get a posher one when I get back to the parlour."

He then fished out a trolley from an underfloor compartment and assembled it by stretching out a series of concertinaed metal bars. He then dragged the coffin onto it and, as Ellie held the double doors to the mortuary open, he pushed the trolley into a window-less, brick lined family waiting area.

Fred nodded to the mortician, a thin man of about forty-five, and asked, "Where's his wife?"

The mortician pointed to Ellie.

"But she's Colin Foster's wife."

"That's correct," said Ellie, "though widow to be more precise."

Fred took a few moments to take this in before the penny dropped. "Oh poor old bugger. I am sorry. When did it happen?"

"This morning, heart attack."

Fred came to his senses. "Hopefully you'll still regard me as your funeral director of choice."

"I will that, but Smoking Chimneys was destroyed in an explosion this morning after Colin had succumbed. So it may be some time before I'm up and running again."

"Good lord. How–"

"So you said the basic package was a thousand?" asked Ellie, interrupting Fred.

"Yes. But I thought you said the family…"

"I'm his family and I've just had a change of heart. Here's the thousand," she said, returning the brown envelope to him.

"What?"

"I just want the basic package."

"But this is the grand I just gave you."

Ellie cocked her head to one side. "Gave me for what?"

Fred glanced to the mortician and whispered, "Gave you outside."

"Do you want it all over town that you've been paying sweeteners to my husband?" whispered Ellie.

"You wouldn't dare."

"Try me. Get him cremated ASAP and we'll say no more about it. I'll keep passing work your way but I want fifteen percent in future."

45

"Right," said Home Secretary, Toby Peers. He looked along the table at the three chief constables of Shire Force and hoped this, their fifth meeting, would be the last. In fact he hoped never to see any of them again. The office of Home Secretary was playing havoc with his nerves; if the Prime Minister found cause to ask for his resignation he didn't plan to argue his case.

"Thank you once again gentlemen," he continued. "Things have taken an interesting turn. Stephen Mentall is in custody and we are holding him on charges of stealing exhibit money from the East Castle Street robbery trial, manslaughter and the wilful destruction of a care home–"

"You haven't prepared an agenda?" interrupted Bertie Hamilton-Smith, representing the National Crime Agency.

"No," Peers replied cautiously. "This is just a short meeting to wind things up. Why do you ask?"

"Oh, no reason," he replied.

Peers was only too aware why Hamilton-Smith had asked if there was an agenda. He'd bloody well enjoyed the three chief constables hijacking these meetings with their own issues. First it was a squabble over their driver, then their parking space, then their office and finally their secretary. He'd thought of Hamilton-Smith as an ally, but now he realised he was nothing short of a shit-stirrer. The office of Home Secretary came with no allies. "So, as I was saying," he continued, "we have Stephen Mentall under arrest on three charges."

"What exactly were the circumstances of his arrest?" asked Edgeson.

"As far as we can tell," said Peers, glancing down at his briefing paper, "the fire service were on strike, and the army received a call at 0457 yesterday morning, reporting a massive gas leak in the Smoking Chimneys care home. That, as I'm sure you'll all recall, is the place Robert and his team had tracked Stephen Mentall down to. When the army arrived the place blew up injuring numerous of their personnel. That's the testimony of the army captain who was the skipper on the day."

Peers looked around the room before continuing. "Some hours later Judge Stephen Mentall was apprehended at Albridge Railway Station and claimed to be a missing person with amnesia. The proprietor of the home, one Ellie Foster, has positively identified Stephen Mentall as having been a resident. It appears this Ellie Foster lost her husband, Colin Foster, in the incident. Hence the manslaughter charge."

"Robert didn't need to plan the raid after all," said Edgeson gleefully.

"I think," continued Peers choosing to ignore Edgeson's remark, "you can all be relieved with this turn of events, a raid could easily have been botched."

Nortly shuffled uneasily in his seat.

"Something the matter, Simon?" asked Peers.

"No, no," Nortly replied hurriedly before adding, "They didn't mention any police attendance at Smoking Chimneys did they?"

Peers flicked his eyes over his briefing paper and shook his head. "Nothing logged here. Why do you ask?"

"Oh… I thought it a bit odd."

"Whole things a bit bloody odd if you ask me," said Hamilton-Smith.

"Well, I wasn't asking you," Nortly snapped.

"Okay, okay, gentlemen please," said Peers, raising a hand. "Let's be grateful for how things have turned out. We now need to decide what to do with the judge."

"Why can't we just let him go?" asked Edgeson.

"Because," began Wytton, "we don't know what he was up to. If we send him down we silence him and, given he's under arrest, it's going to look just a little odd if we drop all charges. Our reputations are at stake here – we put it out he was wanted so we've got to go through with it."

"Thank you, Robert," said Peers. "So what do you suggest?"

Wytton straightened himself. "Instruct the CPS to go ahead and prosecute him with the wilful destruction of an old people's home, manslaughter of this Colin Foster fellow and the theft of the East Castle Street exhibit money."

"Are we all agreed?" asked Peers. He made a point of looking around the room until he'd received a nod from each of his colleagues. "Very well then, I'll ask the Attorney General to instruct the CPS."

"I thought the CPS were supposed to be independent," said Hamilton-Smith.

"Look," said Peers, his voice full of anger, "I think I know how to handle things."

"You need to do this properly, Home Secretary," said Wytton. "If it came out later that you'd influenced the CPS he could appeal his conviction."

Peers shot Wytton a look of venomous anger. "I don't think he'd get very far with that."

"Don't forget the Supreme Court and the Human Rights Act, Home Secretary."

"Isn't the Human Rights Act being repealed under Brexit?" asked Nortly, sounding surprised.

Peers turned to Nortly. "It appears the Human Rights legislation will remain on the statute books. The PM won't entertain its repeal."

"Typical," huffed Nortly, "I only voted Leave to get rid of it."

46

Mentall spent two months on remand before convincing a bail-hearing, at the Albridge courthouse, that he wasn't about to disappear again. He was then escorted by a Group 4 security guard to his chambers where he collected a spare set of keys and a bundle of well-thumbed ten pound notes that he kept there for such emergencies. He then took a taxi to the Northbridge Industrial Estate where he'd parked his Mercedes C-Class car some three months previously.

There was a long scratch down the passenger side, the driver's door mirror was hanging loose and somebody had written 'Wanker' in black marker pen on the windscreen. But otherwise the car was intact. Mentall pressed a button on the key-fob and smiled with relief when the indicators flashed in response.

He opened the door and slipped into the driver's seat. The squeak and smell of the luxurious leather interior reminded him of where he belonged. The engine started at the push of a button and the automatic gearbox slipped effortlessly through the gears as he drove across town.

His road, Oak Hill Drive, was deserted: he was glad that the local busybody, Margaret Wainscott-Bruce was nowhere to be seen. He parked and stepped out onto his driveway.

The flower borders were overgrown and the lawns had gone to seed. *So much for neighbourhood watch*, he thought. He turned the key in the front door lock and pushed against a mountain of junk mail. With the door partway open he squeezed past, turned on the hall light and froze with shock at what lay before him. The hall and the lounge were stripped bare apart from turned out drawers of paperwork, rotting pizza boxes and the DVD of his appearance on Panorama. *Bloody tenants*, he thought.

The kitchen lino was covered in scraps of food, the hall carpet was matted with mud and the lounge carpet was giving off a solvent like smell. He knelt down to sniff it and noticed it was ingrained with an odd looking white powder.

He spent the evening tidying up as best he could and then spent an uncomfortable night trying to sleep on the lounge carpet.

He woke feeling a bit odd and spent the morning going through his paperwork. His household insurance had expired and a recent bank statement showed he still had a modest amount of savings. But with no career, and probably no pension, they wouldn't sustain him for long.

He phoned around the local estate agents enquiring if they had let his house. None of them had, but each agent insisted on sending him details of their terms and conditions should he subsequently choose to let his property. He read them through and pitted his legal mind against the charges they imposed on the landlord in return for dumping years of grime and decay upon the tenants.

He left phone messages for some of his fellow freemasons. Not one returned his calls. *So much for the old boy network*, he thought. He felt pangs of injustice but he knew things could have been worse. He could be dead or still in that confounded Smoking Chimneys. He believed the charges wouldn't stick so he set about turning his house back into a home.

The curtains had escaped his kidnapper's attentions, and the interior walls he painted himself. He bought a new bed and ordered a television. For the exterior pebble dashing he employed the services of a local decorating firm. Leaving a Post-it note declaring 'This Colour' next to 'Apple White' on a Dulux colour chart, he set off to reacquaint himself with Madam Suzie's House of Pleasure.

The softly lit interior was familiar, but there was now a reception desk staffed by a woman he'd not met before: blond hair shaped to her shoulders, a tinge of grey at the roots, large brown made up eyes, a slim body with a waist length jacket and a tight, black top showing off a firm breast line. Above her head was a sign which read, "Ask About Our MILF Deal."

"How can I help you?" she asked.

"What's that all about?" asked Mentall pointing to the sign.

"Oh, we are doing mother and daughter twosomes. Well three-somes including the client."

"Good lord. How much?" asked Mentall, coming to his senses.

"One fifty, you get half an hour."

"And I get both?"

"Yup."

"How many have you got in?"

"All the other mothers and daughters are busy so you'd have to put up with me I'm afraid," she said, smiling.

"Okay."

"You sure?" she asked.

"Yes, quite sure," he said. His eyes feasted on her body and his heart prayed there'd be no hiccup. This would start to compensate for the loss of his career, the kidnapping and any conviction put together. And the daughter? *My God*, he thought, *if the mother looks like this at her age how fit must the daughter be?*

She picked up the phone and pressed an intercom button. "Mum, get ready, we've got another taker. Oh and send Petronella down to take over the desk?"

As she hung up Mentall stuttered out, "I've changed my mind. I'll take Petronella."

"I thought you wanted the MILF deal," she replied.

"I've changed my mind," said Mentall.

"Okay, have it your way. Go on up, Petronella's third on the left if she's not already on her way down."

*

Five hours later Mentall slipped out of the brothel's main door and headed home feeling relaxed and fulfilled.

He pulled up on his drive, stepped out of his car and was met by an angry-faced Margaret Wainscott-Bruce, chairwoman of the local neighbourhood watch.

"Don't you think it's embarrassing enough for us to have to live alongside a disgraced judge?" she asked.

Mentall wiped the back of his neck and wondered how she'd rumbled his visit to the parlour. The phrase 'disgraced judge' also bothered him a bit.

"Now we have to put up with this!" she continued. "Whatever you

207

do inside your own house is your own business but any midlife issues you have we'd appreciate you didn't inflict upon your neighbours."

This was a bit strong thought Mentall, a discreet visit to a parlour was hardly inflicting anything on one's neighbours. A visiting pro maybe, but he had stopped all that after Margaret Wainscott-Bruce had asked some awkward questions about the old bangers parked on his drive overnight. The old bangers that were driving them was also something Margaret Wainscott-Bruce had commented on.

"I can assure you I'm a very discreet man."

"Discreet, discreet! Call that discreet." Margaret Wainscott-Bruce flung her arm in the direction of his house.

Mentall, realising perhaps there was a bit more to this than a simple parlour visit, turned his head in the same direction. His eyes fell on the ghastly sight of a painter putting the final touches to a Post-it note yellow pebble-dashed exterior.

Wandering in disbelief towards his house, pursued by Margaret Wainscott-Bruce ejaculating a stream of abuse, he met the painter descending his ladder.

"Had a spot of bother matching the colour, but got there in the end," said the man, pointing to the Post-it note with 'This Colour' written on it. "Had to mix marigold with spring morning daffodil, but we've got there. Proper job, might do my garage with what's left."

Mentall stood dumfounded. The painter collapsed his ladder, attached it to the roof of his Citroen Berlingo van and called out, "I'll drop the bill round in the morning."

After that fiasco Mentall laid low for a few days and turned his attention to the filthy carpets.

In Mentall's eyes it was no surprise the tenants had not looked after the place. Having never lived in rental accommodation he viewed all tenants as Reds. How could you ever expect some long haired-hippy, who hadn't changed his underpants for three weeks, to clean a carpet?

Mentall pondered how he could get the carpets cleaned on the cheap and was hit by a stroke of luck when Isabel Longtree, of the

Fibre Lover Vacuum Cleaner Company, called at his door one evening.

"Do you worry about your pile?" was her opening line. Mentall was just about to get rid of her for such an impertinent remark when he caught sight of her demonstration model Fibre Lover. He invited her in and said he would welcome a demonstration.

"Nice colour your house. You're just moving in I see," said Isabel.

"Ah yes," Mentall replied, happy to play along with her misunderstanding.

"You see most people use cheap vacuum cleaners," said Isabel, setting up the demonstrator, "and that is where most of the fibre damage occurs."

Mentall sat back on his sole deckchair and allowed her to begin the demonstration. Realising she wasn't going to fall for shampooing the entire lounge carpet, let alone the whole house, he asked for a go.

"What's it like on the stairs?" asked Mentall after he'd raced around the lounge.

"Brilliant," exclaimed Isabel, "with the built-in multi-valve double filtration cleansing system your stair carpet will be as good as new in no time at all."

He hurried up the stairs, grunting at additional claims of brilliance beholding the Fibre Lover. On the landing she positioned herself in front of him and took back control of the machine.

"How long are you hoping these carpets will last?" she asked.

"They'll be good for many years," Mentall replied.

"Well they've been done with a conventional cleaner, you can tell."

"How's that?" asked Mentall convinced the only difference between one vacuum and the next was the price tag.

Isabel bent down and plucked a fibre from the carpet. "Deep pile lifting," she said straightening her back.

Mentall observed the fibre she held between thumb and forefinger. "Deep pile what?"

"Lifting," explained Isabel. "You're using a cheap vacuum cleaner.

I'd give these carpets no more than a year, two at the most, then you will have to replace the lot."

"Really?" asked Mentall, his voice full of doubt.

"Do you know what this is?" asked Isabel bringing the curled shaped fibre, she had plucked from the carpet, closer to Mentall's face. Mentall was about to reply when Isabel added, "That's your deep pile, breaking away from the backing."

"It's actually one of my pubic hairs," said Mentall.

"Eghhh!!" exclaimed Isabel, shaking the object from her grasp. "You *are* a disgusting pig. Don't you ever vacuum your bloody carpets?"

She gathered up the Fibre Lover, ran down the stairs and opened the front door.

"I'm sorry," he called after her.

She briefly turned her head towards him before stepping outside, slamming the door behind her whilst shouting, "And it's a fucking terrible colour your house."

47

Mentall's next brush with a member of the public was when Jane Millerson of 'Hello' magazine phoned.

"Hello, this is Jane Millerson from Hello magazine."

"Why Hello," Mentall replied, clearly pleased with his quick wit.

"Quite," Millerson replied, drawing a sharp breath. "We are doing a series entitled 'The Fall from Grace' about eminent people whose careers have been ruined by scandal."

"Oh yes," Mentall replied.

"And we've selected you for one of the articles," she explained.

"No thank you," said Mentall.

"In your case my editor has instructed me to offer you ten thousand pounds."

"When do we meet?" asked Mentall.

*

On the morning of the interview Mentall shaved, showered and dressed then shaved again before he heard a car pulling onto his drive. From the landing window he watched two people get out of the car and walk towards his porch.

He raced down stairs and opened the door before they could ring the bell. "Jane?" he asked, eyeing up her slim, forty-something body.

"Stephen," she replied, offering her hand. "And this is Tom my photographer," she added, casting a hand towards a bearded, leather jacketed man.

"How do," said Tom offering no hand. "If it's all the same to you we'll get the outside shots now. The light's about right."

Mentall stepped outside and, with his back to his house, presented his most regal pose. Tom looked down at his light meter. "Bloody things convulsing all over the place with those awful yellow walls."

"Have you just had them painted?" asked Millerson.

"Yes," Mentall replied.

"Could you relax a bit?" asked Tom.

"How do you mean?" asked Mentall.

"Stop looking like you've got a rod up your back and permanent smell under your nose."

Working class yobo made good, thought Mentall, *thinks he's something important.*

Tom took a succession of shots. "Right, I suppose that'll do."

"Please come in," said Mentall to Millerson.

"You been burgled?" asked Tom, following on behind.

"Why?"

"Well, where's all your stuff?"

"In storage," Mentall lied.

"No point me hanging around – a photo needs a backdrop. I'll go down that pub we saw on the way in and pop back at two."

"Okay," said Millerson.

Tom let himself out the front door. *That's got rid of the opposition*, thought Mentall, gesticulating that Millerson should sit on the deckchair.

"Where will you sit?" she asked.

"I'll make do on the floor."

She looked around the room then asked, "Why's all your stuff in storage?"

"I'm having the place redecorated."

Millerson began by asking him about his career. He was happy to fill her in on his rise to becoming a judge; she smiled, nodded and took notes.

Mentall managed to make up suitable reasons for the events leading up to his kidnapping then stuck to the truth. The interview was only interrupted by a ring at the doorbell.

"Excuse me," said Mentall, getting to his feet. He then walked into the hall and opened his front door.

"One television," said a delivery driver, "I'll put it down here shall I?"

"Yes."

"Sign here then, sir."

Mentall took the offered clipboard and started to read the

agreement. "It states that I'll be accepting the unit is undamaged and fully working."

"That's right. If you can just put your moniker there and date and time it."

"But we need to open it to check it," Mentall protested.

"I haven't time for that. Sign there or I'll pop it back on the van."

Mentall signed and returned to the interview.

"What are your plans for the future?" asked Millerson.

"If they acquit me I intend to offer my services to the charity sector."

He watched Millerson smile and nod with pursed lips. *She'll print that all the same*, he thought.

"Right, I think we're done?" she said.

"Oh that's a shame," said Mentall.

"Why?" she asked cautiously.

"It's not often I have such charming company."

"Right," said Millerson, shoving her notebook into her bag. "I hope you get your house decorated and your furniture back soon."

"It's not all in storage, the bed's upstairs."

"I think we'll leave it there, Mr Mentall."

"Dinner?" he enquired.

"A gentleman would have offered me dinner first."

"Well, I could stand you that."

"Mr *Mentall,* this is my workplace and you have some serious charges pending. What bloody century are you in?"

"In my day a young lady would be delighted with the company of a member of the establishment."

"This is *not* your day."

Mentall rued the truth in that statement then said, "You know where I am if you change your mind."

"I can honestly and sincerely tell you there's no danger of that."

The awkwardness was broken by the doorbell.

She opened the door, Tom stood there, the froth from his last beer still on his moustache. "Get me away from this creep," she said.

*

Mentall had beans on toast for his supper and then turned his attention to the television. He unwrapped it and found a deep chip in the black surround. He cursed, peeled off the helpline label, picked up his landline's handset and dialled.

"Hello, you're through to Kenny. How can I help you?" asked a man with a broad Scottish accent.

"I have received a television set and it has a chip in it."

"They all have chips in them, sir," replied Kenny cockily.

"I mean it's damaged. The black surround has a nasty chip on it."

"Okay. What's the first two letters of the order reference number? It's on the pink slip of paper in the box."

"E I," said Mentall.

"E for Edinburgh, I for independence?" Kenny replied.

"Yes," Mentall replied ruefully.

"Next two letters?"

"S O," Mentall replied.

"S O for Scottish Oil?"

"Or Sassenach Oppressor if that makes you happy," Mentall replied, thinking the telly's not the only thing with a chip on it.

"And finally what's the last letter?"

"W," Mentall replied.

"W for–"

"I could certainly help you with *that* one," said Mentall.

"W for William Wallace?"

"Yes," sighed Mentall.

"I have your name here as Stephen Mentall."

"Yes, that's right."

"You're nae that judge who's in a spot of bother are ye?"

Mentall didn't reply.

"Aye you were on the news this evening. Did you nae see it?"

"I don't have a television."

"I thought the television was with you?"

"Yes, but it has a chip on it and I want to return it," Mentall replied testily.

"Did you nae check it when the delivery driver dropped it off?"

"There wasn't a chance. He wouldn't wait."

"Did you buy it on your credit card?"

"No, I paid cash at the store," Mentall replied with the distinct feeling this was not going to have a good outcome.

"Aye well, you've accepted the goods. It'd be different if it was broken. We could replace it under warranty. But we aren't responsible for superficial damage that you could've caused yourself."

"It was damaged when I opened the box," Mentall protested.

"Aye well, we can't take your word for that."

"But I'm a judge."

"Were a judge by the last reckoning. The news didnae paint you as a very trustworthy character. Did you know you're on Panorama tonight? More revelations apparently."

"I don't have a televi, no forget it," Mentall replied and hung up.

Mentall hooked up the damaged television, retrieved the Waterloo Porn Trial DVD, 'Wet Girls Clam Up', from behind the tins of paint in the potting shed and spent an hour enjoying a lesbian romp. He then played the DVD of his eminent Panorama interview on 'The East Castle Street Robbery' and at ten p.m. watched a live episode revealing stories of blown up care homes, missing exhibit money and, with Mentall closing his eyes in disbelief, call girls. Mentall knew it'd be unlikely he'd get prosecuted on the latter but the revelations would encourage the jury to convict on the others.

Mentall came back to the moment with a sharp rat-tat-tat at his door.

He opened the door to reveal a thunder-faced Margaret Wainscott-Bruce. "You disgust me."

"You can't believe everything you see on the television," Mentall replied.

"But it was the BBC."

Mentall slammed the door in her face, stuck a coat hanger into the ventilation grill of the television, waited for a satisfying spark and a trail of smoke then called the helpline and reported it faulty.

48

Detective Chief Inspector Marjorie Stainthwaite took the witness stand at the second hearing of Tadler's disciplinary.

The chair, Chief Constable Robert Wytton, consulted his notes then began. "Can you describe to the hearing what your relationship with DS Peter Tadler was?"

"I can assure you there was no relationship," stated Stainthwaite.

"I mean professional relationship."

"I was his superior officer."

"And he reported to you on all matters?"

"That is correct Sir, yes."

"And can you describe his abilities as a police officer and what you saw of the incident in question?"

"I found his police work decisively deficient. His record keeping was appalling, his attitude to senior officers insubordinate and his ability to keep appointments with me rather lacking. In fact, I found him a rather disgusting and ignorant individual prone to sexism and I feel he resented reporting to a female officer."

"And on the day in question?" Wytton asked, making notes.

"I needed to check up on something with DS Tadler and, knowing he was prone to not taking my calls, walked down to his office for a brief meeting. On opening the door, I found him with his right hand down the front of his trousers. He was, and I'll make this as polite as I can, having a good rummage around."

"You mean he was groping himself?"

"Yes, and when I challenged him he withdrew his hand and I noted ejaculate on his fingers. I found this sickening. I've seen a few things in my time as a serving officer but I have never been exposed to anything like this. He is a disgusting, ill bred, loathsome, ignorant, sexual pervert."

"Anything else?" asked Wytton.

"Well I don't want to be too hard on him."

Tadler explained that the white substance was in fact haemorrhoid cream, but Wytton dismissed this in his summing up and demoted him back to the rank of police constable.

"Furthermore," continued Wytton, "I further demote you for your previous offensive behaviour in front of this tribunal panel."

"But there's nothing lower than a police constable," said Tadler.

"Correction, there's nothing lower than you. However, as I think you were trying to point out, this demotion takes place from your now current rank of police constable and as this is the lowest rank in the force, I hereby dismiss you. Your salary will be paid up to today and your entire pension contributions will be returned to you."

One of the other tribunal members leaned over and whispered into his ear.

"I've just been informed there's a settlement pending due to a petition from your estranged wife who, for whatever reason, has seen fit to sue for divorce. Therefore your pension contributions will be withheld and you'll be additionally liable to the force for whatever the appointed actuary deems your estranged wife's entitlement is."

Tadler shook his head in disbelief.

"The police pension is a generous scheme," continued Wytton.

Too right, thought Tadler: the tribunal panel members were made up of a mix of retired senior officers, sporting gold fillings, sun tanned complexion and tailor made suits.

"Therefore I advise you to hold onto what reserves you have until your divorce is settled."

*

Sat in his car Tadler knew he'd been suckered and knew he'd suckered himself. Being put under DCI Stainthwaite, a turn of phrase on which he did not wish to dwell, had come at the worst moment of his divorce. Her persuasive techniques were so similar to his wife's that he'd adopted the same half-hearted attitude to anything asked of him. Leaving aside the innocent email about 'Horse Face', the opportunistic misunderstanding of the administering of haemorrhoid cream, and the dumping of the Judge Mentall case upon him, he knew he'd not played things well. The police force was a tough place to work and you had to play along, bite your

217

lip and just put up with things. But he hadn't, he'd fought against "Yes ma'am, no ma'am" whereas he'd done well before with "Yes sir, no sir."

But something still bothered him about the Judge Mentall case. Something didn't add up.

49

Mentall stirred, he'd fallen asleep on the deckchair in his lounge and the front doorbell was now ringing. *Please don't let it be that bloody Margaret Wainscott-Bruce woman*, he thought. He staggered into the hall, opened the door and took a moment to recognise the familiar figure now stood before him.

"I had no idea," began Ellie Foster.

"No idea what?" asked Mentall while trying to comprehend this unexpected visitor.

"That you were not a real old person in need of the home."

"Well I did try to say," Mentall protested.

"But your family?"

"Not my family," Mentall replied.

"But it was all so convincing," she said in a low voice.

"I think you wanted to be convinced," said Mentall.

"I guess so, but I'm so sorry. I was asked to identify your photograph after the explosion, then I read that article in Hello magazine, and couldn't believe my eyes. It said you've lost everything apart from this big empty house."

"Yes," Mentall replied, "and I'm pending a trial."

"Is there anything I can do?"

Mentall noticed that Margaret Wainscott-Bruce was standing at the entrance to his driveway. "Do you want to come in for a minute?" he asked, standing aside.

She stepped into the hall, he quickly closed the door behind her and then led her into the lounge. "I don't suppose you have a contact number for that Daniel O'Donnell impressionist do you? I passed him a note saying I was being held captive. Nothing came of it but it would corroborate my story if he could testify to that."

Ellie paused for a moment then said, "No. Everything was destroyed in the explosion and, if I remember correctly, his agent cold called Colin and he booked it there and then. We paid cash on the night. I'm really sorry."

"Okay, I've tried to find the fellow but can't track him down."

"Is the trial likely to be bad?" she asked.

"I think there are some powers at play against me."

"How terrible for you. And you such a respected judge and everything. But surely if you're innocent…"

"It's not always as easy as that."

"Isn't the law innocent until proven guilty?"

"Something like that," Mentall replied.

"I believe in you, you strike me as a man of great character."

Mentall looked at her in a new light. She'd always dressed blandly at Smoking Chimney, and he'd never taken much notice of her. But now, stood in his lounge, he saw an attractive woman. He imagined her with her hair down, dressed in a red skirt and a pair of heels: she could pass as a classy piece.

"Would you like some supper?" he asked.

"Would love some," she replied, smiling.

Mentall nodded: this was going to solve the problem of funding the visits to Madam Suzie's House of Pleasure.

*

A month later, wrapped in his dressing gown and sipping coffee at the breakfast table, Ellie began to gaze around the kitchen. "You know this'd make an ideal old people's home, just a few select customers. We could run it together. I should get the insurance money from Smoking Chimneys soon and I have a few savings too."

"I'll give it some thought," Mentall said cautiously. "But why don't you have Smoking Chimneys rebuilt?"

"It'll take ages. Anyhow I'm handing it over to the insurance company and they plan to sell it on as a housing development. They're due to pay me its full market value immediately prior to the explosion."

She's being taken for a ride, thought Mentall.

"And I need to move on from the family home where Colin, and so many of my relatives, died."

Sentimental fool, thought Mentall.

"So I was thinking we've five bedrooms here, plus three reception rooms downstairs. We can start by converting the bedrooms upstairs, one reception room can be the dayroom and dining area, the other can be our room and the final one the office."

Cheeky bitch, thought Mentall.

"We'll need to install a lift," added Ellie, "our room already has an ensuite so it'll just be a case of knocking through from bedroom two into the main bathroom and adding wet-rooms to the other three."

"Are all these ensuites necessary?" asked Mentall, suspicious at the speed at which her plan was taking shape.

"You don't know old people, best to always have them near the porcelain."

"Right. Well I won't rule it out," Mentall replied.

They spent the day in the garden, tidying borders, dredging out the pond, mowing the grass with an ancient Flymo (the cocaine snorting Poles having sold the tractor mower) and pruning the roses.

Mentall watched Ellie and pondered her idea. *She's a good worker*, he thought. It sounded a solid plan but tying himself up financially bothered him. She'd be putting in the majority of the money, he'd prefer it the other way but knew that'd cause him a whole set of different anxieties. His thoughts were interrupted by the delivery of the replacement television. This time, as the delivery driver bitterly complained, he insisted on unpacking and inspecting it before signing the delivery note.

"You're very thorough," said Ellie as he carried it through to the lounge.

"Well you've got to be," Mentall replied, hooking it up to the mains, aerial and DVD player.

"I suppose in your line of work, seeing the worst in people, makes you mistrustful."

"It can get like that."

"I hope I didn't worry you going on about making this into a care home?"

"No, not at all. It's just a lot to think through."

"If it's the profitability that worries you we can extend the house to make more rooms. And we can make you the main proprietor. You've been treated badly, I thought you might like some status back?"

Mentall looked at her and thought this is the first woman he'd ever met that had actually got inside his head.

"Shall we watch a DVD?" she asked.

"The tenants stole them all apart from my first Panorama appearance."

"The philistines," Ellie commiserated. "I'd like to see it."

Mentall took the DVD from its sleeve, put it in the player and pressed the play button. Each time he appeared on the TV screen he glanced to see Ellie's reaction. When it came to an end Ellie remarked, "You're very eminent."

Mentall smiled. "Well that's my DVD collection gone through."

"What about porn?" she asked.

Mentall was surprised, "No, bloody filth. Wouldn't have it in the house."

"Is that why you keep it in the potting shed then?"

"Must have been my wife's," Mentall stumbled out.

"With 'Waterloo Porn Trial' written on the disc? Wasn't that one of the cases you did?"

Mentall was lost for words until Ellie added, "Go and get it you daft fool. I'm no prude, never know it might warm me up."

*

Sat up in bed, with the window open, Mentall felt relaxed. Ellie was doing a word search in a folded newspaper, and the sheets were pulled up to her waist leaving her breasts exposed. This was quite different to his usual experiences: his ex-wife always got up and busied herself with chores after intimacy and the parlour girls always counted the cash.

"What's the prize for the word search?" he asked.

"I just like seeing my name in the paper as the winner. I cut it out and put it in my scrapbook."

"You keep a scrapbook!"

"Don't you keep a scrapbook of your trials?"

"I don't trust the paper's versions."

"But the prize is fifty quid, I don't win often and it doesn't go far."

"Fifty quid is fifty quid," said Mentall thinking that'd buy him twenty minutes at Madam Suzie's House of Pleasure.

She lowered the paper into her lap. "You've got no other source of income have you, love?"

"No. But if I get acquitted I'll be able to work again."

"What are the chances of that?"

"Well I didn't destroy the home."

"And the East Castle Street exhibit money?"

Mentall paused then said, "There's no proof I took it."

"But did you?"

Mentall did not reply.

"You did take it didn't you!" she said, turning to him.

Mentall raised his eyebrows.

"Oh God," said Ellie, raising a hand to her mouth, "I've been called as a witness at your trial. They're going to make me give evidence against you."

"If you say there was a police raid they can't find me guilty of destroying the house."

"And the East Castle Street exhibit money?"

"I don't think they'll ask you about that."

"What if they do? What if they find out about us?" Ellie began to weep.

"Steady on girl," said Mentall, patting her on the leg.

"I don't want them to take you from me. I wish we could run this place together as a care home and be happy. My knowhow, your house and my money. I think you'd be good at it too, you've a real presence and you could use your legal knowhow to advise client's families on taking out powers of attorney and clever things like that."

Mentall allowed her to weep and cuddle into him while he thought. This woman *was* keen on him and the insurance money from Smoking Chimneys would be substantially more than the value of his home. And she mentioned some savings too. With her breathing slipping into sleep he gently extracted his arm, stepped out of the bed and pulled the bedroom door closed behind him.

He stepped into the spare room next to the bathroom and surveyed her worldly goods stacked against the far wall. *Where would she put it?* he thought. He then nodded and smiled as his eyes fixed on a box file marked 'Savings'.

Opening her building society pass book he let out a long whistle. "Like taking candy from a baby," he whispered. *Top that up with the insurance money and this was looking the real deal.*

Having dealt with many a prenuptial he knew the party with the smallest stake always gained; if all went pear shaped he'd still have his house. And with Ellie preoccupied with running the home, visits to Madam Suzie's House of Pleasure could be reintroduced.

He slipped back into bed and took her hand. She stirred and murmured, "Hello."

"Yes, let's make this a care home if that's what you want," he whispered.

"They won't make me give evidence against you will they?" she asked, beginning to sob gently. "Tell me they won't."

"Not if you were my wife."

"Is that a proposal?" she laughed through her tears.

"If you want it to be."

"Oh thank you," she said, hugging him. "We can call it the Foster-Mentall home."

"Perhaps just the Mentall Home," he replied.

"We can't call it that!" Ellie replied.

"Judging by that bunch of characters at Smoking Chimneys it would hardly be against trade descriptions," said Mentall.

"We can't call it the Mentall Home, nor the Foster Home for that matter," she replied, "and I suppose Foster-Mentall might get us into trouble too."

"What about anagrams?" asked Mentall.

"Strange name for a home?" she asked, pulling away to look at him.

"Anagrams of our names."

"Oh. Well an anagram of mine is Forest."

"Mantell," Mentall replied.

"Mantell Forest?" suggested Ellie.

"Yes," Mentall replied, pleased that she'd put his name first.

"The Mantell Forest Rest Home," said Ellie, testing the words.

50

Sandra Pughes surveyed her husband from across the breakfast table. "I'm going to stay at my mother's for a few days."

"Whatever for?"

"We're a bit crowded here with Wayne recuperating, and I need to get on and sort her place so I can get it on the market."

"We could do with the cash," said Jack.

"No, Jack, no," she replied, shaking her head. "That money is for mum's care and if there's any leftover you're not getting your thieving hands on it."

"But you've got power of attorney," exclaimed Jack.

Sandra shook her head in utter disbelief. "You just don't get it do you?"

"Get what?"

"That my poor old mum deserves a decent home and that has to be paid for. Left in your hands the money would get wasted on some scam and she'd end up in a place like we put that judge in."

"But if we invest it shrewdly we can all win," said Jack.

"And if the investment fails she'll be living with us. You thought about that Jack? Are you up to changing the bedding five times a day while engaging in pointless conversation?"

"No."

"Well, to be frank I'm surprised Jack because any conversation with you is fucking pointless."

"There's no need to get personal."

Sandra's face turned black as she glowered at him. "All your schemes turn to disaster. You're not getting anywhere near mum's money."

"In that case I won't be sharing my latest venture with you."

"And what might that be?" asked Sandra with a pronounced sigh.

"My campaign to get Bernard Bresslaw posthumously knighted."

"What! I don't believe this. You can't be serious."

"I am," Jack replied proudly.

Sandra raised both hands to her forehead. "As your harebrained schemes go this must be the worse. For one I should imagine half the population have never heard of him. For two you can't knight the dead and for three, supposing there was a miraculous change in the law, can you think of any reason why the Prime Minister or Her Majesty The Queen would take it on themselves to knight a bit part actor from the Carry On Films?"

"That's the beauty of it. He's never going to get knighted so my Just Giving page can run and run in the background."

"You've setup a Just Giving page?"

"I have," Jack replied proudly. "And it's taken us twenty quid so far."

"What! You mean there's suckers out there who've actually given you money for it?"

"Well, not exactly," said Jack, screwing up his face.

"What do you mean, *not exactly*?"

"Well," he admitted reluctantly, "the twenty quid was actually me testing out the page."

"So, Jack," said Sandra, briefly closing her eyes, "let's get this straight. You have sponsored yourself twenty quid to get Bernard Bresslaw posthumously knighted?"

"Well I was just testing the page before I sent it viral on Facebook."

"Jack this is an ultimatum – all cash through this house, our bank accounts, any bank accounts you might have and your pockets from now on must be legit. Got it? We could have gone down for a very long stretch over that judge. And with his trial coming up I'm still a bit concerned but I think we've just got away with it. You're riding your luck and if you've any interest in this marriage, and God knows why I'm suggesting this, you're getting a job. And that's a proper job with a weekly pay-packet with tax and national insurance deductions."

"What about you? Why must I always be the bread winner?" asked Jack.

"Because I'm sorting my mum's house so she can stay in that care home. Remember?"

Jack winced.

"But yes, okay, afterwards I'll get a job too. And we can go out on Friday nights and have holidays without watching over our shoulders for the old bill."

"But what if I take a job and something big comes in?"

"Such as?"

"Well, I've got a few things out there, a few ears to the ground."

"Jack do you want a divorce?"

"No."

"Well it's my way or the highway. Which is it to be?"

"Well..."

"Jack, which is it to be?"

"Your way," he sighed.

"Right, here's last night's Evening News. I suggest you turn to situations vacant and start looking."

"The what?"

"The job pages, Jack. The job pages."

Jack flicked through the newspaper then stopped. Sandra caught his line of sight. "The jobs pages, Jack *not* the for sale and wanted ads."

He flicked through a few more sheets until he found the situations vacant page. She watched him going down each advert.

"They're all trades, I'm not a bricky a plumber or a chippy."

"Any driving jobs?"

"I don't have a license thanks to somebody."

"Anything else?"

"There's one for a handyman."

"Read it out."

"Handyman required for a new care home in Albridge. Gardening and general maintenance. Good rates of pay, hours to suit."

"Let's have a look at that," said Sandra, taking the paper.

"Did you read the entire advert?" she asked.

"Yes."

"What about the contact details, did you read those?"

"It was just an email address," Jack replied.

"Yes, Ellie.Foster@SmokingChimneys.co.uk."

"Oh."

"Oh indeed, Jack."

"But Smoking Chimneys has been destroyed."

"Oh Jack, you're such a cretin. She's obviously starting up again. It says *in Albridge*, no mention of Maston where Smoking Chimneys was. And it might just, just occur to you that after Wayne's little escapade with his cigarette lighter, Smoking Chimneys may take more than an odd job man to sort out."

"You'd have thought she'd have changed her email address," said Jack.

"Not necessarily. I expect she's got enough on her hands without worrying about that. And you never know she might be calling the new place 'Smoking Chimneys'."

"Well it's a bit strange."

"A bit lucky more like. You imagine turning up there for interview. She'd recognise you straightaway and who knows where that might lead."

"Well there's nothing else."

"Okay Jack, get yourself down the job centre, or whatever they call themselves these days, and see what they've got. And sign on at one of those agencies where they find you work. But just do something and have it found before I get back from my mother's."

"How many days will you be?"

"I'm not telling you Jack. The deal is when I get back you'll be in legit employment. Got it?"

"Yes," Jack replied sounding defeated.

51

In the week before Mentall's trial the press, now referring to his arrest as 'his capture', dutifully ran stories on how he'd stolen exhibit money and then taken refuge in a care home.

More than one high court judge opened their trials with quips that they were there for the duration and wouldn't be going into hiding, or absconding with the evidence.

The Home Secretary announced reforms to make it easier to track the whereabouts of trial judges, BBC Radio Four's Woman's Hour ran an episode devoted to judicial misogyny and Panorama repeated their documentary discrediting Mentall.

The judge, chosen for Stephen Mentall's trial, was a prominent women's rights advocate, and the prosecuting barrister was selected from a list who harboured a personal grudge against him. Top of that list was Juliet Framson, a black feminist who had joined the legal system to try and enforce change after Mentall had sent her younger brother down for six months for affray while giving his white accomplice, and the alleged ringleader, fifteen hours community service.

Mentall decided to defend himself. At the opening of his trial he stood impassively while the charges were read out: the theft of exhibit money and the wilful destruction of Smoking Chimneys and in so doing, the manslaughter of the proprietor, Colin Foster.

"How do you plead on the first count?" asked the clerk of the court.

"I do not recognise this court," Mentall replied.

Judge Mandy Stenbark removed her glasses and stared at him. "Well we've had it decorated since you last presided in it, Mr Mentall."

There were some smirks from the press box and an audible guffaw from the jury. Mentall eyed up the jury: another typical bunch of middle-class do-gooders basking in their self-importance of being called as a juror. This was their day and they were going to get their money's worth.

Juliet Framson opened for the prosecution and, remembering

how he had patronised her as a junior counsel, gripped her lapels, straightened her back and began. "Mr Mentall, you claim in your statement you were kidnapped."

"There is no *claim* about it. I *was* kidnapped."

"Here in Albridge?"

"Yes, that's right."

"Whereabouts exactly in Albridge?"

"On the Northbridge Industrial Estate."

"And, according to your evidence," she continued, turning a page, "this alleged abduction occurred on an evening of the trial of PC Edward Sawman."

"Yes," Mentall replied.

"What was your business on the Northbridge Industrial Estate that evening?"

"I was taking a neighbour's dog for a walk," Mentall replied.

"Any particular reason?"

"They were away, and I was looking after it."

"Are you aware the Northbridge Industrial Estate is some five miles from your home?"

"I've never measured it."

"Well I have, making it at least a ten mile circular walk. Why so far?"

"He wanted to stretch his legs."

"Does your neighbour's dog enjoy walking on the Northbridge Industrial Estate?"

"I didn't ask him."

"This is quite some dog that belongs to your neighbour. He is able to ask for a ten mile walk to 'stretch his legs' and seemingly, if posed, is able to answer questions on his favourite areas of town."

"I *never* said that. I didn't enter into conversation with the dog."

"Very wise, I'm sure. No doubt the dog would've found the quality of the conversation somewhat lacking."

"Objection," called Mentall.

"Sustained," said Stenbark with a sigh, "the prosecution will refrain from unnecessary personal remarks."

"I withdraw the remark," said Framson. "What were you really doing on the Northbridge Industrial Estate that evening?" asked Framson.

Mentall wiped the back of his neck and dropped his head.

"Let me see if I can help you," continued Framson. "Are you aware the Northbridge Industrial Estate has a house of ill repute trading as a massage parlour?"

"I have heard talk of that," Mentall replied.

"Let me put it to you – you were visiting a brothel that evening." Mentall paused.

"Well, Mr Mentall?"

"I was visiting it, yes, but not for the reasons you're insinuating."

"And what might I be insinuating?"

"That I was there for the purposes of soliciting sexual intercourse with a female."

"And were you there for the purposes of soliciting sexual intercourse with a female?"

"No."

"A male then?"

"No, I *was* not!"

"Surely you don't expect the jury to believe there was another reason."

"If you must know I had a bad back and had booked a massage."

"You had a bad back and had booked a massage?"

"Is there a bloody echo in here or something?" barked Mentall.

"You must be blessed with a high degree of stoicism to walk ten miles with a bad back to get a massage."

"Is your back troubling you now?" enquired Stenbark.

"No."

"It's just I was unaware you had a bad back?"

"It's quite all right today thank you," Mentall replied.

"I'm sure we're all glad to hear that," said Framson raising her eyebrows. "So you claim you were on the Northbridge Industrial Estate, possibly walking your neighbour's rather talented dog and visiting a brothel for an orthopaedic massage."

"How was I supposed to know it was a brothel?"

"Do you think the jury are stupid?"

"I wouldn't know."

"This isn't one of your trials," interjected Judge Mandy Stenbark, "your influence over the jury is very different as the defendant. You'll be advised not to cast doubt on their intelligence."

"Thank you, your honour," said Framson.

"I've *never* sought to influence a jury," Mentall protested.

"So you maintain, on the evening in question, you visited a brothel on the Northbridge Industrial Estate for the purposes of an orthopaedic massage."

"I just said that, yes."

"And at what point did you realise you'd made a mistake?"

"When I saw what the young ladies were wearing," Mentall replied.

"Presumably not very much?"

"That is correct. I was disgusted and left immediately."

"And were promptly kidnapped?"

"That is correct, yes."

"Mr Mentall," interrupted Judge Stenbark, "what I don't understand is why you didn't say all this in your statement to the police. You must realise that it is inadvisable to rely on evidence in court that you didn't previously offer."

"Well it was a bit embarrassing."

"What was?"

"Visiting a brothel."

"So you admit it then?" asked Framson.

"Don't try and get clever with me my girl. I didn't realise it was a brothel until I got there."

"You weren't tempted by the attractive young women then?" asked Framson.

"What attractive young women?" asked Mentall.

"The ones you chanced across in the brothel where you claim you'd gone for an orthopaedic massage."

"No, I was not."

"Come, come, now, Mr Mentall. You, a divorced, late middle-aged man faced with the opportunity to have sex with an attractive young woman turned the chance down?"

"They weren't attractive. They were a bunch of hags that I wouldn't touch with a barge pole," fumed Mentall.

Mentall looked around the court and was shocked by the shocked faces. Nobody spoke, the moment hung in the air and Mentall's legs felt like they were about to give way.

The silence was broken by a press portrait artist turning the pages of his art book and scribbling the scene before him.

"I think we'll have a twenty minute recess," said Stenbark.

*

"Let's move on shall we and return to your evening on the Northbridge Industrial Estate," said Framson after the resumption. "Where did you see the advert for the brothel?"

"Objection," Mentall snapped.

"On what grounds?" asked Judge Stenbark.

"Surely it's obvious? The question presumes I knew it was a brothel when I phoned and booked."

"Very well, counsel please rephrase the question," said Stenbark.

"Where did you see the advert for the establishment offering an out-of-hours massage service?" asked Framson.

Mentall pursed his lips and took a moment to begin his reply. "In the back pages of the Albridge Evening News."

"In the back pages of the Albridge Evening News," Framson repeated, "did that not strike you as suspicious?"

"Not in the slightest."

"I have here a copy of the Albridge Evening News," said Framson wafting a paper in the air for the court to see. "I'd like to read you some of these adverts," she continued. She then opened the paper and read, "Bunnies All Night Massage. Girls Always Wanted. Relaxing Massage in Discrete Surroundings. Massage. Out Calls Available. Ten p.m. to Three a.m. Massage Service. Live Girls Available to Chat."

"Well I don't know about those. The one I phoned didn't have an advert like that."

"What sort of advert did it have?"

"I don't recall."

"But not like the ones I just read out?"

"No. That's what I've been saying," Mentall replied with clear frustration in his voice.

"Would you like to examine the paper and point out to the court which advert you responded to?"

"It was too far back. There's no point in playing these silly games."

"How about this one, Madam Suzie's House of Pleasure. Companion and Escort Agency in Albridge?"

"It wasn't that one," said Mentall, rather too quickly.

"Well it has the telephone number of the one on the Northbridge Industrial Estate."

"Haven't you considered there's probably more than one on the Northbridge Industrial Estate?"

"We telephoned them all for directions. This is the only one on the Northbridge Industrial Estate."

"They have probably changed their advert," snapped Mentall.

"This copy of the Albridge Evening News is dated the day you allege you were kidnapped."

"I used an older copy," Mentall replied dismissively.

"We've been back four years, their advert has never varied."

Mentall flinched. "Well I don't know about that."

"Do you still maintain you were kidnapped?"

"My dear girl," said Mentall patronisingly, "how many times do I have to tell you, I *was* kidnapped?"

"Can you describe these alleged kidnappers?"

"They put a bag over my head."

"Very convenient."

"It darned well wasn't very convenient for me," hissed Mentall.

"How many kidnappers were there?"

"I'd say approximately three."

"Give or take three no doubt," replied Framson. "Now, do you have any idea why the police have not pursued your kidnapping as a line of enquiry?"

"I've no idea."

"I put it to you it's a tissue of lies. You conveniently disappeared and hid in a care home to avoid the issue of the theft of the exhibit money from the East Castle Street robbery."

"No," Mentall replied.

Framson paused for a moment. "Let me return to your alleged kidnappers. Where did they take you after the kidnapping?"

"I don't know."

"Let me put it a different way. Can you describe where you were held?"

"It was a room off a bathroom. I was chained to a wall and brought food and water."

"And made to wear a bag over your head?"

"Only when the kidnappers were present," Mentall replied.

"Do you often take to wearing a bag over your head?" asked Framson.

"Only when I've been kidnapped."

"Not perhaps when visiting a lady on the Northbridge Industrial Estate?"

"Your honour, I object," said Mentall.

"Objection overruled, please continue."

"Thank you your honour," said Framson, clutching her lapels. "How many days were you held in this room?"

"I'm not sure, possibly as much as a week. I was then collected by a man and a woman and taken to a care home."

"You say in your statement they deposited you as a resident in the Smoking Chimneys care home."

Mentall wiped his brow. "That is correct, yes."

"Didn't that strike you as a bit odd?"

"Completely bloody odd if you ask me," Mentall replied.

"I was indeed asking you. Why didn't you immediately make it known that you were a kidnapped judge?"

"I did but no one listened. I tried to escape on numerous occasions but was thwarted every time. Nobody would believe me when I said who I was. I didn't know the setup so I was cautious as to who I approached. I found Smoking Chimneys a sinister place, high fences, darkened cellars and bathtubs screwed to the floors."

"Did the cellars have windows?"

"No."

"Did they have lights permanently on?" asked Framson, raising the pitch of her voice.

"No."

"Hardly surprising they were darkened then is it Mr Mentall?"

"No, put like that I suppose–"

"And bathtubs screwed to the floors. Aren't most bathtubs screwed to a floor?"

"Well I suppose–"

"I think you suppose we can't see you're trying to paint Smoking Chimneys as some sinister place of incarceration when in fact it was a friendly, well run care home for the elderly you chose to destroy."

"No."

"Either way, if we're to believe your account, I find it hard to comprehend you took so much time to approach the proprietor, Colin Foster."

"I did approach him."

"Did you also approach his wife, Ellie Foster?"

"No."

"Or any other member of staff?"

"No."

"Or a family member visiting a relative perhaps?" asked Framson with a threatening smile.

"I did ask a couple for a lift to Albridge."

"But you didn't say who you were."

"No, I saved that for when they were stopped by the police."

"Yes, I note that in your statement. However, the police have investigated and can find no record of this."

"Well they're probably too embarrassed to admit their mistake," Mentall replied.

"And Colin Foster, the one person you claim you did speak to, is conveniently dead is he not?"

"I doubt if it's very convenient for him," Mentall replied.

"But dead nonetheless?"

"Yes."

"Dead as a result of your actions," said Framson, nodding.

"No."

"I put it to you Mr Mentall, to avoid the scandal of the theft of the East Castle Street exhibit money, you paid a husband and wife team to deposit you in the Smoking Chimneys care home on the pretext of you being the woman's father."

"No," Mentall protested.

"And when you'd had enough you engineered a gas explosion to destroy the home and make your escape."

"No. There was a police raid. I escaped through the gates they'd opened. I only heard later that an explosion had occurred."

"This police raid you refer to," said Framson, flicking through her notes, "Shire Force have no record of a raid taking place on the day in question or any other day for that matter."

"Lies!" barked Mentall.

"Indeed they are lies, Mr Mentall. Lies indeed," and with that Juliet Framson sat down.

Judge Stenbark addressed Mentall, "Do you wish to cross-examine yourself?"

"No."

"Very well, does the counsel for the prosecution wish to continue?"

"Yes," said Framson, getting to her feet. "If it pleases your honour I'd like to present to the court Exhibit One, a DVD of a recent Panorama documentary on the affairs of the defendant."

"Objection," bellowed Mentall.

"On what grounds?" asked Stenbark.

"Oh, come on, surely it's obvious. A television programme is no more than rumour and conjecture. This court's role is to determine the facts," Mentall replied, hoping that perhaps not all the facts would be determined.

"Counsel, what are your motives for showing this documentary to the court?" asked Stenbark.

"While I accept the defences concern that a television programme may contain an element of conjecture, I wish to simply present the Panorama episode and then ask the defendant to confirm or deny a critical point."

"Can't you just show the critical point you want me to confirm or deny?" asked Mentall.

"Your honour I think we need the full context to be fair to the defendant," said Framson.

"Very well, please show the episode," Stenbark replied.

The blinds were pulled and a large screen television was wheeled into the court. As an aged clerk battled with the technology Mentall sighed and drummed his fingers.

The jury watched with interest as the DVD repeated stories of blown up care homes, missing exhibit money and, with Mentall closing his eyes, call girls. As the DVD came to a close the blinds were raised and the television was pushed to one side.

Framson rose to her feet, and Mentall prepared himself for whatever critical point she wanted him to confirm or deny.

"Mr Mentall, can you confirm whether the subject of the documentary, one Stephen Mentall, is or is not you?"

"It is me," Mentall replied.

"Thank you, no further questions your honour," and with that Framson sat down.

"Is that it?" asked Mentall.

Stenbark glanced down at Framson who returned a nod.

"That's a bit rich," said Mentall, "I thought there was to be some clarification against Panorama's allegations."

"It appears not," Stenbark replied.

"In that case, with the courts permission, I'd like to present my own exhibit of an earlier Panorama documentary in which I gave an interview about the East Castle Street Case."

"That'd be the case you're charged with stealing the exhibit money from?" asked Stenbark.

"I did *not* steal the money."

"It's the same case is it not?"

"Yes," Mentall replied.

"Very well."

The clerk wheeled the television back to centre stage, took the DVD from Mentall and, after a further tussle with the technology, the screen flickered into life and, as Mentall prepared himself for a half-hour of self-indulgence, the credits rolled with the title, 'Wet Girls Clam Up'.

The jury leant forward, one or two were seen to quickly remove and polish their glasses.

As Stenbark's eyes were glued to the screen Framson rose to her feet and stated, "For whatever reason this despicable and discredited man now sees fit to disrespect this court with this pornographic filth."

"What, oh, yes, quite right," said Stenbark, "switch this filth off at once."

The clerk withdrew the DVD, the screen went blank and the jury leant back in their seats. As he went to return the DVD to Mentall, Stenbark interjected, "I'll take that if you don't mind. I'll need it for erm a contempt of court charge."

"I don't know how this has happened," said Mentall, "I can only apologise."

"But this was the DVD you presented to the court?" asked Framson.

"Well yes, but I was expecting it to be the first Panorama documentary I appeared on," Mentall replied.

"Clearly it wasn't," said Framson.

"No."

"But you accept this filth is a DVD you brought into court today?"

"Yes, but–"

"That's all, thank you, Mr Mentall."

"But–"

"Thank you, Mr Mentall."

"But–"

"With your permission your honour, before we recess for lunch, I'd like to call Isabel Longtree of the Fibre Lover Vacuum Cleaner Company."

Mentall tried to figure out the purpose of her testimony. Her statement included an odd reference to her cat having got sick following the vacuum cleaner demonstration she had made at his house. He didn't like the smell of this so he objected.

"On what grounds?" sighed Stenbark.

"There's nothing in her witness statement connected with what I am on trial for."

"Counsel for the prosecution, do you wish to comment before I make a decision?"

"Thank you your honour. I think if the witness is allowed to give her evidence all will become clear," said Framson.

"Very well, objection overruled."

As Mentall couldn't remember making a pass at her or saying anything improper, he decided to protest no further. There was always the chance he could discredit this witness and weaken the prosecution's case.

After the preliminaries Framson asked, "Please explain to the court what occurred on the evening in question."

"I called at the house," began Longtree, "and was invited in to demonstrate the Fibre Lover. It was a bit of an odd demonstration because the house was virtually empty, and I got the feeling the occupier was using me to get his carpets vacuumed and shampooed on the cheap."

"Did the defendant purchase a vacuum cleaner?"

"No," replied Longtree. "I terminated the demonstration early as I found him rather gross."

"Did the defendant make an improper advance upon you?"

"No, it was just the general hygiene of the house. The hall carpet was caked with mud and there was a strange white powder ingrained in the lounge carpet."

Those bloody tenants, thought Mentall.

"What did you do after you left the property?"

"I decided to make that the last call of the day and returned home. I emptied the vacuum cleaner bag into my kitchen pedal bin and retired to bed."

"Then what?"

"At around three thirty a.m. I awoke to a commotion in my kitchen. I went to investigate and found the pedal bin tipped up and my tabby cat, Bingo, crashing around the kitchen."

"Alarming I'm sure," interjected Framson. "Can you elaborate on the point 'crashing around the kitchen'?"

"Well, he's fourteen and usually a little docile. He has trouble with his kidneys you know." She then paused and looked towards the jury like she was waiting for a sympathetic nod. "But," she continued, "that night he was literally flying off the walls, crashing into everything like a mad thing. And his pupils were terribly wide eyed and dilated. I had trouble calming him down. It took me an hour and a half to get him into his basket. I took him straight to the vet first thing."

"And what was the vet's analysis?"

"At first he was unsure but they took a blood test and found he was high on cocaine."

A murmur from the public gallery was curtailed by Framson asking, "And where do you think he got hold of the cocaine from?"

"Well my pedal bin of course."

"Are you sure of this?"

"The vet asked me to bring it in and he confirmed the dust contained cocaine."

Mentall eyed her. He didn't like the sound of the way this was going. Clearly the strange white powder, left ingrained in his lounge carpet by the tenants, was cocaine. However, without proof his house had been let, this was not an avenue he could pursue.

"Did you contact the police?" asked Framson.

"No. Not straightaway."

"And why not?"

"Well Bingo appeared to be making a good recovery – it was not until I saw the defendant was being prosecuted that I came forward."

"And what of Bingo now?" asked Framson, lifting her voice, "Is he well?"

"I wouldn't know. He's left home and moved in next door with a bunch of students."

"No further questions, your honour," concluded Framson.

"Your witness, Mr Mentall," said Stenbark.

Mentall rose to his feet and stared at Longtree. "How many demonstrations of the Fibre Lover had you made on that day?"

"Four or five I suppose."

"And you say you emptied the bag into your pedal bin."

"Yes, that's right," replied Longtree.

"So how can you be sure the cocaine came from my house?" asked Mentall in a tone that clearly suggested he thought he had got the better of her.

"I always change the bag before each demonstration."

"And why is that?"

"It's part of our training to."

"Any particular reason?" asked Mentall suspiciously.

"The Fibre Lover gives better suction on an empty bag."

"So you admit to deceiving the public. In reality an owner of the said product wouldn't change the bag on a daily basis."

"As I said it's part of our training."

"Very well. How can you be sure the bag you emptied into your pedal bin was not one you'd filled earlier in the day?"

"I'm quite sure it wasn't."

"How so?"

"Well," and Isabel Longtree looked uncomfortable, "I deposited the empty ones into your wheelie bin before knocking your door."

"That wasn't very professional of you was it?"

"I suppose not."

"Can you be sure the cocaine wasn't already in your pedal bin?"

"If it was I wouldn't know how on earth it got there."

"But nonetheless there's no absolute proof that the bag from cleaning my carpets contained the cocaine."

"I suppose not."

"Your honour, I request the jury be instructed to ignore this evidence. I'm not indicted with the possession of cocaine and even if I were the prosecution have failed to prove the cocaine came from my house. I feel this whole charade is no more than a stunt to stain my character."

"Very well," said Stenbark, "the jury will ignore this evidence."

"Thank you, your honour," said Mentall knowing full well he'd been stitched up; the jury would have made their minds up about bad character.

*

242

First up after lunch was the former Ellie Foster.

"You are Ellie Foster a former proprietor of the Smoking Chimneys care home?" asked Framson.

"I was co-owner of the Smoking Chimneys care home, but I'm not called Ellie Foster."

"What is your name then?"

"It's Ellie Mentall."

"This court is not a place for guessing games, madam."

"No, my name is Ellie Mentall, short for Eleanor Mentall."

"Oh I see. Are you some relation of the defendant then?" asked Framson cautiously.

"I'm his wife."

"You're his wife!"

"Yes."

"But you were formerly Ellie Foster?"

"Yes."

"Since when have you been married to the defendant?"

"Two months ago."

Mentall smiled. He was enjoying this.

Judge Stenbark interrupted. "Are you still happy to give evidence in this case? You aren't compelled to give evidence against your husband."

"Yes, I am."

Mentall glanced across to her. He didn't like the sound of that.

"The jury," said Stenbark, "will take note of this unusual situation. Mrs Mentall is giving evidence in the trial of her now husband for the wilful destruction of her former home and the manslaughter of her previous husband, Colin Foster. You may proceed."

"Thank you your honour. So Mrs Mentall, can you cast your mind back to the unfortunate morning of the explosion in which you lost your home and your husband?"

"Yes, I can."

"Was there a police raid on your premises?"

"No."

Mentall's eyes widened in utter disbelief.

"But you claim in your statement there was a gas leak?"

"Yes."

"Caused by?"

"I don't know," Ellie replied evasively.

"I mean caused by what, not whom," clarified Framson.

"It came from one of the gas cookers in the kitchen."

"And where was Stephen Mentall during all this?"

"He was nowhere to be seen," she replied in a tone that cast suspicion.

"What did you do, Mrs Mentall?"

"I called the fire brigade, but the army attended."

Judge Mandy Stenbark interrupted, "Why did the army attend?"

"The fire service were on strike your honour," explained Framson.

"And I suppose the army do have a record of this?"

"Yes, your honour."

"Thank you. Proceed."

Framson directed her questioning back to Ellie. "Then what happened?"

"We evacuated the premises and the army took control."

"And did you see Stephen Mentall during any of this?"

"No," Ellie replied.

"Is it possible, having sabotaged a gas appliance, he was hiding in the home poised to strike a match?"

"It'd be possible I suppose, yes."

Mentall stared at his wife, shocked and horrified by this turn of events.

*

As the army captain, having offered no explanation of what might have triggered the explosion, left the courtroom Framson rose and asked, "If it pleases your honour I'd like to recall the defendant to the stand."

"On what basis?" asked Stenbark.

"Given it has come to light he's married one of the key witnesses, I'd like to put some further questions to him."

"Very well," Stenbark replied, "Mr Mentall please return to the stand."

Mentall took up his place and gave Framson a long stare: he had a good inkling of what was coming.

"Mr Mentall why did you marry Ellie Foster?"

"For love," he replied.

"Not money?"

"No."

"I put it to you that you married Ellie Foster to get your hands on the insurance money from Smoking Chimneys."

"That is not correct."

"Oh come, come Mr Mentall. You played Ellie Foster's vulnerability to your advantage. You destroyed her home, conveniently killing her husband, then groomed her into matrimony. A marriage giving you unfettered access to her assets."

Mentall, knowing the only assets of Ellie he'd so far got unfettered access to were not monetary, shook his head and replied, "The insurance money has not come through. I took Ellie in penniless."

"But you saw her as a woman of wealth did you not, Mr Mentall?"

"No."

"Were you aware there would be an insurance pay-out?"

"Yes," Mentall admitted.

"Then I put it to you that your sole motivations for marrying this poor woman were to get your hands on her money."

"No."

"Yes, Mr Mentall. You went into hiding when charges against you were about to be made for theft of exhibit money. You then found yourself without work and you hatched this plan to destroy a respectable care home."

"No!"

"Yes, Mr Mentall," replied Framson.

"The place was destroyed in a police raid," barked Mentall.

"Mr Mentall I think the court has established that there was no police raid."

"What about the four sets of handcuffs found on the drive?"

"Shire Force have no record of a raid and no record of any missing equipment on the night in question. And on examining the handcuffs they state, and let me quote, 'This type of handcuff has not been in use since the nineteen-sixties'. I suggest Mr Mentall, that you planted those handcuffs."

"Rubbish," barked Mentall.

"Rubbish indeed," replied Framson before pausing and adding, "Mr Mentall, what plans do you and your wife have?"

"How do you mean?" asked Mentall.

"For money. What plans do you have?"

Mentall hesitated then said, "We are starting up a business at home."

"Your home?"

"Yes."

"And for the benefit of the court can you reveal what that business is?"

Mentall's eyes flicked around the court; a beam of afternoon sun from the top window exposed dust in the air.

"What type of business, Mr Mentall?"

Mentall gripped the imitation light oak of the witness stand.

"Mr Mentall, we are waiting."

"It's a care home," he replied.

Juliet Framson straightened herself, gripped her lapels, took a step back and smiled; murmurs came from the public gallery.

"A care home, Mr Mentall? A care home? Let me put it to you that you have an expensive lifestyle of visiting ladies of doubtful morals which you funded by the theft of exhibit money from the East Castle Street case and, when that was running out and about to be exposed, you went into hiding and, without a career to look forward to and your only asset being your home, you saw the model of Smoking Chimneys as a means to secure your future so you set about destroying the said premises to firstly see off any competition, and secondly to offer rescue to Ellie Foster and in so doing take advantage of her finances and business knowledge."

"No!"

Mentall sat cross-legged in a cell below the courtroom. A Group 4 guard appeared at the barred window. "Your jury didn't hang about," he said, "you're back up for the verdict."

A bit too quick, thought Mentall flicking an empty sandwich carton onto the cell floor. The guard unlocked the door and led him back to the courtroom. The jury were then called in. Mentall eyed them one by one. As a judge he used to pride himself on guessing the verdict based on their posture and facial expressions. Things didn't look good at all.

The clerk of the court asked the jury foreman to stand.

A bespectacled, sharp featured woman, rose. "Typical," grumbled Mentall.

"Have you reached a verdict on the charge of theft of exhibit money from the East Castle Street robbery trial?" asked the clerk.

"Yes."

"And do you find the defendant guilty or not guilty."

"Guilty."

Stenbark made a note.

"Have you reached a verdict on the second charge of the wilful destruction of the Smoking Chimneys care home and in so doing the manslaughter of the proprietor, Colin Foster?"

"Yes."

"And do you find the defendant guilty or not guilty."

"Guilty."

Stenbark made a note. Mentall sat down and dragged his hands across his face.

52

Ellie Mentall emerged from the courthouse dabbing her eyes and lowering her head to a volley of waiting cameras.

"Mrs Mentall," called out a reporter, "how is your husband?"

None too pleased, thought Ellie slipping into a taxi. The driver tried to engage her in conversation but, other than telling him her address, she remained silent.

As the cab turned onto the drive she surveyed her new venture. The builders were making good progress with the care home conversion, the garden was coming along and the building was freshly repainted.

She let herself in, sat down in the lounge and switched on the evening news. It relayed the events she knew only too well. When the coverage of the trial ended there was a sharp rat-tat-tat at the door.

She made her way to the hall and opened it. Stood before her was Margaret Wainscott-Bruce.

"You on your own this evening my dear?"

"Yes," Ellie replied.

"Do you fancy coming to mine for a sherry?"

"No, I just want time to myself thank you."

"Well you know where I am. Eight years is going to be a long time."

"I'll get used to it."

Wainscott-Bruce smiled thinly then said, "Well if you ask me he was a bit wayward dear."

"I wasn't."

"Wasn't what?" asked Margaret Wainscott-Bruce.

"Asking you."

"Oh," she replied, sounding distinctly put out. "Well I brought you the Albridge Evening News, it reveals more of his misdemeanours. I suppose they can print it now he's convicted."

Ellie took the paper and shut Wainscott-Bruce out of her world. She read the headline, "Judge Gives Judge Eight Years."

She slept fitfully until the new hall clock chimed eight a.m. She showered, drew back the curtains and gave a wave to her new handyman coaxing leaves into a pile on the lawn.

*

Ex Detective Sergeant DS1553 Peter Tadler looked up to her window and returned her wave. The job advert with contact details of Ellie.Foster@SmokingChimneys.co.uk had been too tempting. It meant another woman boss but needs must if he wanted to clear his name and get his job and pension back.

He'd supplied the information of the Judge's whereabouts at his first tribunal and within days the place had been flattened. He'd also heard rumour that somehow SOAP, from the old Northshire Constabulary, were involved.

He was now biding his time, waiting for the right moment to ask if there had been any police involvement in the destruction of Smoking Chimneys. If he could prove that then he could embarrass the force in to reinstating him. But then there had been the trial. Stephen Mentall claimed there'd been a police raid and yesterday his new wife claimed there hadn't. This was a new twist. She was up to something, he was now sure of that. *Not quite a smoking gun,* he thought, *but certainly a smoking chimney.*

He continued to rake but the sweeping action was playing havoc with his piles. As he paused, to rub trouser fabric into the offending area, he was interrupted by Ellie carrying a tray.

"Cup of tea, Peter?" she asked.

Close call, don't want to get sacked for that again, he thought.

"Thank you, Ma'am," he said, clenching his buttocks and rocking from side to side to ease the itching.

"Penguin?" she asked.

"No, just a bit of discomfort, Ma'am."

"I meant do you want a Penguin biscuit to go with your tea?"

"Oh I see, I thought you meant, well never mind," and he took the biscuit.

"Why do you keep calling me Ma'am, Peter? It's so formal."

"Well I've been in service all my life, Ma I mean Mrs Mentall. Sort of a force of habit," Tadler replied knowing his cover required his best behaviour.

"Well as long as I don't have to start calling you 'boy' or anything we'll get along fine."

"No, that won't be necessary, Mrs Mentall."

"How about Ellie?" she suggested, "or Eleanor if you need to be a bit more formal."

"Very good, Ellie. I'd just like to say how sorry I am about the outcome for Mr Mentall yesterday."

"It's going to be a long eight years."

"He'll be out in four if he behaves himself."

"I have grave doubts whether that'll be possible," she replied. "Anyhow I'm off into town for a couple of hours, the builders will be here at nine to finish the ensuites. Can you let them in?" she asked.

"Yes, of course."

He watched her depart across the garden and rued the tragedy of the situation. She was good looking but he was here for greater things. He waited until he heard her car reverse off the drive, and then he walked across the lawn to the house and let himself in. He went upstairs and started his search with the dresser in her room. He found nothing. He then searched her wardrobe, still nothing.

He scratched his chin, he knew women. Whenever they had a warrant to search a premise, females invariably concealed items in something a man would never have cause to look in. He tried the bathroom cabinet, the Tampax box, the makeup bag. Still no joy. He carefully put everything back before heading downstairs. The kitchen was scant but one of the cupboards contained boxes of women's shoes. He went through each and finished by sitting on his haunches and shaking his head.

He checked his watch, ten minutes before the builders were due. Only enough time left to give the lounge a quick look over. Not wishing to disturb the drawn curtains he clicked on the light. Tadler smiled when he saw a tray with an empty mug and a half eaten biscuit perched on the top of a sewing box.

Concealed below balls of wool and reels of cotton was a scrap-book. Years in the force had told him to look for things out of place. He opened it at a piece cut from the Albridge Evening News, "Judge Gives Judge Eight Years".

"Last night's headline," he muttered. "This is fresh."

He flicked back through the pages and glanced at newspaper articles covering the destruction of Smoking Chimneys. He then froze in amazement as he read headlines concerning care homes she'd run with her previous two husbands. "Wife Awarded Care Home in Divorce Case – Society wouldn't tolerate the elderly turned out of their familiar surroundings says judge" and "Husband Drops Case and Allows Wife to Keep Care Home After Protests From Families."

"Well, well, well," he whispered, "the poor old judge. This'll do nicely for my pension."

A voice came from behind him. "Don't be so sure of that, Peter. Or do you prefer Mr Tadler or even ex-Detective Sergeant Tadler?"

Tadler rose slowly and turned to face Ellie.

"Do you think I was so stupid to have employed an ex-police officer with a grudge?"

"How did you find out?"

"I vet all my employees."

"I suppose with what you're up to you have to be extra diligent."

"What exactly am I up to?"

"Deception, fraud."

"That's a rather slanderous remark isn't it? And on the subject of deception it didn't take long to see through your phoney CV. A few minutes on Google and I had you rumbled."

"Why did you employ me then?"

"I wanted to know what you were up to."

"Keep your enemies close, I suppose," offered Tadler.

"Something like that," she replied with a guarded nod of her head.

"So what are we going to do?" asked Tadler.

"We are going to do nothing. You're going to put those articles back, go home and I never want to see or hear from you again."

"Hold on a moment. These newspaper articles are incriminating," said Tadler.

"Tell me why they're incriminating?"

"Well just look at them. Wife Awarded Care Home in Divorce Case. Husband Drops Case and Allows Wife to Keep Care Home After Protests From Families."

"Just what law have I broken?"

"Well…" and he knew he was beat.

"Well what?" asked Ellie. "I admit it could look a bit embarrassing but it's all legal and above board. You planned to blackmail me didn't you?"

Tadler didn't respond.

"I had a great deal of fun watching you on the security cameras going through my underwear drawer. Do you have a warrant?"

"I don't need one."

"Of course, I was forgetting you aren't a policeman anymore. So we've an illegal search of my house, including routing through my underwear drawer, deception and attempted blackmail."

"You can't prove it."

Ellie pointed to a camera in the corner of the room, "Still filming and recording I'm afraid." And with that she pulled out her smartphone, tapped the screen a few times then added, "But not any longer."

"What did you do that for?" asked Tadler.

"Just wondering how much you'll pay me to wipe out the evidence?"

53

It was just before noon on the day after his trial when Mentall was collected from his courthouse cell and ushered into the rear of a Group 4 prison van. A guard took his details, checked a clipboard and then pointed him towards a seat. He dutifully sat on it and clipped on the lap-belt. Other prisoners boarded, he didn't recognise any professionally but he recognised them all as a bunch of typical good-for-nothing descendants of the once working classes who blamed everybody but themselves for their predicament.

The rear doors were slammed shut and the engine started. The van pulled out into the lunchtime traffic. Mentall shielded his face until the van had gathered speed and reached the outskirts of Albridge. As the hedgerows flashed by he cast his mind back to Ellie's evidence. She'd explained it, in a brief visit after the trial, as a ruse to stop the insurance company from shifting the blame onto the police.

"Thanks to you denying there was a police raid I've been sent down for eight years," he'd said.

"You'll be out in four and the slate will be clean," she'd replied. "We're now guaranteed the insurance money and you won't have to worry about your past catching up with you."

He thought through the conversations when she'd raised the idea of converting his house into a care home. How the plan had formulated, how she'd stroked his ego by suggesting he'd be the figurehead and how easy it was to find her 'Albridge Building Society' pass book to confirm she had the funds. He'd always prided himself on being able to judge a character, to spot a phoney but, without him realising, she'd pursued him, studied him and portrayed herself as needy while hunting out his soft under belly. She'd set herself up as the mug but all the time it was him. He felt more unnerved by this than the loss of his career, reputation and liberty put together.

A voice snapped Mentall from his thoughts. "Don't I know you?"

Mentall looked towards an unshaven, thin man, around forty-five, with short, dark cropped hair and fingers full of rings. 'LOVE' and 'HATE' were crudely tattooed across his knuckles.

"I don't think so," Mentall replied.

"You weren't in the Scrubs five years back?" asked the man.

"No."

"On the Moor in the nineties?"

"No, you're mistaken," Mentall replied returning his gaze to the barred window and the countryside beyond.

"Oh bloody hell, it's just come back to me. You were the bleeding judge that put me in the Scrubs. Barely recognised you without the lady tickler."

Mentall took a moment to realise the man was referring to his moustache. He turned back towards him and said, "I'd appreciate it if you didn't let on."

"Incognito are we?"

"I'd rather keep it quiet," Mentall replied, not wishing it to become common knowledge that he was a judge.

"How long will you be with us for?"

"Eight years if my appeal fails," Mentall replied.

"Oh, I thought you were just visiting." He paused and then added, "Do you smoke?"

"No, thank you."

"Right. I'll keep schtum in return for your snout allowance."

"What?" asked Mentall, sounding alarmed.

"Deal?" he asked, offering the hand with 'LOVE' tattooed across the knuckles.

"Deal," Mentall replied, giving a half-hearted shake and hoping this would end the conversation.

The man grinned and exposed his few remaining teeth. "You've a lot to learn, mate."

"Why?"

"You should've haggled. You should've offered only half your snout allowance."

"I don't smoke."

"But you trade it. Chocolate, radio batteries, razor blades. Swap it for something you need. Tell you what, I'll take half your snout allowance if you help me with my appeal."

"What are you in for?"

"Arson, GBH, threatening to kill a police officer and dealing in heroin. But I was provoked."

"I'll think about it," said Mentall.

*

The van pulled up at a set of tall, solid metal gates. To the right, screwed to a tall brick wall, was a sign which read, 'WELCOME TO HM PRISON SOUTHSHIRE'.

The driver lowered the window and spoke into a faceless microphone. The gates slid open and Mentall could see a curved concrete drive which led to an imposing, Victorian red brick prison. Lines of barred windows frowned down in the gloom of the stormy afternoon. *Smoking Chimneys all over again*, thought Mentall.

The rear doors opened, and Mentall and the other prisoners were ushered into a reception area. A guard, standing behind a waist height desk, was processing each prisoner in turn. Another was searching each man after he had exchanged his civilian clothes and possessions for a prison number, a pile of bedding, a prison uniform and a pair of black shoes.

Mentall parked himself as the last man to be processed. He didn't want to annoy his fellow inmates but didn't want to share with them either. He listened to the questions asked of each prisoner:

"Are you dependent on cigarettes, alcohol or any class A or B drugs?"

"Do you have any medical conditions?"

"Have you any preference to the type of person you share with?"

When all the other prisoners had been processed Mentall stood and approached the desk.

He confirmed that he was not dependent on any drugs, alcohol or cigarettes but when asked if he had any personal preference to the type cellmate he requested a single cell.

255

"That won't be possible," replied the guard.

"Well I'm a professional man, if you see what I mean. I might not get on with the normal inmates."

"From your particulars it looks like you sent half of them here."

"That's what concerns me," Mentall replied.

"Let me see," said the officer tapping into a computer and dragging his hand across his chin. "Professional you say?"

"Yes, if possible," Mentall replied.

"Okay I'll put you on third floor E Block, cell thirty two."

"Thank you."

"Do you want a shower before you're escorted there?"

"No, that won't be necessary, thank you."

"Okay, strip and bend over for the search."

The other guard pulled on a fresh pair of latex gloves. He closed his eyes with the indignity and thought of the role play he'd acted out with Petronella where she would play the prison guard and him the new inmate presenting for a search.

Mentall dressed in the coarse material of the prison uniform before being led away by two prison officers. As each set of steel doors were unlocked and locked a crescendo of doom gathered within him.

He walked between the guards up the open lattice stairs, passing walls of gloss painted bricks and cell doors: some closed, some open with pale faced men looking out.

The door to cell thirty two, third floor E Block was open but nobody was in.

"Your cellmate will be back shortly," said one of the officers. "He's down in the first aid room getting patched up. We'll leave you to settle in and introduce yourself."

"What's happened to him?" asked Mentall, alarmed this so called fellow professional might be predisposed to picking fights.

"Don't worry, we wouldn't put you with anybody violent. Sawman was a copper so nobody likes him. It'll do him good to have a friend."

Somehow Mentall doubted that.

Acknowledgements

Many thanks to the following who gave me tireless feedback during the development of this book: Suzanne Bellenger, Steven Hampton, Jon Stock, Gisella Storm and Jill Todd.

37660871R00153

Printed in Great Britain
by Amazon